New Perspectives on Anthropological and Social Demography

Series editors:
David I. Kertzer and Dennis P. Hogan (Brown University)

Associate editors:
Jack Caldwell, Andrew Cherlin, Tom Fricke, Francis Goldscheider, Susan Greenhalgh, and Richard Smith.

Demography deals with issues of great social importance, and demographic research fuels some of the central current policy debates of our time. Yet, demographic theory has not changed much over the years, and old and sometimes inappropriate models are still being applied to new problems. Increasingly, however, demographers have become aware of the limitations of standard surveys and statistics, and are moving to incorporate theoretical and methodological approaches from other disciplines, in particular anthropology. For their part, anthropologists have generally failed to take account of the advances in modern demography, but they are now beginning to take part in the central debates on questions of theory and policy in population research. A new wave of interdisciplinary research is emerging, combining the interests and approaches of demographers, anthropologists, and other social scientists. Some of the most interesting products of this new wave will be published in **New Perspectives on Anthropological and Social Demography**.

Census and Identity

*The Politics of Race, Ethnicity, and
Language in National Censuses*

Edited by

David I. Kertzer and Dominique Arel

CAMBRIDGE
UNIVERSITY PRESS

PUBLISHED BY THE PRESS SYNDICATE OF THE UNIVERSITY OF CAMBRIDGE
The Pitt Building, Trumpington Street, Cambridge, United Kingdom

CAMBRIDGE UNIVERSITY PRESS
The Edinburgh Building, Cambridge CB2 2RU, UK
40 West 20th Street, New York, NY 10011-4211, USA
477 Williamstown Road, Port Melbourne, VIC 3207, Australia
Ruiz de Alarcón 13, 28014 Madrid, Spain
Dock House, The Waterfront, Cape Town 8001, South Africa

http://www.cambridge.org

First published 2002

Printed in the United Kingdom at the University Press, Cambridge

Typeface Plantin 10/12 pt.   *System* LaTeX 2_ε [TB]

A catalogue record for this book is available from the British Library

Library of Congress Cataloguing in Publication Data
Census and Identity: The politics of race, ethnicity, and language in national
censuses / edited by David I. Kertzer and Dominique Arel.
     p.   cm. – (New perspectives on anthropological and social demography)
Includes bibliographical references and index.
ISBN 0 521 80823 5 – ISBN 0 521 00427 6 (pbk.)
1. Census – Methodology – Case studies.   2. Race – Case studies.
3. Ethnicity – Case studies.   4. Linguistic demography – Case studies.
I. Kertzer, David I., 1948–   II. Arel, Dominique, 1959–   III. Series.
HA179 .P65   2001   306.2 – dc21   2001037352

ISBN 0 521 80823 5 hardback
ISBN 0 521 00427 6 paperback

Contents

Contributors

DAVID ABRAMSON
Office of International Religious
    Freedom
US Department of State

DOMINIQUE AREL
Watson Institute for International
    Studies
Brown University

ALAIN BLUM
Institut national d'études
    démographiques
Paris

CALVIN GOLDSCHEIDER
Program in Judaic Studies and
    Department of Sociology
Brown University

DAVID KERTZER
Department of Anthropology and
    Watson Institute for International
    Studies
Brown University

MELISSA NOBLES
Department of Political Science
Massachusetts Institute
    of Technology

PETER UVIN
Henry Leir Chair of International
    Humanitarian Studies
Fletcher School of Law
    and Diplomacy
Tufts University

Preface

A surge of interest in how collective identities are produced and, in particular, in the role of political actors and governments in fostering such identities has been evident for a number of years now. Yet scholarly interest in the intersection of these identities with state-level politics has a long pedigree. In the nineteenth century, scholars were heavily involved in the efforts of various European empires (Habsburg, Russian, and Ottoman) to categorize and hence better control their heterogeneous populations. Later, following World War II, attention shifted to the efforts of new post-colonial states to create national identities amidst a welter of competing "tribal" and racial identities.

Census and Identity arose from an interest in these questions of states and collective identities shared by a group of scholars based at the Watson Institute of International Studies at Brown University, under the aegis of the Institute's Research Program in Politics, Culture, and Identity. We became fascinated by the ways in which states entered into the struggle over collective identity formation, and saw the state-sponsored census as an especially promising vehicle for examining these processes. Academic interest in the role of censuses in the projection of state power is, of course, not new. A large number of country-specific studies of identity categorization in censuses have now been published, some with a historical focus and others with a more contemporary bent. Notable, too, is Benedict Anderson's decision to add a chapter to the second edition of his now classic book, *Imagined Communities*, devoted to the role of censuses (along with maps and museums) in the construction of national identity.

But to date no one has attempted a comparative study of the role of censuses in collective identity formation that has ranged across all types of states. This is what we have set out to do here, by bringing together scholars with diverse geographical specialties – from central Asia to central Africa, from Israel to North and South America – and different disciplinary backgrounds – from anthropology and sociology to political science and demography. Throughout we adopt a broad historical view.

After incubating this project by bringing in a series of distinguished experts in this field to speak with us at Brown in 1996–1998, we organized a conference at which the first version of the chapters in this book were presented. Held at the Watson Institute February 4–6, 1999, and co-sponsored by the Institute and Brown's Population Studies and Training Center, the conference helped the chapter authors tremendously in re-thinking their contributions and in crafting a unified volume. Credit must go to the discussants at that conference for the insight they provided. We thank William Beeman, Thomas Biersteker, Virginia Dominguez, Matthew Gutmann, Michael Herzfeld, Francine Hirsch, Dennis Hogan, Michael Omi, Brian Silver, Peter Sinnott, Jacqueline Urla, Aristide Zohlberg, and Alan Zuckerman.

Following that conference, new drafts of the chapters were prepared by the authors, and on June 16–17, 1999, they gathered again at the Watson Institute for an intensive discussion of each chapter. A new series of revisions followed.

Before the first conference, a preliminary draft of what has now evolved into the first chapter of this volume, written by the volume editors, was circulated to all chapter authors to help provide a common theoretical framework for the volume. This chapter represents the editors' own attempt to provide a theoretical synthesis of the role of censuses in collective identity formation. It became clear soon enough, however, that some of the chapter authors had different views on these questions. Clearly not all agreed with all aspects of our own perspective and conclusions. We believe that the result is an especially provocative and lively volume, accomplishing the difficult feat of offering a well-integrated and tightly focused book that offers complementary perspectives on a common set of issues.

The book has a three-part structure. Chapter one offers an overview of the major issues involved, and a general theoretical perspective for understanding them. There then follow three chapters which examine, in turn, three major modes of categorizing citizens: race (chapter two); ethnicity (chapter three); and language (chapter four). Each of these chapters approaches the question comparatively: Melissa Nobles offers a historical analysis of the use of racial categorization in the censuses of the United States and Brazil; Calvin Goldscheider examines ethnic categorization in censuses by comparing Israel, Canada, and the United States; and Dominique Arel focuses primarily (but not exclusively) on the countries of Western, Central and Eastern Europe, again viewed historically.

The final section of the book consists of three chapters that focus on the uses of the census in categorizing citizens in particular parts of the world in which problems of such categorization have been (or are becoming) especially acute. In chapter five, Alain Blum, himself a major participant in the highly charged current debates in France over the use of ethnic categorization in censuses and other government statistic-gathering, offers a view of the issues at stake there. In chapter six, Peter Uvin addresses the sanguinary example of Burundi and Rwanda, where division of the population into ethnic categories has produced horrific results. Finally, in chapter seven, David Abramson examines the case of the new states of the former Soviet Union (FSU), with a particular focus on Uzbekistan, as, in mounting their first censuses since independence, they confront the legacy of the Soviet policy of dividing all citizens into distinct nationality categories.

Mention of this last chapter brings up the happy fact that this book represents not the end of our efforts to explore these questions, but rather the first milestone on a longer road. The Politics, Culture, and Identity research program at the Watson Institute is now in the midst of a field-based study of the experiences of the FSU states in conducting their first censuses. This project involves an international network of scholars. Over the course of the past two years these colleagues (especially Francine Hirsch, Brian Silver, and Peter Sinnot) have done much to enrich Kertzer and Arel's understanding of census and identity issues, as we believe is reflected in the introductory chapter to this book. We would like to thank the Mellon Foundation for its support of this project, and especially thank program officer Carolyn Makinson. Thanks, too, to the National Council for East European and Eurasian Research, and program officers Morris Jacobs, Jon Mogul, and Kim Righter, for their support. For those readers interested in learning more details of this new phase of our work, please consult the Watson Institute web site (http://www.brown.edu/Departments/Watson_Institute/).

Finally, we are grateful to Jessica Kuper, anthropology editor of Cambridge University Press, for her support and encouragement. We also thank Neil de Cort at the Press for his work with the manuscript, and Kate Bowman, who prepared the index.

1   Censuses, identity formation, and the struggle for political power

David I. Kertzer and Dominique Arel

The past decade has seen a great outpouring of interest in the nature of collective identities of various kinds. Within the United States, both popular and academic interest in identities that divide the population have not only spawned heated debates but have also had substantial social consequences and public policy implications. Fueled in part by the legacy of racism and the still daunting problems of racial division, and nurtured as well by recent and ongoing waves of immigration, the issue is frequently framed in terms of "multiculturalism." In this version, the American population is presumably divided into a fixed number of different "cultures," each deserving of equal respect and some, perhaps, deserving of special aid.

Beyond the American shores, interest in issues of collective identities, their nature, and their consequences, is scarcely less acute. Nineteenth-century theorists of nationalism – riding the Europe-wide wave of state-creation according to principles of national identity – gave way in the twentieth century to theorists who predicted that such national identity would soon be supplanted by supranational allegiances. The European Union was, for some, viewed as the very embodiment of these processes. Yet events of the recent past have sent these evolutionary internationalists into retreat and ushered in a new concern for the continuing – some would say growing – strength of national and ethnic loyalties. Moreover, from the Balkans to central Africa, ethnic conflict and violence have been interpreted as evidence that people's collective identities do not necessarily match national borders. Accordingly, states that are ethnically heterogeneous – the great majority of states in the contemporary world – are under pressure to take measures to prevent the escalation of ethnic tensions and the development of internal lines of social division.

These tensions are all the more on people's minds as a result of the huge movements of peoples that characterize the world today, movements that are likely to continue to reshuffle the human population in the decades to come. Huge differentials in wealth are drawing people from the poorer to the richer countries, just as low fertility means that, in many cases, the wealthier countries cannot maintain their population without such immigration. The many other well-known sources of instability in much of the world – wars, famines, political fragility, environmental degradation – mean that even within what used to be known as the Third World people are continually in motion, producing a new mix of peoples lacking any common sense of identity.

All of this may be granted, yet what does it have to do with national censuses? Censuses are, after all, generally viewed as matters of bureaucratic routine, somewhat unpleasant necessities of the modern age, a kind of national accounting. Yet it is our argument that the census does much more than simply reflect social reality; rather, it plays a key role in the construction of that reality. In no sector is this more importantly the case than in the ways in which the census is used to divide national populations into separate identity categories: racial, ethnic, linguistic, or religious. It is our hope that the chapters in this book will establish this point and show how collective identities are molded through censuses.

State modernity and the impetus to categorize

The significance of official state certification of collective identities through a variety of official registration procedures can be gleaned by contrasting these government efforts with the situation that existed before such bureaucratic categorization began. Collective identities are, of course, far from a recent innovation in human history. However, before the emergence of modern states, such identities had great fluidity and implied no necessary exclusivity. The very notion that the cultural identities of populations mattered in public life was utterly alien to the pre-modern state (Gellner 1983). That state periodically required some assessment of its population for purposes of taxation and conscription, yet remained largely indifferent to recording the myriad cultural identities of its subjects. As a result, there was little social pressure on people to rank-order their localized and overlapping identities. People often had the sense of simply being "from here."

The development of the modern state, however, increasingly instilled a resolve among its elites to categorize populations, setting boundaries, so to speak, across pre-existing shifting identities. James Scott refers to this process as the "state's attempt to make a society legible," which he regards as a "central problem of statecraft." In order to grasp the complex social reality of the society over which they rule, leaders must devise a means of radically simplifying that reality through what Scott refers to as a "series of typifications." Once these are made, it is in the interest of state authorities that people be understandable through the categories in which they fall.

"The builders of the modern nation-state," Scott writes, "do not merely describe, observe, and map; they strive to shape a people and landscape that will fit these techniques of observation" (1998:2–3, 76–77, 81).

The emergence of nationalism as a new narrative of political legitimacy required the identification of the sovereign "nation" along either legal or cultural criteria, or a combination of both. The rise of colonialism, based on the denial that the colonized had political rights, required a clear demarcation between the settlers and the indigenes. The "Others" had to be collectively identified. In the United States, the refusal to enfranchise Blacks and native Americans led to the development of racial categories. The categorization of identities became part and parcel of the legitimating narratives of the national, colonial, and "New World" state.

States thus became interested in representing their population, at the aggregate level, along identity criteria. The census, in this respect, emerged as the most visible, and arguably the most politically important, means by which states statistically depict collective identities. It is by no means the sole categorizing tool at the state's disposal, however. Birth certificates are often used by states to compile statistics on the basis of identity categories. These include ethnic nationality (a widespread practice in Eastern Europe); mother tongue, as in Finland and Quebec (Courbage 1998: 49); and race, in the United States (Snipp 1989: 33). Migration documents have also, in some cases, recorded cultural identities. The Soviet Union, for instance, generated statistics on migration across Soviet republics according to ethnicity. The US Immigration Service, from 1899 to 1920, classified newly arrived immigrants at Ellis Island according to a list of forty-eight "races or peoples," generally determined by language rather than physical traits (Brown 1996).

Parallel to the need for statistical representation was the need for control. In order to establish a "monopoly of the legitimate means of movement" (Torpey 2000: 1), states imposed the use of personal identity documents to distinguish the citizen from the foreigner (Noiriel 1996) and, in some cases, attempted to control the internal migration of their population through residency permits and internal passports (Matthews 1993). In a number of cases, such identification documents contained an identity category beyond the civic or legal status of the individual: for example, the Soviet Union, where citizens had their "nationality" (in the ethnic sense) indicated on their internal passports (Zaslavsky and Luryi 1979); Rwanda, with Hutu or Tutsi ethnicity (actually called "race") appearing in identity cards (Uvin, this volume); Greece, Turkey, and Israel, with religion recorded in identity cards (Courbage 1997: 114; Goldscheider, this volume)[1]; and apartheid South Africa, with racial categories inscribed on identification papers (Petersen 1997: 97).

The categorization of identities, along culturally constructed criteria, on *individual* documents can serve nefarious or well-meaning purposes. In the United States, a racial category in birth certificates was long used to discriminate against Blacks and Indians. Following the rigid principle of the "one-drop rule," according to which a single Black ancestor, however remote, made one Black, birth certificates were often used in Southern states to bar individuals of racially-mixed ancestry from marrying Whites (Davis 1991: 157). The rise of affirmative action, based on the notion that achieving true equality required special consideration to be given to historically disadvantaged minorities in access to jobs and education, implied the bureaucratic categorization of "minorities." As a consequence, particularly in the case of Blacks and Indians, it has meant continuing commitment to the determination of race according to "objective" ancestry, as opposed to simple self-definition. Thus, the Indian Health Service of the Bureau of Indian Affairs continues to hold that eligible patients must have a minimum of one-fourth "blood quantum," which in practice entails that they must prove that at least one of their grandparents appeared on tribal enrollments (tribal rolls) of recognized tribes (Snipp 1989: 34).

A similar policy was employed by Nazi Germany to identify both Jews and Germans. In spite of the shrill propaganda on the physical alienness of Jews, the criterion actually chosen to separate the Jews eventually targeted for destruction was a mixture of religion and descent, and not anthropometric measurement. Those with at least three Jewish grandparents were categorized as Jews. Ancestry, in turn, was determined by birth certificates issued by religious institutions (Hilberg 1985). At the outset of World War II, when the Nazi government sought to transfer German-speaking populations from the East (Baltics, Ukraine, Romania) to newly annexed territories from Poland, the question of defining German identity arose. In this case, religion was not deemed determinative and ethnicity did not appear on birth certificates. In Estonia, where a liberal minority law in 1925 had established officially recognized ethnic associations, claimants had to show a certificate, delivered either by their German association or by the Estonian Ministry of the Interior, attesting to their German ancestry (Institut national de la statistique 1946: 80).[2] Interestingly, since post-war Germany has adopted a kind of Law of Return, granting automatic citizenship to ethnic Germans from abroad, the issue of legally documenting one's ethnic German affiliation remains germane today. After apparently relying on the self-declaration of applicants during the Cold War, the German state devised a complex questionnaire in the early 1990s to determine who can be deemed "German" (Brubaker 1996).

The practice of inscribing cultural categories on personal identification documents can clearly affect an individual's own sense of identity. In the Soviet Union, the ethnic nationality in one's internal passport was also determined by descent (i.e., one's parents' nationality), as with the cases of the Jews, Germans, Blacks, and Indians cited above. In such a context, it seems likely that people whose passport certified them to be of "Ukrainian" ethnic nationality, yet spoke Russian as their first language, would nevertheless associate "Ukrainian" with their ethnic identity, at least by force of habit. However, a literature is lacking on the relationship between state-enshrined identities on personal documents and collective identity formation or, for that matter, between categories used on the census and in private documents. Clearly, comparative research on the politics and bureaucratic implementation of identity categorization practices in state documents is needed. Yet, while cognizant that the census belongs to a larger family of state categorizing practices, the current volume focuses its gaze on the census and its relationship to identity formation. Our goal in doing so is both to reconcile various strands of emerging literatures, which to date have often been regionally segmented (New World, colonial experience, France, East-Central Europe), and to help provide a theoretical framework for further comparative research. The universality and political salience of the census dictated our selection of the census as a fruitful point of departure.

The rise of population statistics and the construction of identities

Much of the most influential literature on the role of statistics gathering in extending state control has focused on the colonial state. Anderson, in his influential book *Imagined Communities*, pointed to the census as one of the primary devices employed by the colonial state to impose a "totalizing, classificatory grid" on its territory, and hence make all inside it its own. For Anderson, the key was the ability to make distinctions, to draw borders, to allow governments to distinguish among "peoples, regions, religions, languages." The very boundedness of the state meant that its component objects were countable, and hence able to be incorporated into the state organization (Anderson 1991: 184). The state's goal here, as Scott (1998:65) put it, is to "create a legible people."

In short, the use of identity categories in censuses – as in other mechanisms of state administration – creates a particular vision of social reality. All people are assigned to a single category, and hence are conceptualized as sharing, with a certain number of others, a common collective identity. This, in turn, encourages people to view the world as composed of distinct groups of people and may focus attention on whatever criteria are utilized to distinguish among these categories (Urla 1993). Rather than view social links as complex and social groupings situational, the view promoted by the census is one in which populations are divided into neat categories. Appadurai's (1993: 334) comment is apropos here: "statistics are to bodies and social types what maps are to territories: they flatten and enclose."

In Europe, national statistics-gathering was developing in the nineteenth century as a major means of modernizing the state. International congresses were held where the latest statistical and census developments were hawked to government representatives from across the continent. Knowledge was power, and the knowledge of the population produced by the census gave those in power insight into social conditions, allowing them to know the population and devise appropriate plans for dealing with them. As Urla (1993: 819) put it, "With the professionalization and regularization of statistics-gathering in the nineteenth century, social statistics, once primarily an instrument of the state, became a uniquely privileged way of 'knowing' the social body and a central technology in diagnosing its ills and managing its welfare."

Such language, not coincidentally, brings to mind Foucault, and his view of the emergence of a modern state that progressively manages its population by extending greater surveillance over it. In examining state action in the construction of collective identities, we enter into the complex debates over what is meant by "the state." The state itself is, of course, an abstraction, not something one can touch. Such a perspective impels us to examine the multiplicity of actors who together represent state power, and discourages us from the view that "the state" necessarily acts with a single motive or a single design. An inquiry into censuses and identity formation, then, requires examination of just which individuals and groups representing state power are involved, and how they interrelate with one another as well as with the general population. Pioneering research of this sort has been done on the impact of various advocacy groups. Especially valuable work has been done on the Census Advisory Committee on Spanish Origin Population in formulating the "Hispanic" category in the 1980 US census (Choldin 1986). Similarly important work has been done on the role of ethnographers, geographers, and party activists in devising an official list of ethnic "nationalities" for the first Soviet census of 1926 (Hirsch 1997). Sorely needed are more ethnographic efforts at examining the workings of state agencies of various kinds – from legislatures to census-takers – in their interactions with each other and with the people under their surveillance.[3]

That the kind of counting and categorizing that goes on in censuses is an imposition of central state authorities, and thereby a means of extending central control, has long been recognized. Indeed, ever since the first census-takers ventured into the field, struggles between local people and state authorities over attempts to collect such information were common. Such was the case in mid-eighteenth-century France, when various attempts to collect population data by the central government had to be abandoned. Opposition came not only from a suspicious populace but also from local governments. Each feared that the information was being gathered to facilitate new state taxes (Starr 1987: 12–13). These first population enumerations were typically identified with attempts to tax (often newly acquired) populations, as well as to conscript them for labor or military service.

Given such purposes, those undertaking these early censuses sought not to achieve a complete enumeration of the population, but only to register the part of most direct interest to state authorities. That segment generally was a taxable unit, such as the household, and not the individual *per se*. Moreover, since several social groups were exempted from taxation – in the case of the first enumerations of the Ottoman Empire in the fifteenth and sixteenth centuries these included religious orders, the military, and judges (Behar 1998: 137) – pre-modern censuses were neither comprehensive nor standardized. Regional implementation tended to vary enormously, both in time and form.

Churches, too, have long been involved in this process, indeed in parts of Europe long predating the state in attempting comprehensive population enumerations. For example, the Lutheran Church in Sweden began a full registration of its population in the 1600s (Willigan and Lynch 1982: 123). Similarly, one product of the Roman Catholic Church's counter-Reformation efforts to solidify its control over its far-flung population was to order parish priests to take an annual census of their parishioners. This practice, begun in the sixteenth century, continues in many areas to this day.

Full, regular, periodic state-sponsored enumerations of individuals apparently date to 1790, when the United States began its decennial censuses. Within a century, they would become a defining feature of the modern state, with most European/New World states and colonial possessions having experienced their first modern census by the latter part of the nineteenth century. The decision to enumerate individuals, however, brought up the question of *which* individuals to include. Should the enumeration be limited to citizens, or should it encompass all individuals residing within the boundaries of a given state at the time of the census, irrespective of civic status? The United States, for example, did not count Indians remaining in reservations, who were not considered citizens and therefore subject to taxation, until the 1820 census

(Nobles, this volume). The question of whom to count was debated several times by the International Statistical Congress, a body that met every three years or so in Europe between the 1850s and the 1880s, and its recommendation to count the *resident* population became standard practice.

States thus sought to count everyone on their soil, and among the first categorizations introduced on the modern census was the division between citizens and non-citizens or the related – but distinct – division between those born within the state and those born abroad. The French case, in this respect, is of particular interest. The French republican state had an organic conception of "la nation," a civic body regarded as indivisible. French discourse became philosophically opposed to any subcategorization of the nation in the census or other state-sponsored practices. This conception, however, called for a strict separation between those who were part of the *nation* and the others. As a result, "the citizen and the foreigner became the two principal categories of analysis" (Blum, this volume). "Foreigners" were categorized according to their country of origin, a criterion eventually extended, from 1962 on, to the "naturalized French."

British, American, and Australian census-designers have also long been interested in ascertaining the country of origin of their residents. A census question on birthplace has appeared on the censuses of these countries from the beginning in the United States, since the middle of the nineteenth century in Britain, and since 1911 in Australia. In Britain, a question on nationality (citizenship) was likewise included from 1851 to 1961 (Booth 1985: 256). The German census had questions on both place of birth and citizenship, while Austria and Hungary – which administered separate censuses – were only interested in ascertaining citizenship (Tebarth 1991). The information on the foreign-born was sometimes used to calibrate immigration policy. When legislation was passed after World War I to restrict immigration to the United States, an annual quota (2 percent) was established for each country of origin according to the census figures of foreign-born for 1880 (Simon 1997b: 16).[4] This remained in force until the 1965 immigration law abolished country-specific quotas.

The development of cultural categories

While the practice of distinguishing the enumerated by civic status or place of birth became generalized, no such consensus emerged over the merits of using *cultural* categories in the census. With the rise of the "nationality question" in Europe – i.e., the legitimization of political demands based on the cultural markers of territorially concentrated groups – two representations of the "nation" came into conflict. On the one hand there was the French model of a political nation that was coterminous with the boundaries of the citizenry (the "nation-state"). On the other there was the German model of a cultural nation (in practice defined by language) not necessarily corresponding to state boundaries. States of Western Europe (France, Britain, Spain) professed the ideology of the "nation-state," while to the east (Germany, Austria-Hungary, Imperial Russia and the Ottoman Empire) leaders embraced a model of the multinational state (with religion serving as a marker of identity in the Ottoman lands).

At the sessions of the International Statistical Congress, statisticians from the Western "nation-states" argued that the concept of cultural nationality, as developed in Eastern Europe, did not apply to them. Their Eastern counterparts argued that the concept was not geographically restricted, and they held extensive discussions on which particular categories would best represent people's cultural "nationality." A consensus emerged among Eastern census-makers that the question of cultural nationality should not be asked directly, but rather be derived from a question on language. With a few minor exceptions to the rule, this became the practice in the first wave of periodic censuses in Eastern Europe before World War I. The main objection to directly asking individuals about their cultural nationality was that, at a time of low national consciousness, many would have been confused about what to answer (Kleeberg 1915: 42; Roth 1991). In other words, while certain nationalist elites were arguing that national groups existed and needed to be statistically represented, many of the putative members of these groupings were unaware that they had such an affiliation.

Meanwhile, as new colonial territories were conquered, or modern administrative practices brought to old ones, censuses were introduced to the colonies as well. One of the major elements of this attempt by colonial state authorities to make populations knowable, to link them to the state and thereby make them governable, was the Herculean effort to divide the people into mutually exclusive and exhaustive identity categories. This represented a decisive break from precolonial enumerative practices. Appadurai contrasts the European practice with that of the earlier conquerors of South Asia, the Mughals, who did much to map and measure the land they controlled, as part of their efforts to tax it, yet showed no interest in enumerating the whole population. "Enumeration of various things," he writes, "was certainly part of the Mughal state *imaginaire* as was the acknowledgment of group identities, *but not the enumeration of group identities*" (1993: 329).

The European colonial powers (France, Britain, Belgium), who rejected cultural categorizations in their metropolitan censuses as incompatible with their imagined "nation-states," had no such qualms when faced with the daunting task of counting their colonial subjects (Kateb 1998: 105; Appadurai 1993: 317–18). There is little doubt that racial ideologies, popular in Europe in late nineteenth century, influenced the thinking of colonial census-makers regarding the enumeration of Asian and African communities (Hirschman 1987). Yet another important factor was the absence of any idea of common citizenship uniting the colonial settlers with the locals. Since the "nation-state" construct was restricted to the relatively tiny number of colonial settlers, other categories had to be devised for the vast majority of the population (Anderson 1997: 58).

Censuses and the construction of race

As a product of the ideology of colonial and modern states, the project of dividing populations into separable categories of collective identity inevitably intersected with the division of populations into racial categories. The two efforts share a common logic, a kind of categorical imperative, in which people must be assigned to a category and to one category alone. The history of racial thinking is a history of cultural categorization, of seizing on certain physical characteristics and inventing a biological category for those people who manifest them.

In devising "racial" categories, imperial census-makers used names from the existing repertoire of cultural and geographical markers, but the categories themselves reflected the perception of the European rulers rather than that of the natives. Anderson (1991: 165–6) writes that few recognized themselves under the early "racial" labels of "Malay," "Javanese," "Sakai," "Banjarese," etc. in the 1911 Indonesian census. In the same vein, Hirschman (1987: 567) argues that the "Malay," "Chinese," and "Indian" categories in the Malaysian census were much broader than socially understood. That these categories reflected subjective values is hardly distinctive. Identities being by definition subjectively determined, their conceptual representation in *any* census can only reflect subjective processes. What distinguished colonial from non-colonial censuses, however, was that the formulation of categories in the colonies was unilaterally done by the ruling officials, while European categories of cultural nationality and language were already being negotiated, to some extent, with social groups.

Even more significant was the belief, fundamental to a racist conception of the world, that racial categories were rank ordered according to aptitude. Imperial races, unlike colonial ones, were fit to rule, while certain colonial races were better equipped to assist the colonial project than others. Such a conception of group categories was initially foreign to the natives in most areas. In Rwanda and Burundi, for instance, the Belgian colonial state ruled through the minority Tutsi, in keeping with the widespread colonial practice of indirect rule. The Belgians legitimized Tutsi dominance by creating a racial distinction making the Tutsi superior Africans, due to an alleged "Hamitic" origin, while the Hutus were relegated to the bottom of the racial scale. What was new was not the naming itself, since the colonial categories of Tutsi and Hutus overlapped with pre-existing ones, "but rather the colonial policy of indirect rule and the racist ideology associated with it. It was those factors that crystallized the categories and erected them against each other." (Uvin, this volume.)

It is the United States, however, that has the longest continuous history of placing its entire population into mutually exclusive racial categories based on pseudo-scientific theories of race. As Nobles shows in her chapter in this volume, the categories and criteria have evolved over time, with categories once thought natural – such as that of "mulatto" – eventually being regarded as not only unscientific but morally reprehensible. In societies such as the United States, where the ideology of racial categorization has had tremendous social and political consequences, the census is a cauldron of racial construction. By pigeon-holing people into official governmental categories, the census gives a legitimacy to the categories and to this mode of thinking about people. Moreover, in so far as the census is presented as an instrument of scientific inquiry, racial categorization in censuses provides an aura of scientific legitimacy for the racial project as well.

The confusion between race and ethnicity

The compulsion to divide people into racial categories has never been far from the drive to divide them into ethnic categories. In fact, the two concepts are often blurred, a confusion having largely to do with a belief that identity can be *objectively* determined through ancestry. We have already discussed how racial categorization in the United States continues to be linked, in courts and government agencies, to "blood quantum." Yet the primordialist discourse of nationalism, with its emphasis on the timeless "essence" of the nation, also implies a genetic transmission of identity across the ages. "National consciousness," rather than phenotypical traits, constitutes the inherited trait for primordialists. Nationalist literature is replete with assumptions about presumed members of the ethnic nation who do not know who they *truly* are, that is, whose authentic and transmitted national identity is, as it were, buried within themselves. To give an example among many, Lithuanian nationalists consider the Polish minority of Lithuania to be "polonized Lithuanians." As Snyder (1998: 10–11) points out, "On this line of thinking, national identity is treated as a question of race rather than of history or personal choice."

This explains why, prior to World War II, European ethnic nationalities were routinely referred to as "races" in public and scholarly discourse. For instance, when the renowned British historian R. W. Seton-Watson published *Racial Problems in Hungary* in 1908, a book chiefly on the Slovaks, he was mostly employing categories that would now be called "ethnic." The Slovaks formed a different nation, in his view, because of such cultural traits as their distinct language and their belief in sharing a common descent. Moreover, it was widely believed at the time that nations had unique "characters." The "national character" of the British was deemed to be different from that of the French or Germans. Even the nations espousing a so-called civic conception of themselves, such as the British, were commonly referrred to as "races" as well. The common thread to this semantic jumble of nations, nationalities, and races – the term ethnicity was rarely used before World War II – was a notion that what these "races" passed along through heredity was largely expressed through *cultural* traits. These included not only language and religion but also "character," denoted by work ethic, collective personality, and so forth.[5]

This is not to say that the colonial emphasis on inherited physical traits was absent from the European landscape. Yet, until the rise of fascism in the 1920s, the biological idea of race remained marginal in nationalist discourse and, even more importantly for the purposes of this volume, was entirely discarded from pre-World War I censuses in Europe. However pervasive in popular discourse, "race" was found, by censusmakers of the era, to be totally inadequate to capture cultural nationality (ethnicity). Crucially, these census-makers shared a belief that nationality was *subjectively* determined, and thus contingent on one's sense of identity, a notion that contradicted the belief in objectively descended "races." When Nazi Germany introduced racial categorizations based on documented lineage – in the 1939 census, respondents had to indicate whether one of their grandparents was Jewish – it constituted a break not only from the German census tradition of categorizing identity by self-professed language, but also from the entire European census practice of rejecting race as a category (Labbé 1998).

After the Nazi cataclysm, the conflation of biology and culture was discredited and the old practice of calling national, religious, and linguistic groups "races" vanished in Western Europe and the New World. References to "race," which had been routine in the League of Nations, were replaced by references to "ethnicity" in documents of the United Nations. In the colonies, on the other hand, while imperial rule became gradually delegitimized in favor of native "self-determination," racially-based categories often survived decolonization, and not only in the apartheid regimes of Rhodesia and South Africa. We have already mentioned how Hutu rulers in Rwanda continued to highlight the Hutu and Tutsi "races" in censuses, identity cards, and local population registers (Uvin, this volume). That case does not appear to be singular. As Rabushka and Shepsle (1972: 8) pointed out, giving Malaysia as an example, "very often the inhabitants of plural societies subjectively perceive broad cultural divisions as a surrogate for objective phenotypical characteristics." The pre-World War II European confusion between race and ethnicity is still found in various parts of the non-Western world.

That confusion, however, has re-entered Western discourse in recent decades and, for the first time outside of the United States, has become enshrined in official categorizations in a few notable cases. Three developments brought race back to the forefront. First was the unprecedented flow of migrants from Asia and Africa to European countries that previously had relatively little immigration from these areas. Second was the rise of official concerns about combatting discrimination, often leading to policies of "positive discrimination". Third was the mobilization of immigrant groups on the basis of their cultural heritage. Countries that had previously been loath to categorize their populations along a cultural marker were suddenly confronted with a dilemma: how to effectively prevent discrimination without statistically distinguishing the people most likely to be discriminated against? In Britain and the historic countries of immigration (United States, Canada, and Australia), the answer, highly politicized and contested, was to devise "minority" categories – in the case of the United States, to enhance existing "racial" ones, while infusing them with an entirely new purpose. In most instances, the new categories muddled race and ethnicity, despite the consensus among anthropologists and ethnologists on the spuriousness of conflating biology and culture. The case of Britain is illuminative of the recurring failure to distinguish race from ethnicity.

In 1976 Britain passed an anti-discrimination bill, the Race Relations Act, which defined discrimination as the unfavorable treatment of an individual on "racial grounds," that is, on the basis of "colour, race, nationality (including citizenship) or ethnic or national origin" (Simon 1997a: 25). In one fell swoop, the legislation thus mixed together race, ethnicity/cultural nationality, and citizenship. Census officials were instructed to categorize the "minorities" targeted by the Act in order to enable the government to obtain statistical information on them on a variety of social indicators, such as family structure, housing, employment, education, and so forth (White 1979: 333). Various tests were conducted to determine how minority data could best be collected. While people from some minority populations – such as those from India and China – had no objection to checking themselves off as belonging to such a category (e.g., "Indian" or "Chinese") despite the fact that they were born in Britain, others felt differently. Most notably, many of those whose forbears came from the West Indies objected to being officially categorized as "West Indian," arguing instead that they should simply be considered British. To overcome this opposition, census officials proposed using the term "Black British," thus indicating that those so dubbed were indeed British, while distinguishing them by their race, as was done in the United States. Government officials, however, rejected this proposal on the grounds that it placed (politically) unacceptable emphasis on "race" rather than ethnicity (White and Pearce 1993: 274–75).

Political discomfort in Britain with using "race" led to attempts to replace racial terms with ethnic terms. One problem was to find a way out of the use of "White," and so the proposal was made to substitute "White" with two composite categories, separating groups "indigenous" to Britain – "English, Welsh, Scottish or Irish," – from "Other European." Yet whatever terms were used, minority groups objected, and in the end no minority question was asked on the 1981 British census (Booth 1985: 259–60). The matter did not end there, however. After these abortive attempts, the census authorities managed to institute a minority question in the 1991 census by reintroducing the racial categories "White" and "Black," with "British West Indians" becoming a subcategory of "Blacks." The official categories became: White; Black (divided into Caribbean, African, Other); Indian; Pakistani; Bangladeshi; Chinese; Any Other Ethnic Group (Bhrolcháin 1990: 559–60).[6] This amalgam of racial and ethnic categories reflected political pressures. "European" British officials, in line with colonial thinking, viewed the key marker of differentiation between "Europeans" and minorities as racial ("White" versus the Others). Yet those in these minority populations had a different perspective. As Ballard (1997: 185) explained:

So precisely because the visible minorities quite rightly repudiate (in sharp contrast with 'white' majority!) any suggestion that they can be positively identified in biological terms, plain logic suggests that the only kind of question to which they might be expected to offer a positive response would be one about their self-defined ethnic affiliation. And so it proved.

Similar difficulties with collecting data on minority categories were experienced in Canada. Unlike Britain, Canada had an ethnic origin question appearing on its censuses from the start, i.e. since 1871, a century before the rise of the anti-discrimination movement. The reason was that Canada defined itself as a pact between "two founding peoples," largely territorially concentrated – the descendants of French and English settlers. The purpose of the ethnic origin question was to register the changing proportions of these groups in relation to themselves and other groups. The Canadian desire to enumerate groups based on cultural origin was therefore closer to the Eastern European conception of cultural nationalities than to the nation-state premise epitomized by Britain. Between 1901 and 1941, the census question on origins was actually called "race," yet it reflected the sentiment, widely held at the time, that, when applied to European-based groups, "races" were mostly defined through cultural markers.[7]

As in Britain, legislation on the prevention of discrimination forced census-makers to introduce new categories. In 1986, the Canadian government passed the *Employment Equity Act*, requiring employers to report annually on the representation of "designated groups" among their employees. The Act identified four such groups: women, persons with disabilities, aboriginal peoples, and "persons who are, because of their race or colour, in a visible minority in Canada." In a development similar to the British experience, the first efforts to develop a question using racial categories for the 1991 Canadian census floundered, since pre-tests revealed that many respondents found the question offensive (Boyd 1993: 535–36). Amidst continuing controversy, the racial question finally made it to the 1996 census, where respondents were given ten choices: White, Black, Chinese, South Asian, Southeast Asian, West Asian, Filipino, Arab, Japanese, Korean, Latin American, and Other. Aboriginal peoples, the Canadian equivalent of "Native Americans," were counted in a separate question, offering the categories North American Indian, Métis or Inuit (Eskimo). In response to criticisms about instituting racial enumeration, the Chief Statistician of Canada, Ivan P. Fellegi, argued that the question was not about "race," but about "visible minorities," to enable the government to implement its employment-equity legislation (Fellegi 1996).

While adding the new questions on visible minorities and aboriginals, the Canadian census kept its old ethnic-origin question, but the rationale and the categories underwent drastic changes. To counter the rise of nationalism in Quebec, Canada passed the Official Languages Act in 1969, making English and French the official languages of the federal government. The elevation of French as an official language proved unpopular among the increasing number of Canadians of neither British nor French stock who objected that a minority (the French Canadians having been a demographic minority since the inception of Canada) be given more recognition than other immigrant minorities. To assuage the growing opposition to the vision of two "founding peoples," the Canadian government passed the Act on Multiculturalism in 1971 (revised in 1988), which defined the country as a mosaic of cultural groups and provided state funds for the promotion of ethnic heritage. There are important differences between the Multicultural Act and the Employment Equity Act. The former calls for state subsidies of cultural and educational activities of groups including those of European ancestry. Indeed, it was the "Europeans," such as the Ukrainians, who were most involved in mobilizing for such a law in the 1960s). The latter mandates "equitable" representation of certain groups ("visible minorities"), excluding those of European background.

The Official Languages Act, and the subsequent Quebec law making French the sole official language of Quebec, had the effect of shifting the battle between the English and French groups from the ethnic origin to the language question. The ethnic origin question became instead the means of assessing the demographic strength of the groups susceptible to benefit from the Multicultural Act. The question, however, became vulnerable to other emerging political currents. The campaign for gender equality in the 1970s forced the traditional emphasis on paternal ancestor to be dropped from the 1981 census (White, Badets, and Renaud 1993: 229). A decade later, a growing backlash against the "Balkanization" of Canada led to a grass-roots campaign, spearheaded by the *Toronto Star*, urging Canadians of all backgrounds to identify their origins as "Canadian" ("Call Me Canadian!"), a category which had never been allowed by census-makers. In the 1991 census, 3.3 percent entered "Canadian" in the category "Other – specify" of the question on origins, making it the fifth largest "ethnic" group. Since the ethnic categories on the census form must, by law, appear in order of demographic weight according to the previous census, "Canadian" was for the first time listed as an official category in the origin question of the 1996 census, appearing in fifth place. The effect was staggering. A whopping 24.1 percent of the population put down "Canadian," an increase that could be partly be attributed to a semantic confusion among Québécois respondents, since the French term "Canadien" has historically referred to ethnic French Catholics (Goldscheider, this volume; Desjardins 2000).[8]

In the United States, as mentioned earlier, a question on race has appeared in all censuses since 1790. A growing number of categories supplemented this original distinction between White and Black over the years. Indians (in the sense of Native American) and Chinese appeared in 1870, Japanese in 1890, Filipino, Hindu and Korean in 1920 (the last two categories disappearing in 1950), Mexican in 1930 (and only in that year), and Hawaiian, Aleut and Eskimo in 1960. In the 1970s, buffeted by changing political winds, having to respond to civil rights legislation, and facing increasingly vocal "ethnic" or "racial" lobbying groups, census officials found they had less and less control over the categorization system that they administered. In 1977, Directive No. 15 of the Office of Management and Budget (OMB) enunciated a policy for distinguishing races and ethnic groups in all federal statistics including, of course, the census (Nobles, this volume). As a result, several "racial" categories were added to the 1980 census: Korean, Vietnamese, Asian Indian, Guamanian, and Samoan. A separate question on Hispanic ancestry was also added to the census, as mandated by the OMB directive, thanks to intense lobbying from Hispanic groups (Choldin 1986). Twenty years later the categories were largely unchanged. As in Britain and Canada, these categories became linked to specific anti-discrimination legislation: in this case, the Voting Rights Act of 1965, requiring that the decennial redrawing of congressional districts produce a fair representation of selected minorities (Jenkins 2000).

American census-makers have also, in recent years, been tackling the question of ethnic origin. Previous to 1980, the only question about origin had to do with the country of birth of the respondent and their parents, never venturing beyond the second generation. That question is useful to gauge the current wave of immigrants but is a poor indicator of ethnic identity, since most countries of origin are multiethnic. Thus, a study conducted at the turn of the century showed that only 2 percent of the "Russian" immigrants to the United States, i.e., immigrants from (Imperial) Russia, could be classified as ethnic Russians, the great majority being either Jewish or Polish (Petersen 1987: 219), or claimed as such by leaders of Jewish and Polish ethnic organizations in the U.S.[9] The 1980 census marked the first time an attempt was made to attach an ethnic label to every member of the population, regardless of how long a person's ancestors had been in the country. Before that, data on ethnicity were only gathered indirectly, by combining information on place of birth and language (McKenney and Cresce 1993: 176). The census language data, however, were unreliable because the questions were poorly formulated and frequently altered (Crawford 1992: 126).

Beginning in the 1970s, the rise of "multiculturalism" created pressure on enumerative bodies to pay attention to the "ethnic" make-up of the population. The US Census Bureau began to experiment with a question on "ancestry." As happened in Canada, whether an ethnic group was listed or not as an example in the ancestry question made a huge difference in the number of respondents identifying with that particular group.

Thus, the number of Americans of Slovak, Croat, and French Canadian ancestry more than doubled between the 1980 and 1990 censuses, while the number of Cajuns increased sixty-fold – all four categories which were not listed in 1980, but were in 1990 (Passel 1994). On the other hand, no significant popular resistance to ethnic enumeration, in the genre of the "Count Me Canadian!" campaign, arose in the United States (Goldscheider, this volume).

In Australia, another of the historic countries of immigration, similar developments were observed. In preparing for the 1991 census, a government committee found that more than the indirect indicators of place of birth, religion, or language used at home – the questions previously used in Australian censuses – were needed to properly distinguish an ethnic group. Committee members concluded that such was the complexity of ethnicity (involving a sense of history, of cultural tradition, of being "racially conspicuous," etc.) that a specific ethnic question should be asked. Among their arguments was that third and subsequent generation immigrants to Australia could not be distinguished by these indirect indicators, while people born in British colonies who themselves came from British stock were being erroneously assigned to the ethnic category of the colonized (Cornish 1993: 308–11).

Even though the concepts of race and ethnicity tend to be used in a confusing manner in contemporary censuses of the Western countries of the former British Empire, census categories of "race" and "ethnicity" are kept separate (except in Britain) because they serve different political purposes. While the enumeration of "races," or "visible minorities," is directly linked to the politics of entitlement, the enumeration of "ethnic groups" is linked to a renewed pride in one's ancestry, generally without *individual* benefits. (In Britain, as we saw above, the largely racial classification is actually called "ethnic".) Non-White recognized minorities, such as "Japanese," can benefit from policies of implicit or explicit positive discrimination, while Whites of a minority ethnic background, such as Ukrainians, cannot. A key question is whether such political distinctions are sustainable in the long run.

The validity of defining cultural identity in the census

As the discussion has so far amply demonstrated, the formulation of census questions and categories is inextricably embroiled in politics. This raises the question of whether the collection of census data on cultural categories can have any scientific validity. Does the politicization of the census represent the undermining of an exercise that should be left in the hands of scientific experts? Social science does not speak with one voice on the matter, due in part to conflicting disciplinary assumptions and a certain compartmentalization of research.

The assertion that statistical science can stand above politics assumes that the object to be enumerated "exists previous to and outside of statistics" (Labbé 2000). From this perspective, the task of the statistician, and thus of the census expert, is to establish methodological rules protecting data collection from imprecision and sundry distortions, thereby attempting to describe with the greatest accuracy the object under study. The problem with this approach is that, by focusing mainly on the technical aspects of measurement, it takes for granted the existence of the category itself. This is unproblematic when categories refer to objective markers such as "age." But to assume that categories denoting cultural affiliation can be enumerated as objectively as age is to assume that identities can be reduced to an essential core within each individual, a core that exists outside of politics.

The notion that cultural categories can be reduced to an objective core, called "statistical realism" by Labbé, is dangerously close to the primordialist notion of timeless identities, much discredited in recent social science, particularly among anthropologists. Nonetheless, statistical realism appears to have many adherents among demographers. Labbé relates the case of an ambitious project undertaken by the French Institute of Demography, aiming at assessing the reliability of all available demographic data in the Balkans. One of the issues concerns the underregistration of Romas (Gypsies) in the last Hungarian census. The project apparently does not question the criteria used to define the category "Roma" in the first place and whether someone of Roma descent could not legitimately declare him or herself as "Hungarian" (Labbé 2000).

The same mindset characterized the European experts sent to Macedonia in 1994 to devise and conduct a special census aimed at verifying whether ethnic Albanians had been undercounted in the 1991 Macedonian census, as Albanian activists claimed they had been. The experts "thought they were going to be overseeing the technical aspects of a statistical exercise," but were instead shocked by the level of political passion their very exercise reignited, and baffled by the sheer ethnographic complexity of the area (Friedman 1996, 94). How is a Macedonian-speaking Muslim to be counted? As the experts discovered, two diametrically opposed views existed on the matter, and statistical realism was of little help to adjudicate the issue.

Anthropologists emphasize the fact that identities are social constructions, that is, intrinsically dependent on social incentives and political projects, as opposed to deriving from some unalterable kernel that could be discovered in an ideal "state of nature." Some conclude from this that identities are "not real" and therefore inappropriate for enumeration, or for political recognition, for that matter. Others, however, point out that while identities have no reality independent of people's perceptions, the belief by social actors that their identities are real is itself a social fact. In other words, identities are socially "real," inasmuch as socially significant acts are based on ideas of identities (Labbé 2000). For instance, while there is no objective "Macedonian" identity, there is little doubt that social movements and political parties exist whose action is based on the belief in such an identity. The social import of these movements and parties is certainly "real" and, at the same time, likely to affect how individuals define themselves. In this vein, enumerating identities is akin to sorting out how people subjectively define themselves *vis-à-vis* others. As Bulmer claimed, during a debate on the merits of introducing a race/ethnicity question on the British census:

The use of "race" (and the term itself is unsatisfactory and even misleading) in the context of social research refers to the way in which members of a society perceive differences between groups in that society and define the boundaries of such groups, taking into account physical characteristics and skin colour . . . What the ethnic question is trying to do is to find out in as objective a manner as possible how members of British society identify themselves. (Bulmer 1980: 5)

In other words, the census sets its goal as that of *objectively* assessing the state of *subjective* identities. As has already become clear from our discussion of contemporary Western cases, however, the categorization of subjective categories by census-makers is more often than not a matter of political *negotiation*, rather than objective assessment.

While among scholars constructivist approaches have demystified the "scientific" nature of census identity categories, outside the scholarly community many people remain wedded to contrary views. Anthropologists have recently shown consirable interest in the ways that the powerful have attempted to use statistics and quantification to lend themselves the legitimacy of science, to appear to speak truth to the benighted. Urla (1993: 819) refers to this as the equation of knowledge with measurement, and writes of statistics as "technologies of truth production." She herself examines these issues in the heart of Europe, analyzing the fraught political relations of the Basques to the modern Spanish state. In that study, she points out that censuses and social statistics are not simply means of state domination, but also seized on by insurgent political forces to create their own construction of social reality (1993: 837). Far from being a scientific enterprise removed from the political fray, the census is more like a political battleground where competing notions of "real" identities, and therefore competing *names* to assign to categories, battle it out. The prize is a census category which will "scientifically" legitimate the existence of a socially imagined group.

Pierre Bourdieu (1991: 105) discusses this power to create social reality through the use of words. "By structuring the perception which social agents have of the social world," he writes, "the act of naming helps to establish the structure of the world, and does so all the more significantly the more widely it is recognized, i.e. authorized." Although not citing Bourdieu, David Goldberg (1997: 29) echoes him in examining the use of race in the US census, referring to the census as "an exercise in social naming, in nominating into existence." The fiction is maintained – or at least is attempted – that the racial categories used in the censuses, and the process of assigning individuals to each category, simply reflect a pre-existing property of the world, and a scientific effort to capture it objectively. In Goldberg's (1997: 34) phrase, "The census reflects the racializing categories of social formation that it nevertheless at once reifies, which it reproduces as it creates and cements as it naturalizes. The process of objectified nomination thus fixes (at least temporarily and tenuously) what are at best racial fabrications."

Southeastern Europe gives us some of the most dramatic evidence of a political struggle over nominating ethnic groups into existence. At the turn of the twentieth century, political boundaries in the Balkans were unstable, with the Ottoman Empire receding in influence and several states competing over territory. Among the most contested areas was Macedonia, an Ottoman possession claimed by Bulgaria, Serbia, and Greece. At a time when, according to the "principle of nationalities," the legitimacy of territorial sovereignty was determined by the ethnicity (cultural nationality) of the population, the three emerging Orthodox states had reason for adopting a different view. Each sought to define the population in a way that would produce majorities, or at least pluralities, for those claimed ethnically as "theirs." Population figures produced around this time (1889–1905) by Bulgarian, Serb, and Greek authors, and retrospectively by a Turkish author (1975), offered wildly varying accounts of the identity of the population, as can be seen from the collection of figures gathered by Friedman (1996: 85),[10] describing the population of "Macedonia" (see Table 1.1).

Bulgarian, Serbian, and Turkish authors all found that their own ethnic group was in a majority in Macedonia, while the Greek author claimed a plurality of Greeks. One is tempted to impute the huge variations (from 71 percent of Serbs to none!) to willful fabrication, the accusation of choice found in all nationalist literature. "Fabrication," however, while

1.1 *Ethnic Composition of Macedonia, 1889–1905*

Ethnic group by percentage	Source of census figures			
	Bulgarian	*Serbian*	*Greek*	*Turkish*
Bulgarians	52.3%	2.0%	19.3%	30.8%
Serbians	0.0	71.4	0.0	3.4
Greeks	10.1	7.0	37.9	10.6
Albanians	5.7	5.8	0.0	0.0
Turks	22.1	8.1	36.8	51.8
Others	9.7	5.9	6.1	3.4
Total	100	100	100	100

Source: Friedman (1996: 85).

certainly a factor, largely misses the point, since it assumes, in the tradition of statistical realism, a correct and objective method of counting identities, whose process is then spoiled by political elements.

Cultural identities in Macedonia were complex, with much of the population multilingual, religion (Orthodoxy, Catholicism, Islam) crosscutting languages, three Patriarchates (Serbian, Bulgarian, Greek) contending for the loyalty of Orthodox believers, and much of the population having a weak "national" consciousness, in the modern sense of the word. All four competing powers rejected the existence of a "Macedonian" ethnic identity, which explains its absence from Friedman's table, even though archival sources attest that a growing number of people were beginning to define themselves as such at the time (Brown 1996).

The argument of the Bulgarian and Serbian nationalists was that the Slavic language spoken in Macedonia was a dialectical version of their own language, and therefore Slav-speakers were Bulgarian or Serbian, respectively. The Greek position used language as well, but less the vernacular than the language learned at school. Conveniently (if not coincidentally), Greek schools were prevalent in the area, since Greek was the language of prestige and commerce throughout the Balkans. Greek nationalists also used church affiliation as a criterion, counting all those pledging allegiance to the Greek Orthodox Patriarchate as theirs and not recognizing the rival Bulgarian Orthodox Church (the Exarchate). The Albanians, meanwhile, were either a minor or non-existent category in these population figures, being counted as part of the group of each author according to their assumed religious affiliation (Albanian-speaking populations being of Muslim, Orthodox, and Catholic backgrounds).

The "Turks" who constituted a majority in the Turkish source included a number of Albanian-speakers.

The figures cited by Friedman were computed from censuses conducted in Ottoman Macedonia, either by the state or churches, where a *direct* question on nationality (ethnicity) was not asked. The original data, on religion and language, was collected under techniques hardly statistically valid, since the practice was to extrapolate from the number of males in households and the counting itself was capricious (Van Gennep 1992: 120). Moreover, the different authors interpreting the raw data had different conceptions of the geographical boundaries of Macedonia, which probably accounts for some of the important discrepancies in the estimates of "Turks." However scientifically inadequate these numerical exercises were from a technical standpoint, the various and conflicting criteria used to define the categories in the Macedonian case are not the exception but the *norm* of census politics, if perhaps a bit extreme.

The refusal to count

Nominating into existence implies its reverse – the refusal to name. The geographic area of Macedonia was partitioned in 1912. The Yugoslav state, which inherited northeastern Macedonia, eventually recognized a Macedonian "nationality" on its census after World War II. By contrast, the Greek and Bulgarian states refused to recognize such an identity in the Macedonian territories that came under their jurisdictions. In the Soviet Union, which recognized over a hundred nationalities, Hirsch (1997) documents how the definitive list of nationalities was drawn up in the 1920s and 1930s by ethnographers, under pressure from party officials and, to some extent, local ethnic entrepreneurs. The comparative point is that once a decision to count cultural groups is made, there are inevitably other claimants who feel that their group is being denied an existence on the census, and thus in society.

The refusal to count can also be the consequence of a group's fear of being shown to be in the minority and therefore of losing political power. Examples abound. In Burundi, ethnic categorizations have been officially ruled out to mask the domination of the state by the Tutsis, who are vastly outnumbered by the Hutus (Uvin, this volume). In Mauritania, the Moor-dominated government suppressed the results of the 1978 census, a decision interpreted by the ethnic Kewri as an implicit acknowledgment that the Kewri had acquired a majority (Horowitz 1985: 195). In Pakistan, the government postponed the census five times between 1991 and 1998, fearing violence by groups likely to claim that they were undercounted. When the results of the 1998 census finally began to appear, the demographic proportions of the major ethnic groups were virtually unchanged from those of the 1981 census, a highly implausible, but politically safe, outcome (Weiss 1999). The Pakistani exercise amounted to a refusal to count.

The refusal to count can also operate at a deeper level. In various states at various times any use of cultural markers to divide citizens into separate categories has been rejected. Such rejection can arise from an ideological conception of the nation by state elites, or it can result from political pressure. Two of the chapters in this volume discuss cases of modern states that steadfastly refuse to use ethnic categories in their censuses. In Israel, as argued in Goldscheider's chapter, the ideology of Zionism is premised on the notion that ethnic markers among Israeli Jews are the product of the historic exile of the Jewish people. In this view, the return to the "homeland" constitutes a break with the diaspora mentality, and the various ethnic identities of Jewish immigrants will inevitably fuse, within generations, into an Israeli *sabra* identity. Counting ethnicity runs counter to the Israeli nation-building project.

In France, as detailed in Blum's chapter, the republican conception of the "nation," defined as the sum of the state's citizens, admits no other public identity than the civic identity of French. Since national identity is deemed indivisible, the only permissible division on the census is between the nationals (les Français) and the resident foreigners (les étrangers). Unaffected by the evolving international discourse sympathetic to minority rights, France continues to cling to a vision of the nation which, by its very essence, leaves no legal space for the existence of a "minority," and therefore of ethnically defined groups. A 1991 ruling by the French Constitutional Council that the legal term "Corsican people" (peuple corse) is unconstitutional (Rouland, Pierré-Caps and Poumarède 1996: 241), strongly suggests that the French conception is still deeply engrained. By law, questions on ethnicity, language or religion cannot be asked on the census.[11]

Yet in recent years, given the magnitude of immigration from former colonies, an emotional debate has erupted over the merits of introducing ethnic categories into state-financed surveys, a first step that could lead to their incorporation into the census. All parties to the debate invoke the principle of republicanism and the impermissibility of discrimination according to race, ethnicity, language, or religion. The disagreement is over the relationship between cultural categories and discrimination. The traditional republican stance is that any official categorization is discriminatory and runs the risk of politicizing identities and weakening the cohesion of the French political nation. Revisionists reply that discrimination already exists in social interactions and that one has to "identify in

order to act" (Blum, this volume, citing Simon). In this view, the only efficient way to combat discrimination is to assess discriminatory practices
statistically. This is, in effect, the argument of the proponents of positive discrimination in Britain, the United States, Canada, and Australia.
In considering whether or not to categorize identities, census-makers
thus face a dilemma: on the one hand, categorizing can have beneficial
effects on the excluded; on the other hand, the very possibility of linking
group identities to political benefits can provide incentive for "groups"
to mobilize and demand recognition. Far from merely reflecting what is
"out there," the census can be transformed into a mechanism of identity
formation.

Counting fluid identities: the language conundrum

A key argument that has been used to counter the revisionist position
in the contemporary French debate is that reducing ethnicity to a single
census criterion, such as origin or language, greatly distorts the complex
and changing identities of immigrants and their children. In the words
of Blum (this volume), "Ethnicity cannot be defined by a criterion like
origin, whether it is defined by place of birth or descent, since it results
from a combination of multiple criteria, having equally to do with origin,
place of residence, social networks, migratory path, and so forth."

Yet, as we have seen, there is a clear trend in "immigrant" countries
to select the criterion of *origins* in enumerating the ethnic background
of their population. In Canada, the emphasis towards the past is quite
explicit, since the ethnic question on the 2001 census asks: "To which
ethnic or cultural group(s) did this person's *ancestors* [in bold in the
text] belong?" (Census Questionnaire 2001). The question does not directly ask about the ethnic identity of the respondent at the time of the
census, but assumes that this identity coincides with that of his/her ancestors. A similar approach is used in the United States. McKenney,
Farley, and Lewin (1983, cited in McKenney and Cresce 1993: 196)
have justified this new approach by arguing that the new ancestry question minimizes confusion between birthplace and ethnic origin. That is,
if an Italian-origin family lived in Argentina for two generations prior
to moving to the United States, a question about birthplace would be
answered Argentina, while the same individual might reply Italian to
the ancestry question. This is a revealing rationale. While it is true that
birthplace is a weak indicator of ethnicity, it is not clear from its logic
who would qualify as having Argentinean ancestry, as presumably everyone (even the native Americans) at some point had come from some-
where else. The emphasis on ancestry assumes a kind of ethnic purity.

Third-generation immigrant offspring are treated as if they were as ethnically differentiated as their forebears; Italians are viewed as if they were living generation after generation in a closed breeding population within another country. Such a perspective is totally at odds with the consensus in anthropology and political science, which sees unchanging "primordial" identities as a figment of the nationalist imagination.

The movement to privilege the past, and not the present, in formulating census identity criteria has in fact a long pedigree, as old as the first modern censuses in Europe and inextricably linked to the use of *language* categories. As Arel explains in his chapter, while Eastern European statisticians, in the latter part of the nineteenth century, agreed on the desirability of inserting a (cultural) nationality variable in censuses, they long debated which criteria should be used to ascertain the nationality of a respondent. Should nationality be asked directly, as in "What is your nationality?" Or should it be ascertained indirectly, by asking about one's language, and then inferring national identity from the language? All agreed that language was a key component of nationality, although hardly the only one. After much debate, a consensus emerged, with plenty of dissension nonetheless, that language should be selected as an indirect marker of nationality.

Language, however, can be asked in many different ways – as either native language (mother tongue), language of home, or language of use. The 1872 St. Petersburg session of the International Statistical Congress recommended that "mother tongue" be used as the language indicator, but that recommendation was not followed in multilingual Austria where *Umgangsprache* (language of use) was the criterion used in the four censuses administered between 1880 and 1910. Czech nationalists strongly objected to a question emphasizing *current use*, as opposed to *first language learned*, since many people of Czech mother tongue, settled in predominantly German-speaking cities in Austrian Bohemia, might be tempted to answer "German" if the question were posed that way (Zeman 1990: 32–33).

Since language acted as a surrogate for "nationality," Czech nationalists argued that the census *Umgangsprache* data underrepresented them. Someone speaking German outside of the home, but Czech at home, was still a Czech. The opposition to *Umgangsprache*, however, was driven by a sentiment far more essentialist than a plea for statistical precision. The Czech nationalist position could not accept the idea that someone of Czech-speaking parents might actually "become" a German, as this type of language re-identification was portrayed as "forced," resulting from the unjust policies of an imperial state. A "true" count of the Czech nation, from this perspective, had to be "backward-looking." Since linguistic assimilation is seen as unnatural and illegitimate, what must be recorded is the language *that used to predominate*, either earlier in one's lifetime or among one's ancestors.

It is worth recalling here Brubaker's (1996: 79) definition of nationalism "as a form of remedial political action ... [addressing] an allegedly deficient or 'pathological' condition and [proposing] to remedy it". This encapsulates what census identity debates are about: the recognition of "truer" realities over fallacious ones. In this perspective, "mother tongue" reflects less the language of an individual, than the language of the nation to whom the individual is supposed to belong. Similarly, "ethnic origins" in the Western immigrant countries is more about *assumed* belonging (assumed from the outside, that is) than about *felt* belonging. Accordingly, census primordialism – the equation of present ethnic/national identity with ancestral identity – appears to be as potent today as it was a century ago.

Bottom-up efforts to influence census categories

Ever since censuses began, state efforts to pigeon-hole each individual into a single category of identity, and then conceive of the whole population as divisible into these units, have faced resistance. The people so categorized have struggled both to change the categories and to change their distribution across them. Indeed, one of the most important of the topics we probe in this book is the evolution of the locus of power over the construction of identity categories in the census. Who actually decides what categories and what principles are to be employed in generating these collective identities? Are we correct in thinking that there has been a major shift from census categories decided from on high to those crafted through a complex and messy process of political struggle, involving interest groups formed from the people being categorized?

The history of the US census suggests that such a shift has taken place. Whether this observation holds comparatively cries out for research. In the case of the Soviet Union, the evolution of the locus of power over the construction of identities can best be seen as a boomerang cycle. The initial census categories, in the 1920s and 1930s, were shaped to a remarkable extent by national elites and scholars sympathetic to nationality claims (Hirsch 1997). Subsequent debate over the categories was frozen for many years by Party fiat. With the demise of the Soviet Union, the democratizing conditions in several post-Soviet states has once again made their first independent censuses (particularly in Russia, Ukraine, and the Baltics) the political battleground that it has proven to be in so many other countries.

Even when the determination of census categories remained in the hands of imperial bureaucrats in Eastern Europe and in various overseas colonies, a great deal of popular agitation was aroused. Parties and movements acting in the name of ethnic groups sought to convince putative members of the group to register as such. In Austrian Bohemia, for instance, Czech parties campaigned to have people of Czech descent claim "Czech" as *Umgangsprache*, and when the tide began to turn favorably to the Czech language in certain urban areas, German parties began their own campaign in favor of claiming "German" (Arel, this volume).

Another enlightening case concerns Imperial India, where the British went to great lengths to categorize the colonized along a variety of markers, revolving around the fundamental category (in their eyes) of caste. By the time of the 1931 census, as Cohn recounts, the political significance of this process of assigning identities to the Indian population had become so pronounced that some groups organized to promote certain responses to the census-takers questions. A flyer, entitled "Remember! Census Operations Have Begun" (see below), distributed just before the census by one such group in Lahore, entreated the local population to make particular responses (Cohn 1987: 249).

Remember!
Census Operations Have Begun

Question	*You should answer!*
Religion	Vedi Dharm
Sect	Arya Samajist
Caste	Nil
Race	Aryan
Language	Arya Bhasha

This makes the census far closer, in many ways, to a political campaign than to a technical exercise in counting. The activists involved in the agitation generally believe that the identities they are promoting are primordial, and therefore not a matter of choice. Yet they are concerned that many of their co-ethnics are not fully aware of their own "true" identity, and so must be reminded of their roots.

Often, however, people targeted by such campaigning are well aware of their roots, but do not share the backward-looking premise of the nationalist groups. In Belgium, in the post-war period, parents of Flemish mother tongue in Brussels were more interested in claiming French than Flemish as their language on the census, to the despair of Flemish nationalist groups. The parents were motivated by their interest in sending their children to French schools, a desire which they knew would be facilitated by the statistical "finding" of a greater proportion of "French-speakers" in their district (Arel, forthcoming). Statistical realists have decried this confusion between a plebiscite and a census (Lévy 1960). Yet, since identity is subjective and contingent upon social and political factors, one wonders whether it would not be more fruitful to view the census – or, at least, the identity questions of a census – as a type of plebiscite (Labbé 2000).

In many Western countries, efforts to alter the use of ethnic and racial categorization involve not only lobbying respondents to place themselves in one category or another, but lobbying the designers of the census to alter the categories used. Lieberson (1993: 29–30), deliberately overstating the matter, has argued that now "each ethnic group has the potential ability to control its own enumeration – in the sense of a veto on how it is defined, classified and described. However, each group has no veto power over other groups." He argues that these ethnic lobbying groups present their case as a matter of basic morality and, in so far as they are in a position to bring unfavorable publicity to politicians, are a potent force where such matters are concerned.

One of the most significant examples of this process comes from the United States. In 1970, in response to the urgings of various ethnic lobbying groups, the census bureau introduced a question asking a sample of respondents if they were of "Hispanic" origin. Those who answered positively were then asked if they fit into one of five categories (Mexican, Puerto Rican, Cuban, Central or South American, Other Spanish). This effort led to many criticisms, which were taken up by the US Commission on Civil Rights in 1974. Their report, provocatively titled "Counting the Forgotten," blasted the Census Bureau for a poorly conceived effort at counting Hispanics. It urged them to include a newly revised question to be asked of every individual on the 1980 census, which would be "responsive to the needs of the Spanish-speaking background population." The following year, the Census Bureau formed a special advisory committee on the Spanish origin population, having a year earlier established such a committee on the "Black Population." By 1976, political logic had led inevitably to the formation of a third advisory committee, this one devoted to the Asian and Pacific Island population (Conk 1987: 177–78). Controversy has continued to surround the design of these ethnic and racial identity questions. For our purposes, however, what is most notable is the role of the census in the invention and legitimization of such categories of collective identity as "Hispanic".

Census politics undoubtedly has a strong emotional dimension, for it matters a great deal to many people that the groups they identify with are granted official recognition. As Geertz stated in his classic article (1963), "The peoples of the new states are simultaneously animated by two powerful, thoroughly interdependent, yet distinct and often actually opposed motives – the desire to be recognized as responsible agents whose wishes, acts, hopes, and opinions 'matter,' and the desire to build an efficient, dynamic modern state." The historical record has since demonstrated that the desire for such recognition can be as potent among groups in the "old" states as well.

Yet the instrumental dimension of census politics may be just as important since, in the age of the modern state as a provider of social and economic benefits, group recognition in the census entails group *entitlement* to certain rights. Group-differentiated social programs may be directed to certain cities depending on the proportion of their ethnic population. Cross tabulations, with nationality, language, or race as one of the variables, can be used to suggest how some groups lag behind others on certain indicators, leading to demands for further remedial policies by the state.

Since census politics is expressed in numbers, the pursuit of entitlement translates into a contest for achieving the "right" numbers. This may mean remaining in the "majority," according to a politically salient criterion, or at least not falling below a certain numerical threshold. The census can become so politically contested precisely because it is the most important means by which "majorities" and "minorities" can be officialized (Anderson 1998). Identity politics is a numbers game, or more precisely a battle over relative proportions, both within the state and within particular territories of the larger state. Groups fear a change of proportion disadvantageous to themselves, as this often directly affects how political and economic power are allocated. They fear becoming a minority in the territory that matters most to them, which can be conceived either as state, a province, or a district.

The Pakistani case strikingly illustrates how census majority politics is intimately linked to the emotional (identity as self-worth) and instrumental (identity as a tool) dimensions of identity. Pakistan is divided into four provinces (Punjab, Sindh, Baluchistan, and the North West Frontier Province [NWFP]), all containing a majority of the eponymous ethnic group (Pakhtuns, in the case of NWFP). For any of these groups losing its territorial majority is politically unthinkable, as it would call into question the group's legitimacy to rule over the territory that it considers its *own*.[12] Moreover, each ethnic group is given a quota in federal representation and services (including government jobs and university admissions), determined by the relative proportion of the group in the general population as shown in the census. For this reason, falling below their existing quota is also deemed politically unacceptable. This made the government afraid, for security reasons, to come up with results making some groups the relative losers of the entitlement game (Weiss 1999). Lebanon faced a similar dilemma in the post-war period, when its stability rested on a delicate political balance, apportioned by ethnic criteria. Not surprisingly, no census could be conducted.

In states recognizing the existence of language minorities, the census often becomes a major arena of contention in determining where and according to what criteria the minority language will be used in state-supported institutions. Disputes include the minimum proportion of language-speakers necessary for a language to be used in schools and administration (a proportion which varies greatly across cases), the boundaries of the area where the threshold applies (city or province?), and, as we saw above, the very census indicators ascertaining the proportion of language-speakers (mother tongue or language of use?) (Arel, this volume). The fear of falling below the threshold and "losing out" (assimilating) in the long run can become so fierce, and politically destabilizing, that some states have decided to eliminate the census altogether, or at least the questions regarding ethnic identity.

It is useful here to briefly revisit the classic case of Belgium, where the language question was removed from the census in 1960 following political upheaval over the issue of a "threshold." Belgian law mandated that Brussels districts (communes) with a minimum of 30 percent of Francophones had to offer services in French, including schools. The 1947 census, which was the first to apply the law, showed that several heretofore unilingual Flemish districts had become legally bilingual. Flemish parties interpreted this as an inexorable, and intolerable, trend towards their minoritization all over Brussels. The situation became politically untenable and, in 1960, a compromise was achieved preventing the census, or any other state-funded activity, from inquiring about language, thereby "freezing" the language status of communes (Van Velthonen 1987).

The impact of census categories on identity formation

The requirement that each individual be pigeon-holed in a culturally defined category had major implications for how people came to think of themselves, implications that would have a tremendous impact on the creation of politically important interest groups. Bernard Cohn tells how, beginning with the intellectuals of Bengal in the nineteenth century and then spreading to all of the educated Indians in the twentieth century, people began to *objectify* their culture. Not least influential in this process was the need to employ half a million literate Indians to carry out the census of the late nineteenth century. These census-takers were taught to think of the people around them as divisible into clear-cut cultural categories, and taught as well what the crucial distinguishing marks were to be. What previously had been part of the complex web of relationships, practices, and beliefs they shared now became something quite different. An identifiable, distinct culture was distinguished, allowing people to "stand back and look at themselves, their ideas, their symbols and culture and see it as an entity." Once they conceived of themselves as part of a culture in this objectified sense, they could then, as part of the political process, select aspects of that culture, and polish and reformulate them in pursuing their goals (Cohn 1987: 228–29).

The case of Soviet Central Asia is also instructive regarding the impact of state categorizations on the formation of identities. Abramson (this volume) shows how the Soviet system of dividing its population into mutually exclusive cultural nationalities in the 1920s was appropriated by Uzbek elites. After Soviet officials decreed, in 1924, that the "Uzbeks" were a "nationality," it took four years for local elites to agree on who, among the population, should be classified as Uzbeks, largely on the basis of dialects. When Moscow established Soviet republics on the basis of nationality, some newly self-defined Uzbeks ended up on the wrong side of the border. Hirsch (2000: 216) tells the story of Uzbek-identified border villages, assigned to neighboring Kirgizia, whose inhabitants petitioned Moscow to be included in Uzbekistan. She is struck by how adept the petitioners were at using the rhetoric of nationality, which until a few years before had been foreign to the region:

Did the petitioners really *believe* that they were members of a discrete Uzbek nationality? We can never really know. The point is that the petitioners used the language of nationality in their interactions with the state and in doing so helped make official nationality categories real. Indeed, perhaps what is most remarkable is that the petitioners did not question the official assumption that "national identity" was linked to land, water, and other resources. Many of the residents of the new Central Asian republics themselves expressed surprise about how quickly nationality categories took root after national-territorial delimitation.

Even more boldly, Appadurai (1993: 317) has argued that colonial census practices themselves "helped to ignite communitarian and nationalist identities that in fact undermined colonial rule." In the same vein, Kateb has shown how the French colonial state, by denying French nationality (in the sense of citizenship) to Muslims, paradoxically created a national Algerian Muslim identity from a hodgepodge of local affiliations (1998: 105). Zeman (1994: 31), in his study of the Imperial Austrian censuses of this period, observes that the effort to record a cultural nationality for each individual "made a direct contribution to the conflict . . . between the nationalities. A device designed by the civil servants to make the Monarchy more easily governable in fact created a large new area of civil strife." What the relationship is between the modern project of exercising firmer control over populations by extending a more thorough statistical gaze over them and the eventual mobilization of these populations against the imperial/colonial regimes remains a provocative question.

Whether in colonial settings, or in other places where centralized state power is supreme, state-defined identity categories can have a substantial impact on people, altering pre-existing lines of identity divisions within the society. "State officials," writes James Scott, "can often make their categories stick and impose their simplifications." The categories used by the state, he argues, "begun as the artificial inventions of cadastral surveyors, census-takers [etc.] . . . can end by becoming categories that organize people's daily experiences precisely because they are embedded in state-created institutions that structure that experience." The classification of ethnicity, and other forms of state-mandated identity categorization, "acquire their force from the fact that these synoptic data are the points of departure for reality as state officials apprehend and shape it." Where the state is powerful, the "categories used by state agents are not merely means to make their environment legible; they are an authoritative tune to which most of the population must dance" (1998: 81–83).

The realization that governmental statistics-gathering and census-taking have been influential in creating and manipulating identities has led to a new look in the scholarly community at government statistical agencies. In a movement that can be traced in part to the influence of Foucault, some of those social analysts and historians who had previously been least interested in statistics, demography, or governmental record-keeping, have recently come to see the production of statistics as of central importance.

When preparations for the 2000 US census got underway, few topics generated more protest and anguish than the requirement that an individual place him or herself in a single racial category. Revealingly, however, this protest was less politically successful than other, much less visible protests, because it was not linked to any well-organized political lobbying group. Indeed, the demands that have filled the letters-to-the-editor sections of many newspapers, asking that people not be forced to place themselves in a single, neat racial or ethnic category, have been met by strong opposition from those who represent ethnic and racial organizations.

This is a point of great interest in understanding the evolution of censuses and the role they have played in constructing collective identities. What is curious, yet highly revealing, is that while many individuals who feel violated by these rules and practices have voiced strong opposition to them, the leaders of organizations that define themselves in racial terms have strongly backed them. Ironically, given the history of race relations in the US, the continued use of a fundamentally racist ideology ('one drop of Negro blood makes a Negro') has been most effectively championed by African-American organizations. Similarly, both the creation of the ethnic group "Hispanic" and its continued use in the census have been primarily the product of political interest groups who define their membership through such ethnic constructions.

Anthropologists have long been intrigued by the human compulsion to divide the observed world into categories, and by people's discomfort with those people, animals, or other objects who do not seem to fit into a single category (Levi-Strauss 1966; Douglas 1966). This human drive lies behind the universal efforts not only of elites and state officials but also of people of all kinds to divide the social universe into neat categories. In this context, those preferring the blurring of categories confront not only actors whose interests lie in championing their own categorical identities, but a more general difficulty of promulgating identities that fail to fall in any simple category at all.

One other relatively new element of censuses should be considered in this context: the move from census forms filled out by enumerators to those filled out by the respondents themselves. The notion that only the individual has the right to decide which identity category he or she should be placed in is a powerful force in the world today. This can be viewed as part of the western ideology of modern individualism, which Handler (1988: 51) refers to as – following Macpherson – as "possessive individualism." The idea here is that people demonstrate their individuality through making choices for themselves; their identity is something that they themselves produce, and so own.[13]

Self-identification for the census, however, has its practical, and sometimes ideological, limits. As tabulated results can list only so many entries, some identities get either lumped in an "Other" category or subsumed into existing ones. The latter occurs when an identity is unrecognized by census authorities. As Abramson explains in his chapter, in the last Soviet census of 1989 there were almost seven times as many self-identified "nationalities" (823) as recognized ones (128). Thus, even when self-identification is allowed, the recoding of people's responses into a smaller set of categories plays a large role in the statistical representation of groups.

This move to place the respondent in charge of filling out the census form only became possible when and where literacy became universal, and so is still not found in many countries of the world. However, where people now compile their own form, racial and ethnic categorization must cope with a much more chaotic hodgepodge of self-labeling processes. Even, for example, if directions indicate that an individual of mixed "Indian" and "Negro" "blood" should identify with the category reflecting the greatest proportion of "blood," many individuals who identify as native American simply list themselves as native Americans. This reminds us, once more, that what is measured by the census is a particular kind of politicized social construction of reality.

The continuing political and social importance of census categorization

Census categorization of populations by various markers of identity – race, ethnic group, language, religion – has a two-hundred-year history. Today there are few countries which do not have regular population censuses; yet significantly, in those cases where censuses are not held, it is often the very process of enumerating populations by various markers of collective identity that is viewed as most threatening and discourages census enumeration.

The census, although only one of many government information-gathering devices, is arguably the most important and certainly the most universal. As such, investigating the census/identity matrix offers a privileged vantage point for examining such fundamental social and political issues as the growth and evolution of nationalism, ethnic conflict, racism, and transnational identity formation and organization. But these processes should be seen in the larger context of how individuals come to assert certain collective identities for themselves, how they come to assign them to others, and the role that state authorities play in these collective identity processes. This raises a much broader field of inquiry than we have been able to examine in this chapter (or in this book), relating to a newly emerging field of studies. It is a field that includes studies that range from the historical examination of the state's imposition of surnames to the emergence of modern criminology and state surveillance of populations through passports, fingerprinting, and the like (Noiriel 1996; Torpey 2000).

We have seen, too, that the numbers produced through census or census-like categorization schemes can have important political consequences. At its most dramatic, claims to majority status for an "ethnic group" or "nationality" in a particular geographical area can be central to claims for political power. As the case of the Balkans today makes painfully clear, the matter of influencing counts in various ethnic categories is not only a matter of getting people to identify themselves in certain ways when the census-taker comes around. It is also linked to the use of force to empty territories of people associated with other identities, and hence justify a claim to political ownership of the land by those sharing the collective identity deemed to be in the majority.

Examination of the relationship between the census and the formation and evolution of collective identities, as we have seen, involves us in the messy process of politics. We witness the struggle among a multiplicity of actors over that most basic of powers, the power to name, to categorize, and thus to create social reality.

The nature of the contestation over such categorization varies in different parts of the world, as it has over time. Yet, as we have seen, some important parallels can be found when we look at these questions in comparative perspective. It is part of our effort in this volume to examine these similarities, and these differences, to see what general principles are operating, and what their implications are for processes of collective identity formation and for the relationship between states and their citizens.

NOTES

We would like to thank Regine Heberlein and Hamutal Bernstein for their research assistance, as well as all of the participants in the Conference on Categorizing Citizens for their helpful comments on an earlier version of this chapter. We would especially like to thank Michael Herzfeld, Keith Brown, Pamela Ballinger, John Modell, Susan Woodward, Laura Jenkins and three anonymous reviewers for their written suggestions.

1 In Spring 2000, the recently elected Greek government announced that the "religion" entry would be removed from identity cards, to conform with European Union standards. This provoked a storm of protest from the Greek Orthodox church, which argued that, since Greece is the only Orthodox state in the Union, such a policy would imperil Greek identity (Smith 2000).

2 Official certificates of ethnic status were apparently first used to regulate the 1922 transfer of populations between Greece and Bulgaria. Candidates for emigration had to obtain the certificate from the mayor of their commune (Institut National de la Statistique 1946: 77).

3 A good study of the intra-state workings of identity politics can be found in the chapter "Homeland Nationalism in Weimar Germany and 'Weimar Russia'," in Brubaker (1996). The author details how various state and quasi-state agencies, and voluntary associations, competed to formulate a policy *vis-à-vis* the diaspora Germans of Central Europe. For the ethnography of bureaucracy, see Herzfeld (1992).

4 The selection of older census results (1880), as opposed to recent ones (1920) – the final post-war immigration law was passed in 1924 – was made

to greatly diminish the relative proportion of immigrants from Southern and Eastern Europe, compared to those from the then more "acceptable" states of Western and Northern Europe.

5 At the turn of the century, a popular notion held that northern and southern Italians were of such different "character" that they constituted separate "races." In the *Dictionary of Races or Peoples*, prepared for the US Bureau of Immigration (Report on the Immigration Commission 1911), the South Italians were described as "excitable, impulsive, highly imaginative, impracticable . . . [and having] little adaptability to highly organized society." The North Italians were presented as "cool, deliberate, patient, practical, and . . . capable of great progress in the political and social organization of modern civilization."

6 In the 2001 census, the category "White" has been subdivided into "British" and "Irish" for England and Wales, while the questionnaire distributed in Scotland and Northern Ireland will have the sole "White" category along with the various identities of ex-colonials. The three territorially-grounded ethnic identities of "Irish" (in Ireland itself), "Scots," and "Welsh" will thus continue to be absent from the census question, which is officially called the "Ethnic Group question." Interestingly, the category "Irish Traveller" – a group akin to Gypsies in terms of local perceptions – was added to the categories in Northern Ireland (*The 2001 Census of Population*, 1999).

7 Ryder, quoted by Simon (1997b: 22), claims that the fact that English Canadians spoke of the "founding races," which French Canadians translated as "founding peoples," suggests a misunderstanding in the meaning to be ascribed to the founding communities. Yet, French Canadians also referred to themselves as "la race canadienne-française," in the European turn-of-the-century cultural connotation of the term.

8 The French- and English-speaking groups were originally called "Canadien" and "English." When descendants of English settlers began to identify as "Canadians," the French speakers became the "French Canadians." In the 1996 census, 42 percent of the "Canadians" in the origin question were from Quebec.

9 Since "national" consciousness correlates with urbanization and industrialization, many immigrants to the United States, rural and uneducated, tended to carry a regional identification and have little, if any, sense of a national belonging. Most "Italians," for instance, identified as "Calabrian," "Sicilian," "Neapolitan," and so forth. The "Poles" cited by Petersen also gave regional identities (Connor 1993: 221). After 1899, the US Bureau of Immigration, unlike the US Census Bureau, sought to classify immigrants by "races" (in the cultural sense then prevalent in Europe) and to recode a lot of these regional identities into one of forty-eight "races or peoples" it recognized on its official list (Keith Brown, personal communication).

10 Table A.1, "Conflicting Census Figures for Macedonia 1889–1905" in Friedman (1996: 85) mistakenly gives the figure of 13.86 for the percentage of "Others" claimed by Serbian sources. The correct figure, derived from the absolute figures provided in the Table, is 5.86 percent.

11 As previously mentioned, the French did introduce such cultural categories in colonial censuses, in order to differentiate among the colonized masses

who, perforce, were not citizens. On census practices in Algeria, see Kateb 1998.

12 The same principle operated in the Soviet Union, where federal units were named after the "titular" group (called nationality). The former republic of Kazakhstan, independent since 1992, did not actually have an ethnic majority of Kazakhs in the last Soviet census of 1989. For reasons of territorial legitimacy, everyone expected that the first post-Soviet Kazakhstani census would register a majority of ethnic Kazakhs, whether "true" or not, and it did (Peter Sinnott, personal communication).

13 Although a distinction should be made between whether a census-taker fills out the form (as opposed to the respondent) and who decides what identity category the respondent is placed into. Even when the enumerator filled out the form, at least in the European cases, the question of the appropriate identity category in which the individual should be placed had long been a matter for the respondent to determine. Labbé (1998: 220), in this context, examines the attempts of the Nazi regime to take away from individuals the right to categorize their own race/ethnicity.

REFERENCES

Anderson, Benedict 1991, *Imagined Communities*, New York: Verso.
    1997, "Recensement et politique en Asie du Sud-Est," *Genèse* 26: 55–76.
    1998, *The Spectre of Comparisons*, New York: Verso.
Appadurai, Arjun 1993, "Number in the Colonial Imagination," in Carol A. Breckenridge and Peter van der Veer (eds.), *Orientalism and the Postcolonial Predicament*, Philadelphia: University of Pennsylvania Press, pp. 314–39.
Arel, Dominique 2001, "Political Stability in Multinational Democracies: Comparing Language Dynamics in Brussels, Montreal, and Barcelona," in Alain-G. Gagnon and James Tully (eds.), *Multinational Democracies*, Cambridge: Cambridge University Press, pp. 65–89.
Ballard Roger 1997, "The Construction of a Conceptual Vision: 'Ethnic Groups' and the 1991 UK Census," *Ethnic and Racial Studies* 20: 182–94.
Behar, Cem 1998, "Qui compte? 'Recensements' et statistiques démographiques dans l'Empire ottoman, du XVIe au XXe siècle," *Histoire & Mesure* 13: 135–45.
Bhrolcháin, Máire N' 1990, "The Ethnicity Question for the 1991 Census: Background and Issues," *Ethnic and Racial Studies* 13: 542–67.
Booth, Heather 1985, "Which 'Ethnic Question'?: The Development of Questions Identifying Ethnic Origin in Official Statistics," *Sociological Review* 32: 254–74.
Bourdieu, Pierre 1991, *Language and Symbolic Power*, Cambridge, Mass.: Harvard University Press.
Boyd, Monica 1993, "Measuring Ethnicity in the Future: Population, Policies and Social Science Research," in Gustave Goldmann *et al.* (eds.), *Challenges of Measuring an Ethnic World*, Washington, DC: Bureau of the Census; Ottawa: Statistics Canada, pp. 529–46.

Brown, Keith 1996, "Friction in the Archives: Nations and Negotiations on Ellis Island (NY), 1904–10," Paper presented at the Tenth Annual Conference of the Council for European Studies, Chicago, March.

Brubaker, Rogers 1996, *Nationalism Reframed. Nationhood and the National Question in the New Europe*, Cambridge: Cambridge University Press.

Bulmer, Martin 1980, "On the Feasibility of Identifying 'Race' and 'Ethnicity' in Censuses and Surveys," *New Community* 8: 3–16.

"Census Questionnaire 2001," available on the web site of Statistics Canada, www.statcan.ca.

Choldin, Harvey M. 1986, "Statistics and Politics: The 'Hispanic Issue' in the 1980 Census," *Demography* 23: 403–18.

Cohn, Bernard 1987, "The Census, Social Structure and Objectification in South Asia," in *An Anthropologist among the Historians and Other Essays*, Delhi and New York: Oxford University Press, pp. 224–54.

Conk, Margo 1987, "The 1980 Census in Historical Perspective," in William Alonso and Paul Starr (eds.), *The Politics of Numbers*, New York: Russell Sage Foundation, pp. 155–86.

Connor, Walker 1993, *Ethnonationalism: The Quest for Understanding*, Princeton: Princeton University Press.

Cornish, John 1993, "Australia's Experience with Census Questions on Ethnicity," in Gustave Goldmann *et al.* (eds.), *Challenges of Measuring an Ethnic World*, Washington, DC: Bureau of the Census; Ottawa: Statistics Canada, pp. 307–26.

Courbage, Youssef 1997, *Christians and Jews under Islam*, London: Tauris.

1998, "Survey of the Statistical Sources on Religion, Language(s), National and Ethnic Group in Europe," in Werner Haug, Youssef Courbage, and Paul Compton (eds.), *The Demographic Characteristics of National Minorities in Certain European States*, Strasbourg: Council of Europe Publications, pp. 23–74.

Crawford, James 1992, *Hold Your Tongue: Bilingualism and the Politics of English Only*, Reading, Mass.: Addison-Wesley.

Davis, F. James 1991, *Who is Black? One Nation's Definition*, University Park, Penn.: Pennsylvania State University Press.

Desjardins, Chantal 2000, "La multiplication des Canadiens. En 15 ans, le nombre de personnes se déclarant d'origine ethnique ou culturelle canadienne s'est multiplié par cent!" *La Presse* (Montreal), 5 August.

Douglas, Mary 1966, *Purity and Danger*, New York: Praeger.

Fellegi, Ivan P. 1996, "Question 19. StatsCan Responds to Census Critics," *The Gazette* (Montreal), 5 June.

Friedman, Victor A. 1996, "Observing the Observers: Language, Ethnicity, and Power in the 1994 Macedonian Census and Beyond," in Barnett R. Rubin (ed.), *Toward Comprehensive Peace in Southeast Europe*, New York: Twentieth Century Fund Press, pp. 81–128.

Gellner, Ernest 1983, *Nations and Nationalism*, Ithaca: Cornell University Press.

Geertz, Clifford 1963, "The Integrative Revolution: Primordial Sentiments and Civil Politics in the New States," in Geertz (ed.), *Old Societies and New States: The Quest for Modernity in Asia and Africa*, New York: Free Press, pp. 105–57.

Goldberg, David T. 1997, *Racial Subjects: Writing on Race in America*, New York: Routledge.

Goldmann, Gustave *et al.* (eds.), *Challenges of Measuring an Ethnic World: Science, Politics, and Reality*, Proceedings of the Joint Canada – United States Conference on the Measurement of Ethnicity, April 1–3, 1992, Washington, DC: Bureau of the Census; Ottawa: Statistics Canada.

Handler, Richard 1988, *Nationalism and the Politics of Culture in Quebec*, Madison, Wis.: University of Wisconsin Press.

Herzfeld, Michael 1992, *The Social Production of Indifference: Exploring the Symbolic Roots of Western Bureaucracy*, New York: Berg.

Hilberg, Raul 1985, *The Destruction of the European Jews*, New York: Holmes & Meier.

Hirsch, Francine 1997, "The Soviet Union as a Work-in-Progress: Ethnographers and the Category Nationality in the 1926, 1937, and 1939 Censuses," *Slavic Review* 56: 251–78.

2000, "Toward an Empire of Nations: Border-Making and the Formation of Soviet National Identities," *Russian Review* 59: 201–26.

Hirschman, Charles 1987, "The Meaning and Measurement of Ethnicity in Malaysia: An Analysis of Census Classification," *The Journal of Asian Studies* 46: 555–82.

Horowitz, Donald R. 1985, *Ethnic Groups in Conflict*, Berkeley: University of California Press.

Institut National de la Statistique et des Etudes Economiques 1946, *Les transferts internationaux de populations*, Etudes et documents, Series B-2, Paris: Presses Universitaires de France.

Jenkins, Laura 2000, "Separate Tables: The Census and Social Classifications," Paper presented at the Census Workshop, Watson Institute, Brown University, May 4–5.

Kateb, Kamel 1998, "La gestion statistique des populations dans l'empire colonial français," *Histoire & Mesure* 13: 77–111.

Kleeberg, Rudolf 1915, *Die Nationalitätenstatistik. Ihre Ziele, Methoden und Ergebnisse*, Thüringen: Thomas & Hubert.

Labbé, Morgane 1998, "'Race' et 'nationalité' dans les recensements du Troisième Reich," *Histoire & Mesure* 13: 195–223.

2000, "Censuses, Plebiscites and the Categorizations of Identities," Paper presented at the conference "Whose Self-Determination? Agency and Amnesia in the Disintegration of Yugoslavia," Watson Institute, Brown University, February 4–5.

Levi-Strauss, Claude 1966, *The Savage Mind*, Chicago: University of Chicago Press.

Lévy, Paul M. G. 1960, *La querelle du recensement*, Bruxelles: Institut belge de science politique.

Lieberson, Stanley 1993, "The Enumeration of Ethnic and Racial Groups in the Census: Some Devilish Principles," in Gustave Goldmann *et al.* (eds.), *Challenges of Measuring an Ethnic World*, Washington, DC: Bureau of the Census; Ottawa: Statistics Canada, pp. 23–36.

Matthews, Mervyn 1993, *The Passport Society*, Boulder, Col.: Westview Press.

McKenney, Nampeo R. and Cresce, Arthur R. 1993, "Measurement of Ethnicity in the United States: Experiences of the U.S. Census Bureau," in Gustave Goldmann *et al.* (eds.), *Challenges of Measuring an Ethnic World*, Washington, DC: Bureau of the Census; Ottawa: Statistics Canada, pp. 173–222.

Noiriel, Gérard 1996, *The French Melting Pot: Immigration, Citizenship, and National Identity*, Minneapolis: University of Minnesota Press.

Passel, Jeffrey S. 1994, "Racial and Ethnic Differentiation in the United States: Comments and Observations," Paper presented for the Workshop on Race and Ethnicity Classification: An Assessment of the Federal Standard for Racial and Ethnicity Classification, National Academy of Sciences, February 17–18.

Petersen, William 1987, "Politics and the Measurement of Ethnicity," in William Alonso and Paul Starr (eds.), *The Politics of Numbers*, New York: Russell Sage Foundation, pp. 187–233.

1997, *Ethnicity Counts*, New Brunswick, N.J.: Transaction Publishers.

Rabushka, Alvin and Shepsle, Kenneth A. 1972, *Politics in Plural Societies: A Theory of Political Instability*, Columbus, Ohio: Charles E. Merrill Pub. Co.

Reports of the Immigration Commission 1911, *Dictionary of Races or Peoples*, Senate Documents, Vol. 9, 61th Congress, 3d Session, Document No. 602, Washington, DC: Government Printing Office.

Roth, Brigitte 1991, "Quellenkritische Dokumentation der erfassten Berichtskategorien," in Henning Bauer, Andreas Kappeler, and Brigitte Roth (eds.), *Die Nationalitäten des Russischen Reiches in der Volkzählung von 1897*, Vol. 1, Stuttgart: Franz Steiner Verlag, pp. 135–284.

Rouland, Norbert, Pierré-Caps, Stéphane and Poumarède, Jacques (eds.) 1996, *Droit des minorités et des peuples autochtones*, Paris: Presses Universitaires de France.

Scott, James C. 1998, *Seeing Like a State*, New Haven: Yale University Press.

Simon, Patrick 1997a, "La représentation statistique de l'immigration. Peut-on comptabiliser l'ethnicité?" in Jean-Louis Rallu, Youssef Courbage and Victor Piché (eds.), *Anciennes et nouvelles minorités*, Paris: INED, pp. 11–30.

1997b, "La statistique des origines: 'race' et ethnicité dans les recensements aux Etats-Unis, Canada et Grande Bretagne," *Sociétés Contemporaines* 26: 11–44.

Smith, Helena 2000, "Greece Tackles Identity Issue," *Dawn*, 29 May.

Snipp, Matthew C. 1989, *American Indians: The First of the Land*, New York: Sage.

Snyder, Timothy 1998, "The Polish-Lithuanian Commonwealth since 1989. National Narratives in Relations among Poland, Lithuania, Belarus and Ukraine," *Nationalism and Ethnic Politics* 4: 1–32.

Starr, Paul 1987, "The Sociology of Official Statistics," in William Alonso and Paul Starr (eds.), *The Politics of Numbers*, New York: Russell Sage Foundation, pp. 7–57.

Tebarth, Hans-Jakob 1991, "Geschichte der Volkszählung," in Henning Bauer, Andreas Kappeler, and Brigitte Roth (eds.), *Die Nationalitäten des Russischen*

Reiches in der Volkzählung von 1897, Vol. 1, Stuttgart: Franz Steiner Verlag, pp. 25–87.

The 2001 Census of Population 1999, Presented by the Economic Secretary to the Treasury, the Secretary of State for Scotland, and the Secretary of State for Northern Ireland, by Command of Her Majesty, March, http://www.official-documents. co.uk/document/cm42/ 4253/ whitepap.pdf.

Torpey, John 2000, *The Invention of the Passport. Surveillance, Citizenship and the State*. Cambridge: Cambridge University Press.

Urla, Jacqueline 1993, "Cultural Politics in an Age of Statistics: Numbers, Nations, and the Making of Basque Identity," *American Ethnologist* 20: 818–43.

Van Gennep, Arnold 1992 [1922], *Traité des nationalités*, Paris: Editions du CTHS.

Van Velthonen, Harry 1987, "The Process of Language Shift in Brussels: Historical Background and Mechanisms," in Els Witte and Hugo Baetens Beardsmore (eds.), *The Interdisciplinary Study of Urban Bilingualism in Brussels*, Philadelphia: Multilingual Matters.

Weiss, Anita 1999, "Much Ado about Counting. The Conflict over Holding a Census in Pakistan," *Asian Survey* 39: 679–93.

White, Pamela M., Badets, Jane and Renaud, Viviane 1993, "Measuring Ethnicity in Canadian Censuses," in Gustave Goldmann *et al.* (eds.), *Challenges of Measuring an Ethnic World*, Washington, DC: Bureau of the Census; Ottawa: Statistics Canada, pp. 223–70.

White, Philip H. and Pearce, David L. 1993, "Ethnic Group and the British Census," in Gustave Goldmann *et al.* (eds.), *Challenges of Measuring an Ethnic World*, Washington, DC: Bureau of the Census; Ottawa: Statistics Canada, pp. 271–306.

White, R. M. 1979, "What's in a Name? Problems in Official and Legal Usages of 'Race'," *New Community* 7: 333–49.

Willigan, J. Dennis and Lynch, Katherine A. 1982, *Sources and Methods of Historical Demography*, New York: Academic Press.

Zaslavsky, Victor and Luryi, Yuri 1979, "The Passport System in the USSR," *Soviet Union* 6: 137–53.

Zeman, Z.A.B. 1990, "The Four Austrian Censuses and Their Political Consequences ," in Mark Cornwall (ed.), *The Last Years of Austria-Hungary*, Exeter: University of Exeter Press, pp. 31–39.

2   Racial categorization and censuses

Melissa Nobles

Race and census-taking occupy, at present, two discrete but related fields of study. Historians, sociologists, political scientists, anthropologists, legal scholars, theorists, and, of late, cultural critics have taken up the study of race. They seek to explain what race is (and is not), and how, if not why, it matters socially, culturally, economically, and politically. Census-taking has been treated as the domain of demographers and statisticians who examine and study how census-taking, and hence census data, can be made more accurate. Although never hard and fast, disciplinary and conceptual boundaries have kept our understandings of race and census-taking separate, and have thus impoverished our understanding and study of both. Not surprisingly, the parameters that scholarship has managed to erect bear little resemblance to the very real connections between race and censuses in political and social life. Race, however ambiguous, seems a permanent feature of politics in numerous societies. Policymakers, statisticians, scholars, and the general public treat racial census data as important basic facts, and as raw materials for socioeconomic analyses and for public policies. Given the evident importance of race and racial statistical data in public life, explaining the dynamic between race and censuses is both a necessary and illuminating undertaking.

This chapter argues that censuses help to constitute racial discourse. Racial discourse, in turn, helps to shape and explain public policy outcomes. In this argument, census-taking contributes to the formation and perpetuation of racial ideas; but it is not the only state process to do so. Likewise, racial discourse is not the only determinant of political outcomes. Taking into account complex economic and political interests is indispensable to any explanation of racial politics. The point is that racial discourse has causal weight, and this weight is enhanced by the census. Finally, this argument demonstrates that census bureaus are neither disinterested registers nor innocent bystanders. Rather, they are active, if overlooked, participants in racial politics. American and Brazilian experiences provide the evidence for these claims. At different periods in American history, census-taking has contributed directly to the formation of racial ideas, and throughout American history, census data have been part of larger political processes and policies, both negative (i.e. slavery, racial segregation) and positive (civil rights legislation). Brazilian censuses have partly produced and upheld shifting official discourses about the supposed "whitening" of Brazil's population and the harmonious nature of "race relations." These discourses of "whitening" and "racial democracy" have, in turn, justified the absence of racial, or more precisely, color-conscious policies, either negative or positive. Racial discriminatory policies were not necessary because Brazilians were a racially-mixed people, headed inexorably towards "whiteness." The absence of formal racial segregation and its legacy made positive policies unnecessary.

Despite the evident differences in outcomes – racial segregation in the US and the lack of such in Brazil – the same dynamic between census-taking, race, and public policies exists in both countries. Census-taking supports and reflects racial discourse. Racial discourse affects political outcomes. Not surprisingly, this dynamic continues today, although on dramatically altered political landscapes and with new social actors. The American Civil Rights movement transformed most consequentially racial discourse and public policies. Today, census racial categories are indispensable to the enforcement of civil rights legislation, namely the Voting Rights Act(s). Organized groups also view the census as the proper venue for asserting racial identities. As they demand that the census be a mirror, reflecting America's racial and ethnic diversity, they also seek to use the census to advance a new racial discourse of multiracialism. With Brazil's democratization in the mid-1980s, organized groups have demanded changes in methods of counting by color. Black activists charge that census methods have distorted the truth of Brazil's racial composition and have complicated the development and implementation of positive public policies. If activists succeed, Brazilian censuses will advance a new racial discourse as well, replacing the image of Brazil's racially mixed population with one of a racially distinct population. The close historical examination of these dynamics and their content in the United States and Brazil well illuminates these arguments. But before turning to these cases, it is necessary first to explain the reasons for choosing the United States and Brazil, and then to explain what is meant by "racial discourse."

Why compare the United States and Brazil?

Along key dimensions of political and economic analysis, the United States and Brazil hardly seem comparable. The US's history of democratic and constitutional governance (albeit with long restricted electoral participation for nonwhites and women) and twentieth-century economic and military world dominance contrasts starkly with that of Brazil. Brazilian political history is a story of highly concentrated elite governance: nineteenth-century monarchical rule was followed by twentieth-century oligarchical and military rule, with periodic disruptions in the twentieth century of multiparty competitive politics and elections, first from 1945 through 1963, and then from 1985 to the present. Although Brazil's economy is currently the world's eighth largest, its income distribution is among the most unequal in the world. Indeed, in terms of political economy and politics, the United States and Brazil occupy two discrete, if connected, universes.

On the axis of race, however, comparison has been unavoidable and has seemed utterly appropriate. It is also a comparison that scholars have judged Brazil to have "won," in that Brazilian race relations have appeared far more harmonious and less rigidly stratified than those of the United States. The basis for this comparative scholarship is slavery and its aftermath. The economies of both countries were rooted in African enslavement. Brazil was dominant among Latin American and Caribbean sugar producers in the nineteenth century and was also the largest single participant in the transatlantic slave trade, accounting for 41 percent of the estimated 10 million people transported (Klein 1986, ch. 6; Fogel 1989). The United States, by comparison, imported approximately 693,000 slaves, 7 percent of the 10 million. Although the United States imported far fewer slaves proportionally than Portuguese colonists in Brazil or English colonists in Jamaica, it came to have the largest slave population in the Western Hemisphere by the 1850s, due to the fostering of slave reproduction by American slaveowners and the extremely brutal labor conditions of Brazil and Jamaica (Kolchin 1993; Fogel 1989).

American slavery was finally abolished in 1865 by way of a bloody civil war. After abolition, the Congress passed three constitutional amendments that fundamentally altered American citizenship and politics by formally removing race and former status of servitude as the basis for membership in the political community. The thirteenth amendment abolished slavery, the fourteenth made American citizenship a birthright, and the fifteenth amendment extended the franchise to black males. Constitutional amendments and congressional Reconstruction, however, were unable either to prevent the reconstitution of white political and economic supremacy in the country's southern states or to insure equal enjoyment of the rights and privileges of American citizenship (Smith 1997). By the late 1890s, racial segregation by law and black male disenfranchisement were firmly entrenched in the south; racially discriminatory policies (i.e. in labor, housing, and education) and social customs were widespread throughout the rest of the country. These political and social arrangements would last, more or less intact, for nearly ninety years until the Civil Rights Movement of the 1950s and 1960s.

In contrast, Princess Isabel peacefully ended slavery by decree in 1888, making Brazil the last country in the Western hemisphere to abolish the institution. There was neither *de jure* nor widespread *de facto* racial segregation in Brazil following slavery's abolition. However, there was neither Reconstruction nor any other state-directed efforts to ease the transition for freed people from slavery to freedom. Instead, ex-slaves were left to their own devices. Brazil's rural landowners chose to subsidize the immigration of southern Europeans, mostly Italians, to work on the country's coffee plantations, rather than employ newly freed slaves (Andrews 1991). Coffee cultivation was the foundation of Brazil's export economy and the motor of the first stage of twentieth-century industrialization (Burns 1970).

Comparative scholarship has generally focused on the evident differences in political outcomes after slavery: racial segregation in the United States and its absence in Brazil. Moreover, such scholarship has usually equated the study of "race" with the study of "blacks" and "racial politics" with the existence or absence of discrimination against blacks. These approaches have been profoundly misleading, precisely because they have obscured the commonality of race as a fundamental organizing principle of politics and society in both countries. The United States and Brazil are thus comparable not merely because of slavery and the presence in each country of large numbers of Africans and their descendants; they are comparable because race has been a language and a mechanism of political membership for all Americans and Brazilians. Brazilians are becoming, so the story goes, one "whiter" race due to extensive racial mixture. In the United States, Americans are presumed to be forever racially distinct, and it is on this distinction that privilege and subordination have turned. Comparative scholarship has also obscured the shared role of the American and Brazilian census bureaus in constituting race ideologically and politically. Racial and color categories have not appeared on American and Brazilian censuses as mere demographic markers. Rather, their appearance is tied directly to shifting ideas about race and the political and social significance of race, and thus is also tied to larger political and institutional processes.

Race as discourse

To count by race presumes, of course, that there is something to be counted. Intellectuals, political elites, scientists, and ordinary citizens have considered race an elemental component of human identity, of what it means to be human. The weight of scientific thought about race can hardly be overestimated, especially in census-taking. As the historian Nancy Stepan observes, the modern period of 1800 to 1960 was one in which European and American scientists were "preoccupied by race" (Stepan 1982: x). There have been, and still are, popular understandings of race and of proper racial identifications. These popular understandings are sometimes directly at odds with elite and scientific understandings. They are, as often, informed by them, with variation. Given then that race was (and continues to be) thought elemental to human identity, it would seem no surprise that the census counts by race. The connection between race and census-taking would seemingly end there. Every human body has a racial identity, and population censuses count bodies, so racial data are obtained through the counting of bodies.

But if we question the supposed rigid quality of race and explore its evident plastic qualities, the way is opened to better explaining what race is *and* to understanding the role of the census in creating it. The scholarship that refers to race in one way or another is vast and continues to grow. However that portion of it that examines the concept of race itself is less voluminous, though still substantial. An intellectual consensus exists today whereby most agree that racial categories have no biological basis. This is true even as persons still commonly refer to individuals and groups on the basis of similar and dissimilar physical characteristics, and use the term 'race' and its accompanying discourse, however incoherent, to substantiate these distinctions. With racial categories believed to have no biological basis, the task for scholars has shifted to defining, explaining, describing, and analyzing race. The resulting theories vary as widely as the disciplines.

According to the sociologists Michael Omi and Howard Winant, race is "a concept which signifies and symbolizes social conflicts and interests referring to different types of human bodies" (1994: 55). The historian Evelyn Brooks Higginbotham understands race to have various faces: race, then, is a "social construction"; "a highly contested representation of relations of power between social categories by which individuals are identified and identify themselves"; "a myth"; "a global sign"; and a "metalanguage" (1992: 251–74). The philosopher David Theo Goldberg argues that race is an "irreducibly political category," in that "racial creation and management acquire import in framing and giving specificity to the body politic" (1992: 563). The American Anthropological Association today views race as a concept with little scientific validity, burdened by its association with racist practices, and less useful than ethnicity in capturing the "human variability" of the American people. According to the legal scholar Ian Haney-Lopez, the law constructs race legally by fixing the boundaries of races, by defining the content of racial identities, and by specifying their relative disadvantage and privilege in American society (1996: 10). Literary critic Henry Louis Gates sees race as the "ultimate trope of difference because it is so very arbitrary in its application" (1986: 5). Historians of ideas have traced the development of racial thought in various countries and different historical epochs (Jordan 1968; Horsman 1981; Gould 1981; Barkan 1992; Skidmore 1993). Political scientists view race as a tool, used both by white elites, to insure white domination, and by blacks and other nonwhites, as a potential weapon to resist such domination by blacks and other nonwhites (Hanchard 1994; Marx 1998).

We are a long way, indeed, from seeing race as fixed, objective, and in significant ways, deriving its existence from human bodies at all. Race stems from and rests in language, in social practices, in legal definitions, in ideas, in structural arrangements, and in political contests over power. This chapter builds on certain trends of this theoretical work. It treats race as a discourse, meaning that race is a set of shifting claims that describe and explain what race is and what it means. Although this discourse has various sources in religion, law, and science, it is the latter – science – that has been the most influential in census-taking in the United States and Brazil. Indeed, the influence of scientific thinking argues against viewing racial discourse as merely a tool to be manipulated by elites or masses. While it is true that political and intellectual elites were largely responsible for creating and promulgating scientific racial thought, they did so not only to manipulate and control; rather, they thought that they were adhering to nature's laws of human diversity. However, because scientific investigation results from human endeavor, it is inevitably shaped by larger political, social, and cultural processes. Racial discourse, then, does not exist without its various agents or its institutional channels. Scholars are right in stressing race's discursive nature. Yet their theoretical formulations run the risk of obscuring the institutional sites of its construction, maintenance, and perpetuation. Census Bureaus are such sites because they help to create, maintain, and advance racial discourse.

As we will see, in both countries racial discourse and racial categorization on censuses have focused on the ideas of "whiteness," "blackness," and "mulattoness." However, racial discourse has been applied to other groups as well. In the United States, elite concerns about other "nonwhite" people – the Chinese, Japanese, and especially Native Americans – were also reflected and advanced by the census, although to a far lesser degree. Twentieth-century Brazilian censuses did not enumerate indigenous persons separately (with an indigenous category) until the 1991 census. Racial discourse supplies the boundaries of racial memberships and their content, and is itself context specific. It therefore varies from one national setting to the next. In nineteenth-century colonial Malaysia, for example, race pertained to the broad grouping of Europeans, Malays, Chinese, Indians, and others (Hirschman 1986), and by 1901 censuses counted them as "races" (Hirschman 1987). In Guatemala, Ladinos and Mayas are the two major racial groups. Twentieth-century Guatemalan censuses have supposedly charted the decrease in Mayas, thereby making Guatemala a "whiter, less Indian" nation, according to its political elites (Lovell, Lutz 1994: 137). Likewise, the relation of such discourse to census-taking may vary in its particularities, but the general pattern holds: census-taking reflects, upholds, and often furthers racial discourse.

American censuses: race is fundamental

A race question and racial categories have appeared on every US decennial census, from the Republic's first census in 1790 to the 2000 census. Although the term "color" actually appeared on nineteenth-century census schedules, it was synonymous with "race" in meaning. I divide the history of racial categorization into four periods (see table 2.1). The first period is 1790 to 1840, when categorization was shaped by representational apportionment, slavery, and racial ideas. The second period is 1850 to 1920, when categorization was used expressly to advance the racial theories of scientists. The third period is 1930 to 1960, when census definitions of racial categories were identical to those of southern race laws. The fourth period is 1970 to the present, during which categorization has been shaped most profoundly by civil rights legislation, the implementation of Statistical Directive No. 15, and the lobbying efforts of organized groups. Prior to the introduction of self-identification on the 1960 census, enumerators determined the person's race by visual observation, based on the definitions provided in official instructions.

1790 – 1840 Censuses

The initial reasons race appeared at all in the first censuses were not transparently connected to demographic concerns, because the principal impetus for US census-taking was political. The US Constitution mandated that "an actual enumeration" be conducted every ten years for the purposes of representational apportionment. How slaves would be counted was especially contentious. Delegates of the Constitutional Convention eventually agreed upon the 3/5 compromise, meaning that for apportionment purposes, slaves would count as 3/5 persons. The question remains, then, why did the census count by race? After all, representation depended upon civil status, whether one was free or slave, and whether one was taxed or not. The answer is that race question was included because race was a salient social and political category. Eighteenth-century political elites regarded race as a natural and self-evident component of human identity, in keeping with European Enlightenment thought. Observed differences in physical appearance and cultural practices were the result of differences in natural environment. Humankind was one species, and all were capable of infinite improvement (Horsman 1981: 98). These ideas, most robust in the years immediately preceding and following the Revolution, were gradually subordinated to theories of polygenesis and to the widespread belief in the existence of innately and permanently superior and inferior races. Furthermore, the deepening entrenchment of slavery in economic and political life rendered abstract commitments to universal equality and liberty moot.

To be free and white and to be free and black were distinct political experiences (Kettner 1978). Whites were presumptively citizens. While free blacks were also citizens by birthright, they did not enjoy the same rights and entitlements as whites precisely because blacks were deemed inferior and unfit for republican life, on the grounds of race (Kettner 1978; Finkelman 1986). As for Native Americans, their citizenship status was determined by the particular status of tribes as spelled out in law and treaties. The federal government considered most tribes "quasi-sovereign nations," thereby disqualifying their members from American citizenship (Kettner 1978: 294). The census schedules of 1800 to 1820 explicitly reflected these arrangements in their category "all other free persons, except Indians Not Taxed."

The censuses from the years 1790 to 1840 asked few inquiries beyond those related to population. They counted free white males and free white females, subdivided into age groups; free colored persons, and/or all other free persons, except Indians not taxed; and slaves. The earliest censuses registered race as it was then understood. Race was considered a natural fact, though its political and social significance was still being sorted out. Were Anglo-Saxons, for example, a superior race destined to "bring good government, commercial prosperity and Christianity" to America? (Horsman 1981: 2). Even more disconcerting were the obvious contradictions in ideas about the black race and its place among other races. If all humankind belonged to the same human race, how could one part of it be justifiably enslaved? To be sure, colonial racial discourse had long regarded Africans as different from and inferior to the English, whatever their common humanity (Jordan 1968). Yet political and intellectual elites did not initially regard these differences as permanent. By the 1850s, in this respect, racial discourse changed markedly. So, too, would the role of census-taking.

1850 – 1920

The 1850 census marked a watershed in census-taking in several ways. For our purposes, a large part of its significance rests in the introduction of the "mulatto" category and the reasons for its introduction. It was added not because of demographic shifts, but because of the lobbying efforts of race scientists and the willingness of certain senators to do their bidding. More generally, the mulatto category signaled the ascendance of scientific authority within racial discourse. By the 1850s, polygenist thought was winning a battle that it had lost in Europe. The "American School of Ethnology" distinguished itself from prevailing European racial thought through its insistence that human races were distinct and unequal species (Stanton 1968; Gould 1981). That polygenism endured at all was a victory, since the very existence of racially-mixed persons had led European theorists to abandon it. Moreover, there was considerable resistance to it in the United States. Although most American monogenists were not racial egalitarians, they were initially unwilling to accept claims of separate origins, permanent racial differences, and the infertility of racial mixture. Polygenists deliberately sought hard statistical data to prove that mulattoes, as hybrids of different racial species, were less fertile than their parents of pure races, and hence lived shorter lives.

Racial theorist, medical doctor, scientist, and slaveowner Josiah Nott lobbied certain senators for the inclusion of several inquiries, all designed to prove his theory of mulatto hybridity and separate origins (US Congressional Globe 1850; Horsman 1987). In the end, the senators voted to include only "mulatto," although they hotly debated the inclusion of another inquiry – "[D]egree of removal from pure white and black races" – as well. Instructions to enumerators for the slave population read: "Under heading 5 entitled 'Color,' insert in all cases, when the slave is black, the letter B; when he or she is a mulatto, insert M. The color of all slaves should be noted." (US Bureau of the Census 1989: 23) For the free population, enumerators were instructed: "in all cases where the person is black, insert the letter B; if mulatto, insert M. It is very desirable that these particulars be carefully regarded." (US Bureau of the Census 1989: 22)

The 1850 census introduced a pattern, especially in regard to the mulatto category, that lasted until 1930: the census was deliberately used to advance race science. Such science was a fundamental, though not the only, basis of racial discourse – that is, the discourse that explained what race was. Far from being mere counters of race, the census was helping to create it by assisting scientists in their endeavors. Although scientific ideas about race changed over those eighty years, the role of the census in advancing such thought did not.

The abolition of slavery and the reconstitution of white racial domination in the South were accompanied by an enduring interest in race. Predictably, the ideas that race scientists and proslavery advocates had marshalled to defend slavery were used to oppose the recognition of black political rights. Blacks were naturally inferior to whites, whether as slaves or as free people, and were thereby disqualified from full participation in American economic, political, and social life. Although scientists. along with nearly all whites, were convinced of the inequality of races, they continued in their basic task of investigating racial origins. Darwinism presented a challenge to the still dominant polygenism, but the mulatto category still retained its significance within polygenist theories. How was polygenism able to withstand Darwin's claim that all humankind had descended from a common evolutionary ancestor? Polygenists profited from the fact that Darwin's main claim left unattended two of polygenism's central concerns: the effects of racial mixture and the capacities of races (Fredrickson 1971; Haller 1971; Stocking 1968). As polygenists saw it, common ancestry did not erase the evident fact of human diversity, nor did it explain the content of those differences or the effects of racial intermixture: that whites and blacks could mate did not mean that they should. More information was needed about the physical and psychological effects of racial mixture on whites, blacks, and their mulatto offspring. Moreover, because humankind had evolved from common ancestors did not mean that the races had followed similar or even comparable evolutionary processes. Indeed, polygenists argued that whites and blacks had evolved so differently in the past that it rendered their common ancestry practically meaningless.

By the 1890 census, polygenism and Darwinism came to coexist. Darwinism had not replaced polygenist thought, but rather had combined with it. Race scientists and social theorists were convinced, according to their interpretation of Darwin, that all races were engaged in a struggle for survival. They translated Darwin's biological idea of natural selection into a social theory of racial struggle. Yet, in keeping with their polygenist preoccupation with "mulattoes," these same scientists and social theorists considered mulattoes to be at a distinct disadvantage and thought they would die off. Mulatto frailty would prove that racial mixture engendered racial disadvantage and would result in eventual disappearance or reversion back to the "dominant type." The "dominant type" was, of course, presumed to be black; at no point before or since had mulattoes been considered "mixed whites." Blacks and other nonwhites were mixed; whites were not. These ideas emerged powerfully in the 1890 census, and certain of them persist today. Mulatto data were needed to prove that mulattoes lived shorter lives, and thus that blacks and whites were different racial species. Both the 1870 and 1880 censuses were designed to amass statistical proof for this theory, as enumerator instructions reveal. Enumerators were expected to determine, through visual inspection, the "trace[s] of African blood." The 1870 instructions read:

> It must be assumed that, where nothing is written in this column, 'White' is to be understood. The column is always to be filled. Be particularly careful in reporting the class *Mulatto*. The word here is generic, and includes quadroons, octoroons, and all persons having any perceptible trace of African blood. Important scientific results depend upon the correct determination of this class in schedules 1 and 2 (italics in original). (US Bureau of the Census 1989: 26)

Schedule 1 was for population, Schedule 2 for mortality. The 1880 instructions for "color" were nearly identical.

Congressional documents and enumerator instructions for the 1890 census again reveal scientific interest in the census. Bureau officials and (social) scientists wanted to know "[W]hether the mulattoes, quadroons, and octoroons are disappearing and the race becoming more purely negro" (Congressional Record 1889). Therefore, "quadroon" and "octoroon" were added to the schedule's other categories of "White," "Black," "Chinese," "Japanese," and "Indian." Enumerators were expected to determine, primarily through visual inspection and then through questioning of an individual (when possible and/or necessary), whether that individual was a mulatto, quadroon, octoroon, or one of the other racial designations. The instructions read:

> Write *white*, *black*, *mulatto*, *quadroon*, *octoroon*, *Chinese*, *Japanese*, or *Indian*, according to the color or race of the person enumerated. Be particularly careful to distinguish between blacks, mulattoes, quadroons, and octoroons. The word 'black' should be used to describe those persons who have three-fourths or more black blood; 'mulatto,' those persons who have from three-eighths to five-eighths black blood; 'quadroon,' those persons who have one-fourth black blood; and 'octoroons,' those persons who have one-eighth or any trace of black blood (italics in original). (US Bureau of the Census 1989: 36)

For fifty years, from 1850 to 1900, the census contributed directly to the formation of scientific ideas of race. These ideas were the backbone of a racial discourse that justified and sustained slavery, and then *de jure* and *de facto* racial segregation. At the same time, (social) scientists studied race because of their scientific interest in it, for reasons distinct but not disconnected from larger political, social, and economic developments.

However, in the twentieth century there was a dramatic change, as censuses ceased to play such a prominent role in the formation of racial theory itself. Instead, they have mostly counted by race, presuming race to be a basic fact. Theorizing about race continued in (social) scientific circles, but scientists and theorists did not deliberately enlist the census as they had in the past. Census categorization continued to sustain racial discourse inasmuch as categorizing and counting by race gave race an official existence. The use of the "mulatto" category in racial theorizing until the 1930 census was, however, an important exception to this overall trend. By 1930, the definitions of "nonwhite" categories became consistent with legal definitions of nonwhite racial membership. Since 1970, the census has once again emerged as a venue for directly enabling public policies and for shaping debate about the concept of race itself. The census now supports civil rights legislation, and racial discourse once again turns on the same basic question that nineteenth-century social scientists were driven to answer: what is race? As in the past, the census is being used to answer that question. Compared to the past, however, there is now a much wider circle of participants, including census bureau officials, politicians, social scientists, civil rights advocates, policy makers, and organized groups within civil society seeking recognition.

There were three interrelated, fundamental shifts in American intellectual, institutional, and political life that accounted for the more constrained influence of the census. First, race science settled into a set of ideas that would dominate for nearly forty years and would then be challenged for decades thereafter: discrete races existed; these races possessed distinctive intellectual, cultural, and moral capacities; and these capacities were unequally distributed within and between racial groups. (Social) scientists no longer used the census to sort out the basic questions of race science. Instead, the census registered the evident existence of race.

Second, the Census Bureau's gradual institutionalization changed perceptions about the purposes and limits of racial enumeration. The bureau would eventually become a full-fledged bureaucracy, its methods soundly grounded in statistical science. Its mission was to provide racial data, without explicitly advancing racial thought and without being beholden to political interests (Anderson 1988). Counting by race would come to be widely viewed as an administrative task and technical procedure, and not as a tool of scientific investigation. Moreover, decision-making about racial categorization became an even less public process and purportedly less political one, as Congress deferred to the internal decision-making processes of the Census Bureau. In 1902, the Census Bureau became a permanent federal agency under the Department of Commerce and Labor. In 1918, an Advisory Committee was formed to assist in the development of schedules and inquiries, including the race question. This Committee consulted the Census Bureau until the mid-1940s. In 1954, all census legislation became Title 13 of the United States Code.

Third, the hardening of racial segregation and subordination, both *de jure* and *de facto*, paralleled the hardening of scientific thought. Southern law had largely settled on the "one-drop of nonwhite blood" rule of racial membership by 1930. The definitions of nonwhite categories as spelled out in census enumerator instructions were identical to those of southern race laws, in that any visually perceptible trace of "nonwhiteness" meant that the individual would be designated to the appropriate nonwhite category. It is important to emphasize, however, that the definitions of white and nonwhite racial membership were not limited to the south or its legal regime. They were imposed and assumed nationwide, thereby explaining their appearance on the federal census. However, census categories did not simply reflect race laws, scientific thought, and social customs. The "mulatto" enumeration shows that census-taking followed its own path to the same destination of the "one-drop" rule.

The mulatto category remained on the 1910 and 1920 censuses for the same basic reason that it been introduced in 1850: to build racial theories. (Census officials removed it from the 1900 census because they were dissatisfied with the quality of 1890 mulatto, octoroon, and quadroon data.) The basic idea that distinct races existed and were enduringly unequal remained firmly in place. What happens when superior and inferior races mate? Social and natural scientists still wanted to know. But the Advisory Committee to the Census Bureau decided in 1928 to terminate use of the mulatto category on censuses. The stated reasons for removing it rested on accuracy; if they had had confidence in the data's accuracy or the ability to secure it, mulatto may well have remained on the census. The Advisory Committee did not refer to the evident inability of the mulatto category to settle the central, if shifting, questions of race science: first, did "mulattoness" prove that whites and blacks were different species of humans; and second, were mulattoes weaker than members of the so-called pure races? The exit of the mulatto category from the census was markedly understated, especially when compared to its entrance in 1850 and its enduring significance on nineteenth-century censuses.

Beginning with the 1890 census, all Native Americans (whether taxed or not) were counted on general population schedules (Thornton 1987: 212–16). If racial theorists believed that "mulatto" enumeration would prove their frailty, they also thought that Native Americans were a defeated and vanishing race, headed toward extinction. Given the weight of these expectations in the late nineteenth century, it is not surprising that census methods and data would reflect them. As the historian Brian Dippie observes, "the expansion and shrinkage of Indian population estimates correlate with changing attitudes about the native American's rights and prospects" (Dippie 1982: xv). The idea of the "vanishing Indian" was so pervasive that the censuses of 1910 and 1930 applied a broad definition of "Indian" because officials believed that each would be the last chance for an accurate count. According to the Census Bureau:

> In 1910 a special effort was made to secure a complete enumeration of persons with any perceptible amount of Indian ancestry. This probably resulted in the enumeration as Indian of a considerable number of persons who would have been reported as white in earlier censuses. There were no special efforts in 1920, and the returns showed a much smaller number of Indians than in 1910. Again in 1930 emphasis was placed on securing a complete count of Indians, with the result that the returns probably overstated the decennial increase in the number of Indians. (US Bureau of the Census 1960: 3)

1930 – 1960

With the removal of the mulatto category, categories and instructions for the 1930 census mirrored the racial *status quo* in law, society, and science. Southern statutes that had defined "negro" and other nonwhites by referring to a specific blood quantum now defined them broadly. Any person with any trace of "black blood" was legally black and subject to all the disabilities the designation conferred. Census definitions followed suit, and enumerator instructions in 1930 for "Negroes" read, in part: "A person of mixed white and Negro blood should be returned as a Negro, no matter how small the percentage of Negro blood. Both black and mulatto persons are to be returned as Negroes, without distinction." (U.S. Bureau of the Census 1930) "Other Mixed Races" meant that "any mixture of white and nonwhite should be reported according to the nonwhite parent" (US Bureau of the Census 1930). Similarly detailed instructions, of paragraph length, were provided for "Mexicans" and "Indians." In contrast, legal definitions of "White" did not change, where they existed at all. In general, Southern laws conceived of White as the complete absence of any "Negro or nonwhite blood," down to the last drop and as far back generationally as one could go (Murray 1951). Again, the census reflected legal practices by never providing a definition of White.

The state of racial discourse was more unstable than the 1930–1960 census instructions would lead us to believe. By the 1940s, its scientific foundations had shifted noticeably. Cultural anthropologists, under the guidance of Franz Boas, compellingly challenged the basic tenets of race science. Nazism forced (social) scientists worldwide to re-examine their thinking on race. However, shifting (social) scientific ideas about race alone do not account for changes in racial discourse. The demise of the South's economy, the massive migration of Southern blacks to Northern and Midwestern cities, increased political participation and agitation, successful legal challenges to segregation, and the onset of the Cold War transformed the political landscape. This new landscape was far less nourishing to the prevailing variant(s) of racial discourse. The acceptance of race did not mean that American social, political, and economic life would or should continue to be organized around it in the ways that it had been in the past. Ideas of race, the census, and the attendant (and proper) public policies had long been inseparable; they were no longer. The issue of race itself was detached from how it did and how it should (or should not) matter politically, socially, and economically. If race was believed to have no biological basis, it was easier to loosen the connections.

At the same time, it became increasingly difficult to discuss what race was in a coherent way, other than to state that it did not biologically exist. Civil rights discourse has focused exclusively on racism, discrimination, and equality, leaving aside the question of race itself. Census-taking in the post-civil rights period has reflected this tension: census data are used to remedy racial discrimination while census categories are themselves supported by a decentered, conflicting, and, in certain ways, anachronistic racial discourse.

1970 – 2000

The Civil Rights Movement and resulting civil rights legislation of the 1960s dramatically changed the political context and purposes of racial categorization. Federal civil rights legislation, most notably the Civil Rights Acts of 1964 and 1968 and the Voting Rights Act of 1965, dismantled the most egregious discriminatory mechanisms: namely, black disenfranchisement in the south, rigid residential segregation, and wholesale exclusion from certain occupations and American institutions. These new laws and programs required racial and ethnic data for monitoring legislative compliance and the delivery of new social services and programs. For example, the Civil Rights Act of 1964 and the Voting Rights Act of 1965 and their subsequent amendments, extensions, and court interpretations require population tabulations by race at the level of city blocks for the purposes of redistricting and the possible creation of "minority-majority" congressional electoral districts (Edmonston and Schultze 1995: 140). The now positive benefits of racial categorization and racial data have stimulated and sustained organized attempts to have categories protected, changed, and added. The "Hispanic Origins Question," for example, was added to the 1980 census in response to lobbying by Mexican-American organizations (Choldin 1986), and several Asian categories have been added to the 1980 and 1990 censuses in response to lobbying by Asian-American organizations (Espiritu 1992: 112–87). Civil rights advocates took racial categories (legal and census) as they were, arguing that such categories had been the basis of discrimination and should thus serve as the basis of remedy.

Perhaps most politically consequential for census-taking in the post-civil rights era has been the issuance of Statistical Directive No. 15 by the Office of Management and Budget (OMB) of the Executive Branch. Since 1977, this directive has mandated the standards that govern all statistical reporting by all federal agencies, including the Census Bureau. The five standard categories are defined as:

1. *American Indian or Alaskan Native* – A person having origins in any of the original peoples of North America, and who maintains cultural identification through tribal affiliations or community recognition.
2. *Asian or Pacific Islander* – A person having origins in any of the original peoples of the Far East, Southeast Asia, the Indian subcontinent, or the Pacific Islands. This area includes, for example, China, India, Japan, Korea, the Philippine Islands, and Samoa.
3. *Black* – A person having origins in any of the black racial groups of Africa.
4. *Hispanic* – A person of Mexican, Puerto Rican, Cuban, Central or South American or other Spanish culture or origin, regardless of race.
5. *White* – A person having origins in any of the original peoples of Europe, North Africa, or the Middle East.

The directive defines "Hispanic" as an ethnic category; meaning that there are, for example, "white" hispanics and "black" hispanics. As for persons of "mixed racial or ethnic origins," the directive instructs that such persons be classified according to "[T]he category which most closely reflects the individual's recognition in his community." According to the directive's preamble, these categories were devised to standardize "record keeping, collection, and presentation of data on race and ethnicity" for administrative and statistical purposes. The definitions, the directive cautions, "should not be interpreted as being scientific or anthropological in nature," rather they have been developed to meet expressed congressional and executive needs for "compatible, nonduplicated, and exchangeable" racial and ethnic data. Thus, these categories are both statistical markers and political instruments. Gone is any reference to a purportedly scientific basis of race; whether such a basis exists (or not) is quite beside the point. Federal agencies require racial and ethnic data not only for collection, but for the measurement of compliance with civil rights legislation. This apparent conflation of statistics and politics has made the directive a powerful and highly contentious policy tool. The directive, in its creation and subsequent recognition of official races and ethnicities, acts as a "gatekeeper" to an official statistical existence. Invested with this power and visibility, the directive has become a referent for groups seeking official recognition.

In 1993, the OMB began a comprehensive review of the directive. According to OMB officials, this review was prompted by growing public criticism that the directive was incapable of accurately measuring new immigrants or the offspring of interracial marriages. In its review, the OMB actively sought public comment through congressional subcommittee hearings in 1993 and 1997, and by notices posted in the Federal Register. Not surprisingly, well-established civil rights organizations lobbied against major changes in the Directive, while newly formed organizations of "multiracial" Americans lobbied for the addition of "multiracial" to the directive, potentially making it the sixth official racial category. They argued that the "one-drop rule" of nonwhite racial membership was no longer valid and that census categorization should reflect new understandings of race. Numerous other groups also presented the OMB with their own suggestions, each designed to enhance the recognition of particular groups. For example, the Celtic Coalition, the National European American Society, and the Society for German-American Studies all called for the disaggregation of the white category. The Arab American Institute lobbied for the reclassification of persons of Middle Eastern origin from "white" to a new "Middle-Eastern" category.

At the OMB's request, the National Academy of Sciences, Committee on National Statistics conducted a 1994 workshop that included federal officials, academics, public policy analysts, corporate representatives, and secondary school educators. In March 1994, the OMB established the Interagency Committee for the Review of Racial and Ethnic Standards (ICRRES). This committee included representatives from thirty federal agencies, including the Census Bureau, the Department of Justice, and the Department of Education. In the end, this committee's recommendations to the OMB ruled the day. In October 1997, the OMB announced its final changes to the directive and to census methods. Most significantly, the OMB decided to allow respondents to choose more than one race on their census schedules for the first time in the history of American census-taking. It therefore decided against the adoption of a multiracial category. It also made "Native Hawaiian or other Pacific Islander" a separate racial classification, thereby bringing the total number of racial classifications to five. These classifications were: "American Indian or Alaska Native," "Asian," "Black or African American," "Native Hawaiian or other Pacific Islander," or "White." OMB continues to regard "Hispanic or Latino" as an ethnic classification. The definition of "American Indian or Alaska native" now also includes persons from South and Central America. Finally, the OMB also made slight alterations in the wording of existing categories. The issue of racial categorization is temporarily settled, until preparations for the 2010 census begin.

Brazilian censuses: White is better

When compared to the American experience of census-taking, that of Brazil seems relatively simple, if erratic. The color question has appeared inconsistently on Brazilian censuses from the first modern census in 1872 up to the 2000 census (see table 2.2). The two nineteenth-century censuses, 1872 and 1890, had a color question. Of twentieth-century censuses, the 1940, 1950, 1960, 1980 and 1991 censuses all asked a color question, although the 1960 color data were never fully released. The 1900, 1920 and 1970 censuses did not have such a question. There were no censuses at all in 1910 and 1930. Categorization has itself been more consistent, with the three color categories of white (branco), brown or mixed (pardo), and black (preto) used in nearly every case. I divide the history of categorization into three periods. The first is from 1872 to 1910, when categorization largely reflected elite and popular conceptions of Brazil's racial composition. The second is from 1920 to 1950, when census texts actively promoted and happily reported the "whitening" of Brazil's population. The third is from 1960 to the present, when categorization methods have themselves been questioned and contested by statisticians within the Census Bureau and by organized groups within civil society.

Brazilian censuses have included a color question for the same basic reason that American censuses have included a race question. Brazilian elites viewed race as a natural component of human identity and as an independent factor in human affairs. Brazilian censuses have not counted by race as such, but by color. Color has referred to physical appearance, not to racial origins. Racial origins, however, are not disconnected from color, because color is derived from the "mixture" of Brazil's three original races: Europeans, Africans, and Indians. Color and race are therefore conceptually distinguished, but related: color refers to appearance, race refers to origins (Nogueira 1985). While this distinction is hardly unambiguous, it lies at the heart of Brazilian racial discourse and the support that the census provides for this discourse.

The thinking has gone as follows: Brazilians are racially mixed, of different colors. Such a racial mixture has made counting by race exceedingly imprecise. However, the census questions and categories have themselves organized the fluid boundaries of the very racial mixture presumed to exist. Brazil's intelligentsia, political elite, and census officials have emphasized racial mixture with the same vigilance that their American counterparts have emphasized racial purity. Brazilian social scientists largely accepted the scientific truth of races and their inequality, though not with the same intensity as Americans and Europeans. Like American elites, Brazil's elite, too, were obsessed with racial mixture, but they concluded that Brazilians were becoming a "whiter" race, not a racially degraded and disadvantaged one.

1872 – 1910

Nineteenth-century Brazilian censuses were involved neither in slavery debates nor in directly advancing racial thought, unlike nineteenth-century American censuses. Although the 1872 census was conducted one year after the passage of major abolitionist legislation, neither census inquiries nor census data were marshalled for slavery debates. Likewise, although Brazilian intellectual and political elites were preoccupied with the perceived calamity of racial mixture, they did not use the census to examine the problem. The categories on both censuses were nearly identical: white (branco), black (preto), brown (pardo), and caboclo (mestizo Indian). The 1890 census included these four categories plus the category of "mestiço" (meaning mixture).

Paradoxically, the census was one of the few late nineteenth-century undertakings that was not preoccupied with or used to discern the national disaster that Brazilian elites were convinced would accompany racial mixture. As the Brazilian historian Lilia Moritz Schwarcz has richly documented, museums, historical societies, law schools, medical schools, and scientists all fixed on racial mixture because it was the key to understanding Brazil and its national possibilities (Schwarcz 1993). The silence of the census was likely due to the modest institutionalization of the statistical institute and the underdevelopment of statistical methods. The establishment of the General Directory of Statistics (DGE) accompanied the abolition of slavery of 1888 and the establishment of the Old Republic in 1890. Historians consider all three of the censuses conducted by the DGE (1890, 1900, and 1920) unreliable (Goyer and Dornschke 1983). Brazil's modern federal census bureau, the Brazilian Institute of Geography and Statistics (IBGE), was established in 1938.

1920 – 1950

In the twentieth century the role of the census changed dramatically, as did the Brazilian elites' ideas about racial mixture. In a sharp reversal, intellectuals posited that the disastrous consequences of racial mixture would be averted because Brazilians would become whiter over time. Racial mixture was not degenerative but fortifying for whites and cleansing for nonwhites. The literary critic Silvio Romero argued that racial mixture enabled whites to thrive in the tropics. Through the mixing of Brazil's three founding races, the white race would "predominate through natural selection until it emerges pure and beautiful as in the Old World" (Eakin 1985: 163). Whitening would also be achieved through European immigration.

It is hard to overemphasize the centrality of census data to twentieth-century claims of a racially mixed Brazilian people and the political and social arguments that have flowed from such claims. In the first half of the century, census texts happily reported that Brazilians were becoming whiter. The 1920 census included an extended discussion of the whitening of Brazil's population. In a section of the census entitled "Evolution of the Race" (which was later published separately as a book), the social theorist Oliviera Vianna explained that the "aryanization" of Brazilians was underway (Vianna 1956: 140). Within *mestiço* (racially mixed) groups the "quanta" of "barbaric bloods" was decreasing while the "quanta" of "white blood" was increasing, each time refining the Brazilian race (1956: 183). Given the pervasiveness of the elite's belief in whitening, it is not surprising that this belief was communicated in the census text. However, the text is surprising because the 1920 census did not itself include a color question. Therefore, its predictions of whitening were not based on data collected contemporaneously, however unreliable and ambiguous that such data certainly would have been. Vianna most likely wrote the whitening text to assure elites that Brazil's future as a white country was certain, thereby making the continued recruitment of European workers unnecessary. By 1920, industrialists and politicians were fed up with the militancy of immigrant workers: the honeymoon was over (Maram 1977).

The 1940 census was the first twentieth-century census to ask a color question. Census enumerators were to check either white, black, or yellow. If the respondent did not fit into one of these three categories, the enumerator was to place a horizontal line on the census schedule. These blank lines were later tabulated under "pardo." Indigenous persons were also included within "pardo" as well. The IBGE excluded "pardo" in response to the rise of European fascism. According to IBGE documents, the category's exclusion would assure Brazilians that census data would not be used for discriminatory purposes (IBGE 1950). It is important to note also that the meaning of "pardo" was then and remains ambiguous. Portuguese language dictionaries define it both as "grey" and as "brown." Its connotations are equally ambiguous because Brazilians use it infrequently in common parlance. Its most significant use is as a census term. Although controversy did not then surround "preto" (black), it has also been a peculiar term for the IBGE to use. Brazilians usually use it in the third person, not the first person as the census requires. Even more illuminating, Brazilians use it most commonly to describe objects, not human beings. Black activists raised the issue of terminology most forcefully as the IBGE prepared for the 1991 and 2000 censuses.

The 1940 census also celebrated whitening. The author and esteemed educator Fernando de Azevedo wrote the census text, which was also published separately as a book and (this time) translated into English (Azevedo 1950). Azevedo concluded the chapter entitled "Land and Race" (race, like land, was assigned a natural and fundamental status) with the observation that "[I]f we admit that Negroes and Indians are continuing to disappear, both in the successive dilutions of white blood and in the constant progress of biological and social selection," Brazil would soon be white (1950: 41). The "pardo" category was added to the 1950 census schedule, making the four choices: white (branco), black (preto), brown (pardo), and yellow (amarelo). Self-identification replaced enumerator determination in 1950 as well.

1960 – 2000

From the 1950s onward, census texts spoke little about whitening. The profound shifts in scientific racial thought after World War II largely account for this change. Census texts spoke less aggressively and frequently of both "whitening" and of the regenerative and redemptive powers of mixture. Instead, racial mixture was reported in a matter-of-fact way and was not equated automatically with whitening. However, these texts still disclosed a belief in distinct races, if not in their inherent superiority or inferiority, and in racial mixture. Moreover, Brazilian elites have used color data to promote the image of Brazil as a racial democracy. In this view, Brazilian citizenship has been neither enhanced, diminished, nor stratified because of race. Presumed racial differences are not a way of distinguishing among Brazilians because they are racially mixed. Brazilians are simply Brazilians, with their different colors. The census, in counting by color (and not race), has thus been instrumental to the discourse of racial democracy. Moreover, the IBGE has been reluctant either to

cross-tabulate color categories with socioeconomic variables or to re-
lease color data in a timely fashion. Until the early 1980s, the lack of
such socioeconomic data made it impossible to test the claim that color
was economically and socially inconsequential in Brazil. It also stymied
the advocacy efforts of scholars, policymakers, and activists for remedial
and positive public policies. It was not until the 1976 Household Survey
(PNAD) that the IBGE produced data that pegged color to income,
health, education, and housing. Since then, there has a been a veritable
boom in quantitative research, all of which has clearly shown that color
is a significant variable in determining levels of educational attainment,
employment prospects, and income earned.

The National Census Commission, appointed by the military government, removed the color question from the 1970 census, against
the recommendations of two experts whom the military had itself so-
licited. In the late 1970s, scholars and black activists lobbied to have
the question restored to the 1980 census. It was restored, although the
Census Institute's president remained opposed and called the question
"unconstitutional." Since Brazil's redemocratization in the mid-1980s
(after twenty-one years of military rule), activists and scholars have aggressively challenged the discourse of racial democracy. They have also
necessarily challenged census methods and terminology. Their efforts
have prompted re-examination within the IBGE. In the early 1980s, for
example, a group of statisticians and analysts within the Department of
Social Studies and Indicators (DIESO) decided to unite "pardo" and
"preto" data under the term "negro" (black) in socioeconomic analyses
and tables. They decided that uniting data under "negro" was appropriate because both groups had similar socioeconomic profiles and because
"negro" is the preferred term of black activists and certain academics
(Oliveira 1985: 11–12).

Activists and academics again raised the issue of terminology through
their grassroots campaign around the 1991 census.[1] The campaign,
"Don't Let Your Color Pass in White: Respond with Good Sense," urged Brazilians to check a "darker" color on their census schedules. It
publicly raised two fundamental issues. First, the campaign confronted
the IBGE by asking why "color" was used and not "race", and why
"preto" and "pardo" were used and "negro" was not. Second, the campaign questioned the preferences of most Brazilians to choose "lighter" colors, but especially their decision not to self-select black (preto) on census
schedules.

The 1991 color question was like past questions, with one important
exception: the terms "raça" (race) and "indigena" (indigenous) were

added. The question was rephrased to ask "what is your color or race?";
and indigenous was added to the list of colors white, black, brown, and
yellow. (Since 1940, indigenous persons had been classified as "pardos.")
These two new terms were linked: race applied only to the indigenous
population. Indigenous persons belonged to one race and Brazilians to
another race, with its many colors. The IBGE's decision to include
"indigenous" was reportedly made after consultations with anthropologists and representatives of the Federal Indian Affairs Bureau (FUNAI).
Campaign organizers speculated, however, that it was included at the
request of the World Bank, which wanted demographic information for
Bank initiatives on the protection of indigenous territories.

In the midst of preparations for the 2000 census, there was growing
public and scholarly debate about IBGE methods and terms. In these
debates the IBGE has had to explain and often defend its past and
current methods. The sources of pressure on the IBGE vary. They include demographers, black activists, academics, and politicians. With
the unraveling of racial democracy, the question of who Brazilians really are racially has re-emerged powerfully. There is clear reason for this
connection. The image of a racially democratic and nondiscriminatory
society has hinged on the idea of racial mixture. In fact, a causal link
was drawn that was often presented tautologically: Brazilians are racially
mixed and therefore there can be no discrimination, or there can be
no racial discrimination because Brazilians are racially mixed. The acceptance of discrimination's existence – an existence proven by census
data – has lead unavoidably to the abandonment of the racial democracy
idea and to a rethinking of census terms. The discourses of whitening
and of racial democracy have resided in census methods and texts as
much as they have existed (or not) out in the real world. As Brazilians
now consider whether their society is comprised of distinct racial groups
rather than one racially mixed people, the census will undoubtedly be
involved in advancing a new racial discourse. In the meantime, it now
appears that terminology on the 2000 census will be the same as past censuses: color will be used, not race; "pardo" and "preto" will be used, not
"negro."

Making sense of the American and Brazilian cases

Are the United States and Brazil unique cases of racial enumeration?
What do they teach us? To the first question, the answer is largely "yes."
Although several other countries have at key historical junctures counted
by race, few have developed similarly enduring and pervasive racial

discourses as the United States and Brazil. For example, the 1991 British census was the first to ask an "ethnicity" question; although it was not the first census for which such a question had been considered (Booth 1985; Bhrolcháin 1990; White 1979). The question was introduced for one clear reason: to comply more effectively with the Race Relations Act of 1981, which required racial data in order to measure racial disadvantage. Moreover, the racial discourses of most Latin American societies closely resemble that of Brazil: they are racially mixed populations. Yet, unlike Brazil, few of these discourses have been fully manifested in or advanced by the census. Instead, most other countries have chosen not to count by race (or color) at all. For example, no Venezuelan census since 1854, the year of slavery's abolition, has included race or color questions (Wright 1990). Similarly, neither Colombian, Cuban, nor Dominican Republic censuses count by race or color (Oviedo 1992).

The obvious exceptions to this overall pattern are Nazi Germany and the Apartheid regime in South Africa. It should come as little surprise that in these two cases, the census contained a race question and that such data served the policies of the regimes. However, the extraordinary nature of these regimes and the centrality of racial thought within them have given census-taking in the United States and Brazil, paradoxically, an illusion of ordinariness. American politics, even with its rigid racial segregation, black disenfranchisement, and nonwhite subordination, was not the same as Nazi or Apartheid regime politics. Brazil was the happy land of racial mixture and racial democracy, its deep economic and social inequalities notwithstanding. The irony that Brazil and the United States share company with Nazi Germany and the Apartheid regime in South Africa hardly requires comment.

At the same time, the American and Brazilian experiences richly reveal the sinuous relationship between racial ideas, census-taking, and public policy. They teach us that racial categories on censuses do not merely capture demographic realities, but rather reflect and help to create political realities and ways of thinking and seeing. The categories are themselves intellectual products, social markers, and policy tools. They also teach us that census bureaus must be viewed as the political insiders that they are, not the detached recorders that they purport to be. The recent efforts of Americans and Brazilians to have categories changed, added, or maintained have had the happy effect of forcing census bureaus to account publicly for their methods and rationales. There are no simple, obviously right or obviously wrong, answers to the question of whether American or Brazilian censuses should continue to count by race or color. However, we are better equipped to think about such questions once we understand the complex relationship between race and censuses.

2.1 *US Census Race Categories 1790–2000*
(Presented in the order in which they appeared on schedules)

1790 – 1840

1790   Free White Males; Free White Females; All Other Free Persons; Slaves

1800   Free White Males; Free White Females; All Other Free Persons, except Indians Not Taxed; Slaves

1810   Free White Males; Free White Females; All Other Free Persons, except Indians Not Taxed; Slaves

1820   Free White Males; Free White Females; Free Colored Persons (including all other persons, except Indians Not Taxed); Slaves

1830   Free White Persons; Free Colored Persons; Slaves

1840   Free White Persons; Free Colored Persons; Slaves

1850 – 1920

1850[1]   Black; Mulatto

1860[2]   Black; Mulatto; (Indian)

1870   White; Black; Mulatto; Chinese; Indian

1880   White; Black; Mulatto; Chinese; Indian

1890   White; Black; Mulatto; Quadroon; Octoroon; Chinese; Japanese; Indian

1900   White; Black; Chinese; Japanese; Indian

1910   White; Black; Mulatto; Chinese; Japanese; Indian; Other (+write in)

1920   White; Black; Mulatto; Indian; Chinese; Japanese; Filipino; Hindu; Korean; Other (+write in)

1930 – 1960

1930   White; Negro; Mexican; Indian; Chinese; Japanese; Filipino; Hindu; Korean; (Other races, spell out in full)

1940   White; Negro; Indian; Chinese; Japanese; Filipino; Hindu; Korean; (Other races, spell out in full)

1950   White; Negro; Indian; Japanese; Chinese; Filipino; (Other race – spell out)

1960   White; Negro; American Indian; Japanese; Chinese; Filipino; Hawaiian; Part-Hawaiian; Aleut Eskimo, etc.

1970 – 1990

1970   White; Negro or Black; Indian (Amer.); Japanese; Chinese; Filipino; Hawaiian; Korean; Other (print race)

1980   White; Negro or Black; Japanese; Chinese; Filipino; Korean; Vietnamese; Indian (Amer.); Asian Indian; Hawaiian; Guamanian; Samoan; Eskimo; Aleut; Other (specify)

1990   White; Black or Negro; Indian (Amer.); Eskimo; Aleut; Chinese; Filipino; Hawaiian; Korean; Vietnamese; Japanese; Asian Indian; Samoan; Guamanian; Other API (Asian or Pacific Islander); Other race

---

[1] In 1850 and 1860, free persons were enumerated on schedules for 'free inhabitants'; slaves were enumerated on schedules designated for 'slave inhabitants.' On the free schedule, enumerator instructions read (in part): "In all cases where the person is white leave the space blank in the column marked 'Color.'"

[2] Although "Indian" was not listed on the census schedule, the instructions read: "'Indians.' – Indians not taxed are not to be enumerated. The families of Indians who have renounced tribal rule, and who under State or Territorial laws exercise the rights of citizens, are to be enumerated. In all such cases write "Ind." opposite their names, in column 6, under heading 'Color.'" As in the 1850 census, enumerators were instructed to leave the space blank when the person was white.

2.2 *Brazilian Color Questions and Categories, 1872–1991*

1872 – 1910	
1872	White (branco); Black (preto); Brown (pardo); Caboclo (Mestizo Indian)
1880	No census
1890	White (branco); Black (preto); Caboclo (Mestizo Indian); Mestiço
1900	No color question
1910	No census
1920 – 1950	
1920	No color question, but extended discussion about "whitening."
1930	No census (Revolution of 1930)
1940	White (branco); Black (preto); Yellow (amarelo). If the respondent did not fit into one of these three categories, enumerator was instructed to place a horizontal line on census schedule.
1950	White (branco); Black (preto); Brown (pardo); Yellow (amarelo).
1960 – 1991	
1960	White (branco); Black (preto); Brown (pardo); Yellow (amarelo); Indian (indio)
1970	No color question
1980	White (branco); Black (preto); Brown (pardo); Yellow (amarelo)
1991	White (branco); Black (preto); Brown (pardo); Yellow (amarelo); Indigena (indigenous)

NOTE

1. The 1990 census became the 1991 census because of government mishandling and budgetary battles.

REFERENCES

Anderson, Margo 1988, *The American Census: A Social History*, New Haven: Yale University Press.

Andrews, George Reid 1991, *Blacks and Whites in São Paulo, Brazil: 1888–1988*, Madison: University of Wisconsin Press.

Azevedo, Fernando de 1950, *Brazilian Culture: An Introduction to the Study of Culture in Brazil*, New York: Macmillan.

Barkan, Elazar 1992, *The Retreat of Scientific Racism*, New York and Cambridge: Cambridge University Press.

Bhrolcháin, Máire Ní 1990, "The Ethnicity Question for the 1991 Census: Background and Issues," *Ethnic and Racial Studies* 13: 542–67.

Booth, Heather 1985, "Which 'Ethnic Question'? The Development of Questions Identifying Ethnic Origin in Official Statistics," *The Sociological Review* 23: 254–74.

Burns, E. Bradford 1970, *A History of Brazil*, New York: Columbia University Press.

Choldin, Harvey M. 1986, "Statistics and Politics: The 'Hispanic Issue' in the 1980 Census," *Demography* 23: 403–18.

Dippie, Brian 1982, *The Vanishing American: White Attitudes and U.S. Indian Policy*, Middletown, Conn.: Wesleyan University Press.

Eakin, Marshall C. 1985, "Race and Identity: Silvio Romero, Science, and Social Thought in Late 19th Century Brazil," *Luso-Brazilian Review* 22: 151–74.

Edmonston, Barry and Schulze, Charles (eds.) 1995, *Modernizing the U.S. Census*, Washington, DC: National Academy Press.

Espiritu, Yen Le 1992, *Asian-American Panethnicity: Bridging Institutions and Identities*, Philadelphia: Temple University Press.

Finkelman, Paul 1986, "Prelude to the Fourteenth Amendment: Black Legal Rights in the Antebellum North," *Rutgers Law Journal* 17: 415–82.

Fogel, Robert 1989, *Without Consent or Contract: The Rise and Fall of American Slavery*, New York: W.W. Norton.

Fredrickson, George M. 1971, *The Black Image in the White Mind: The Debate on Afro-American Character and Destiny, 1817–1914*, New York: Harper & Row.

Gates, Henry Louis(ed.)1985, "Introduction," in Gates (ed.), *"Race," Writing, and Difference*, Chicago: The University of Chicago Press, p. 5.

Goldberg, David Theo 1992, "The Semantics of Race", *Ethnic and Racial Studies* 15: 543–69.

Gould, Stephen Jay 1981, *The Mismeasure of Man*, New York: W.W. Norton.

Goyer, Doreen and Dornschke, Elaine 1983, *The Handbook of National Population Censuses: Latin America and the Caribbean, North America and Oceania*, Westport, Conn.: Greenwood Press.

Haller, John S. 1971, *Outcasts from Evolution: Scientific Attitudes of Racial Inferiority, 1859–1900*, Urbana: University of Illinois Press.

Hanchard, Michael G. 1994, *Orpheus and Power: The 'Movimento Negro' of Rio de Janeiro and São Paulo, Brazil*, Princeton: Princeton University Press.

Haney-Lopez, Ian 1996, *White by Law: The Legal Construction of Race*, New York: New York University Press.

Higginbotham, Evelyn Brooks 1992, "African-American Women's History and the Metalanguage of Race," *Signs: Journal of Women in Culture and Society* 17: 251–74.

Hirschman, Charles 1986, "The Making of Race in Colonial Malaya: Political Economy and Racial Ideology," *Sociological Forum* 1: 330–61.

1987, "The Meaning and Measurement of Ethnicity in Malaysia: An Analysis of Census Classifications," *The Journal of Asian Studies* 46: 555–82.

Horsman, Reginald 1981, *Race and Manifest Destiny*, Cambridge, Mass.: Harvard University Press.

1987, *Josiah Nott of Mobile: Southerner, Physician, and Racial Theorist*, Baton Rouge: Louisiana State University Press.

Instituto Brasileiro de Geográfia e Estatística (IBGE) 1950, "Estudos sobre a Composição da População do Brasil Segundo a Cor," *Estudos de Estatística Teórica e Aplicada: Estatística Demográfica* 11: 7–9.

Jordan, Winthrop D. 1968, *White Over Black: American Attitudes Toward the Negro, 1550–1812*, Chapel Hill: University of North Carolina Press.

Kettner, James H. 1978, *The Development of American Citizenship, 1608–1870*, Chapel Hill: University of North Carolina Press.

Klein, Herbert S. 1986, *African Slavery in Latin America and the Caribbean*, New York: Oxford University Press.

Kolchin, Peter 1993, *American Slavery: 1619–1877*, New York: Hill and Wang.

Lovell, W. George and Lutz, Christopher H. 1994, "Conquest and Population: Maya Demography in Historical Perspective," *Latin American Research Review* 29: 133–40.

Maram, Sheldon L. 1977, "Labor and the Left in Brazil, 1890–1921: A Movement Aborted," *Hispanic American Historical Review* 57: 254–72.

Marx, Anthony 1998, *Making Race and Nation: A Comparison of the United States, South Africa and Brazil*, New York and Cambridge: Cambridge University Press.

Murray, Pauli (ed.) 1951, *States' Laws on Race and Color*, Cincinnati, Ohio: Women's Division of Christian Service.

Nogueira, Oracy 1985, *Tanto Preto Quanto Branco: Estudos de Relações Raciais*, São Paulo: T.A. Queiroz.

Oliveira, Lucia Elena Garcia de, Porcaro, Rosa Maria and Araujo, Tereza Cristina N. 1985, *O Lugar do Negro na Força de Trabalho*, Rio de Janeiro: Instituto Brasileiro de Geografia e Estatistica (IBGE).

Omi, Michael and Winant, Howard 1986, *Racial Formation in the United States: From the 1960s to the 1980s*, New York: Routledge.

Oviedo, Rodolfo Monge 1992, "Are We or Aren't We?" *NACLA: Report on the Americas* 4:19.

Schwarcz, Lilia Moritz 1993, *O Espetáculo das Raças: Cientistas, instituições e questão racial no Brasil, 1870–1930*, São Paulo: Companhia das Letras.

Skidmore, Thomas E. 1993, *Black Into White: Race and Nationality in Brazilian Thought*, Durham: Duke University Press.

Smith, Rogers 1997, *Civic Ideals: Conflicting Visions of Citizenship in U.S. History*, New Haven: Yale University Press.

Stanton, William 1968, *The Leopard's Spots: Scientific Attitudes Towards Race in America, 1815–59*, Chicago: University of Chicago Press.

Stepan, Nancy Leys 1982, *The Idea of Race in Science: Great Britain, 1800–1960*, Hamden, Conn.: Archon Books.

Stocking, George 1968, *Race, Culture, and Evolution*, New York: Free Press.

Thornton, Russell 1987, *American Indian Holocaust and Survival*, Norman: University of Oklahoma Press.

US Bureau of the Census 1930, "Instructions to Enumerators," National Archives, Vol. 2 of Scrapbooks, RG 29, Washington, DC: GPO, p. 26.

US Bureau of the Census 1960, *Historical Statistics of the United States: Colonial Times to 1957*, Washington, DC: GPO.

US Bureau of the Census 1989, *200 Years of Census Taking: Population and Housing Questions, 1790–1990*, Washington DC: GPO.

US Congressional Globe 1850, 31st Cong., 1st sess., April 9, 1850, pp. 671–75.

Vianna, Oliveira 1956, *Evolução do Povo Brasileiro*, Rio de Janeiro: Jose Olympio.

White, R. M. 1979, "What's in a Name? Problems in Official and Legal Usages of 'Race'," *New Community: Journal of the Commission for Racial Equality* 7: 333–49.

Wright, Winthrop 1990, *Cafe con Leche: Race, Class, and National Image in Venezuela*, Austin: University of Texas Press.

3 Ethnic categorizations in censuses: comparative observations from Israel, Canada, and the United States

Calvin Goldscheider

Censuses and other official documents gather information to carry out a variety of political, economic, and social objectives. In counting and categorizing residents of the state, the census has to cope in an official way with who is defined as a member of the society and how they should be identified in the count. Issues of counting are elementary but not simple. Who is counted as a legitimate resident of the state (e.g., how are non-legal residents and temporary workers treated in official statistics) and what does residence mean (is it limited to *de facto* residents or are those temporarily living elsewhere included among the state's population) appear on the surface to be straightforward questions, but are at the center of some of the most complex and politically torturous issues facing old and new states. In the global world where movement between states is increasing and taking on new forms, where returning "home" has become more routine, where cases of escape and resettlement can be counted in the millions annually, questions about who are the legitimate residents to be counted in censuses and how they should be classified and categorized are not only technical bureaucratic questions.

Membership in a state involves decisions in the formation of policies. Do particular policies apply only to citizens? Who has representation in local or national governments? Who has rights and entitlements? Questions of how to categorize persons (by simple categories such as age, gender, and marital status – in what category do we place cohabitants? – or even more complex ethnic origin or racial categories, our current focus) always involve decisions that are implicitly political and anchored in ideology and norms. There are no simple, objective census questions, even though researchers often analyze the answers to census questions *as if* the information in the census were unbiased and objective.

Turning the question on its head, official documents reveal the formal construction of categories and groups, and the political contexts in which

This chapter has benefited from the thoughtful comments of David Kertzer, Matthew Gutmann, and Alan Zuckerman.

71

they are shaped. Often the official constructions reinforce a particular view of groups within society and convey a "theory" of groupness. What would we know about ethnicity if we only had the census definition or categories? If our only text about ethnic divisions and categories in a society came from official documents, what would be missing? Historically, if all we knew about ethnicity was derived from census categories and classifications, our understanding of the political, cultural, and social meanings of ethnicity would be severely limited and, indeed, largely distorted. Census definitions of ethnicity tell us more about the construction of ethnic categories within political ideologies than the reality of ethnic divisions.

I focus in this chapter on several illustrations of how these official constructions of ethnic group membership have developed in censuses and other official data collection systems. I draw upon examples from Israel, Canada, and the United States, with some references to European countries. There are, of course, ethnic issues in the statistical collections of most countries.[1] I review illustrations from these three countries not for how ethnic differences are salient in differentiating their populations, in perpetuating inequalities or reinforcing ethnic cultures. Rather my goal is to address the following questions: what do we learn about the construction of ethnic group categories from official data in these countries? Are we constrained in our understanding of ethnicity when we focus exclusively on these official constructions? What is the "theory" underlying what the census categories mean? If we only knew ethnicity from census definitions and categorization, what kind of ethnicity would we be describing? I also want to briefly address how the construction of ethnic categories in the census may define the nature of groups and may reinforce one among several conceptions of ethnic categories.

The census conveys official, contemporaneous understandings of ethnic categories, but it does not create ethnicity any more than it creates regional or gender divisions. There is a reality about ethnic differentiation, often poorly or incompletely captured by census questions. How census categories shape political conceptualizations of ethnicity is an open question, and one difficult to disentangle from the conceptualizations that inform the shaping of the questions themselves. Clearly, what is real about ethnic groups is not simply a function of official definition and construction. Yet particular conceptions of ethnicity are often formed and reinforced by definitions incorporated in official documents. And at the same time, the complexities and multiple dimensions of ethnicity are only partially revealed by official data. Consider the shifts over time and the changing significance in the United States censuses, from "non-white" to "Negro" to "African American" and "Black American." Consider the shift from "Spanish speaking" residents, as used in previous

US censuses, to the category "Hispanic Americans" and in turn the creation of the category "White non-Hispanics." Consider the use of foreign birth, language, religion or ancestry as the basis for ethnic group classification in Canada, or the combined use of all four. Since ethnic categories are often categories of the Other, consider the use of the category "Non-Nordic" in Sweden, to define immigrants from Iran and Turkey and eastern Europe, or "Non-Jews" in Israel, to identify Arabs (Moslems, Christians, and Druze), or "Non-Whites" in the United States, to characterize Black Americans and Asian Americans.

I selected Israel, Canada, and the United States as my illustrations because of their long-term confrontation with issues of ethnic/immigrant group identification in official statistics, their extensive history of immigration from diverse countries of origin, the rich experience in each country of the transition from immigrant to ethnic group among the second and third generations, and the political salience of "origins" in multiple dimensions of social life. In contrast, new ethnic forms are emerging in Europe as the second generation of recent immigrants from former colonies are socialized in France and England. These forms are similar to the reconfigurations that will emerge among recent migrants from east to west Europe, and among the movement of refugees and labor migrants to other western countries. These are complicated cases, where in large part census data attempt to identify immigrants by country of origin (and their children by place of birth or origin of their parents) rather than directly by "ethnic" origin. In this regard, the early distinctions using a "racial" or race/ethnic category in official documents of Europe is a separate issue of political analysis that we shall leave for others to disentangle. One final introductory comment: The nature of states in Europe, with its longer tradition of nationalism and nation-building, makes it difficult in the political sense to refer to recent Turkish immigrants in Sweden as Turkish-Swedes or Chilean immigrants as Chilean-Swedes. Nor are Turks and Italians in Germany referred to as Turkish-Germans or Italian-Germans! We have less difficulty in the United States referring to Italian-Americans, Swedish-Americans, and Turkish-Americans (although we are likely to refer to Chilean-Americans as Hispanics). The multiple ethnic (in the specific sense of national origins) identities that characterize the United States are certainly not unique, but they are peculiar when compared to the European context.

Immigration and the official measurement of ethnicity have been core concerns in all three cases that I examine, embedded politically and culturally in the fabric of society in the process of nation-building. In what follows, I review how ethnicity has been measured in these countries and identify some problems inherent in their conceptualization of ethnicity. We shall pay particular attention to the broader lessons that may be derived from the comparative analysis of official categorizations and measurements of ethnicity over time.

The denial of ethnicity and its official measurement: the case of Israel

Ethnicity captures an odd mixture of national origin and religion in Israel and goes to the heart of who is a member of the society. Ethnic group divisions within Jewish and Arab populations in Israel, as elsewhere, are official constructions, formed from many different sources and linked in critical ways to political, social, cultural, and economic factors. As one of our case studies, the Israeli construction of ethnicity reveals much about the society and reflects significant political and ideological positions. I won't review the details and the nuances of these patterns but rather examine the question of measurement of ethnicity in official publications of Israel. Nevertheless, we need some socio-historical guidelines.

Israeli society has been shaped by immigration, more than most countries. The large number of immigrants to Israel relative to the native-born population, the diverse national origins of the immigrant streams, and the powerful ideological underpinnings of Israel's immigration policies are unique in comparative context. In combination, these features have been critical in nation-building and have had profound implications for the emergence of Israeli society: from the demographic impact of numbers to the complexities of politics; from internal ethnic group formation to the Palestinian-Israeli conflict; from regional developments to social inequalities; from cultural diversity and pluralism to westernization and capitalistic economic development. As for the United States at an earlier point in time, immigration *is* Israeli history.[2]

From the establishment of the state of Israel in 1948 to the end of the twentieth century, over two-and-a-half million immigrants arrived in Israel from diverse countries of origin. They were added to a base population in 1948 of 650,000, in large part with the economic, political, and ideological support of the government. Despite the diversity of immigration sources, immigration has been a major strategy of nation-building and national integration in the state of Israel. The Zionist movement since the nineteenth century and the state from its establishment in 1948 have sought to gather together in one country those around the world who consider themselves Jewish by religion or ancestry. The processes, patterns, and policies of immigration to Israel have been distinctive. The conditions preceding and following the Holocaust and World War II in Europe, the emerging nationalism among Jews around the world, the conditions of Jews in Arab-Moslem countries, and the radical changes in the 1990s in Eastern Europe with the breakup of the Soviet Union, have been among the most obvious external circumstances influencing the immigration of Jews from a wide range of countries to Israel.

Jewish ethnic differentiation in Israel reflects a combination of the social and cultural origins of immigrant groups and the effects of Israeli social conditions. Ethnic divisions among Jews do not derive from Zionist ideological sources or explicit Israeli policies. To the contrary: Zionism denies the salience of ethnicity as a continuing factor for the Israeli Jewish population. National origin differences among Jews are viewed as a product of the long-term dispersal of the Jewish people in the Diaspora. Returning to a homeland, it is argued, will result in the emergence of a new Jew, untainted by the culture and psychology of exile and freed from the constraints and limitations of experiences in places of previous (non-Israel) residence. Zionism's construction of Jewish people-hood therefore involves the assignment of ethnic origin to the minority experiences of Jews outside of Israel and hence requires its devaluation. Zionism rejected both the assimilation of Jews in communities outside of Israel and the retention of ethnic minority status as viable solutions to the position of Jews in modernizing societies. Israel, Zionism posits, is the national homeland of Jews, their ancestry. Their ethnicity is not the source of their identities: Israel is. The recognition of ethnic origins as the country of ancestry would represent the denial of "returning" home for Jewish immigrants since the establishment of the state (although it was not "home" for 2,000 years – an unprecedented stretch in demographic and statistical measurement, but perhaps not in culture or ideology). To recognize the continuing salience of ethnicity would be to treat coming to Israel as *immigration* and not as *Aliya*, the imperative ascent to Israel of Zionist ideology. To deny "returning" to Israel would be ideologically and politically untenable, as would the acknowledgment of the salience and value of ethnic origins.

The continuing distinctiveness of ethnic origin in differentiating key aspects of social life in Israel is viewed therefore as temporary, something reflecting the past, diminishing in the present and expected to disappear in future generations. Thus, Zionist ideology constructs the obvious evidence about ethnic differentiation among Jews in Israel as transitional and largely irrelevant to the longer-term goals of Jewish national integration and nation-building.

The goal of nation-building and the strong ideology about the centrality of immigration build on this Zionist ideology. There is an official anticipated integration, or in Israeli language "absorption," of immigrants from diverse ethnic and socioeconomic backgrounds into the national culture and polity. The language to describe the integration of those from diverse origins in Israel is unusual when viewed in comparative contexts. "Assimilation" in Israel is almost always used to describe what happens to Jews when confronted with choices about integration in countries outside of Israel and almost always has a negative connotation, i.e., the loss of community and Jewish identity. The goal of "absorption" in Israel was to mitigate social splits along lines of national origin and has been among the nation's ideological and political objectives since its establishment. Policies to close the economic and cultural gaps among immigrants were designed in the hope of achieving the rapid integration and equalization of immigrant groups from diverse countries of origin.[3]

Israeli policy-makers fully expect the total assimilation of Jews from diverse countries of origin as the third generation emerges, distant from ethnic origins, socialized into the national polity and culture by exposure to educational institutions and the military, and raised in families where the parents are native-born Israelis. Indeed, the ethnicity of the third generation is expected to be marginal, the cultural remnant of no social and economic significance. Nation-building is expected to remove the diversity of ethnic origins as new forms of state loyalty emerge focusing solely on Jewish peoplehood. Religious similarity, military service, and the collective consciousness derived from Israel's security situation operate to dilute ethnic differences. This is the official and often the social science perspective within Israel. Ethnic cleavage becomes a problem to be solved, not a cultural trait or a source of generational socioeconomic inequality.

This is not the place to evaluate the detailed empirical evidence that strikingly contradicts these notions of the elimination of ethnic differentiation in Israel (Goldscheider 1996). Our goal, instead, is to examine how this ideology is translated and reinforced through official census and related materials.

Nowhere is the ideology that denies the salience of ethnicity more poignant symbolically than in the way ethnic origin is treated in official government statistical publications. Ethnic origin among Jews in Israel is almost always categorized in terms of place of birth of the person (i.e., some "objective" fact that is ascriptive and unchanging). For the Israeli-born, place of birth of parents (usually father) is obtained. This is also an unchanging characteristic. In that context, ethnic origin is simply limited by time (until the third generation needs to be counted) and is descriptive of the immediate past. Using these definitions, it is a simple step to the conclusion that generational distance from foreignness or exposure to Israeli society marks the progress toward the end of ethnic identity and ethnic self-identification. The question of ethnic origin and of "ancestry" of the third generation (the native born of native-born parents) has not so far been addressed officially in Israel. Indeed, to judge solely from the official government publications and statistical bureaus in Israel, this third generation in Israel has no differentiating ethnic origin of significance. They are defined simply as Israelis born of Israeli-born parents, with no need to identify the origins of previous generations. Native-born Jewish-Israelis of native-born parents, unlike their native-born parents, are "just" Israeli without ethnic markers. In contrast, the Arab-Israeli population retains its "ethnic" designation indefinitely.

Persons of mixed ethnic origins are only viewed within the statistical system of Israel, where inter-ethnic marriages are considered the quintessential symbol of the emergence of the new Israeli. Jewish ethnic intermarriage in Israel is a complex puzzle, involving the formation of new ethnic identities among children. Paradoxically, intermarriage often *strengthens* ethnic identity at the group level because of social class and gender trade-offs (Goldscheider 1996: chapter 10). How the children of mixed ethnic marriages develop a set of identities is rarely assessed, since the assumption is that they will be ethnic-less Israelis (Goldscheider 1996; Eisenbach 1992). And data on ethnic origins of the second generation are obtained only through the place of birth of fathers.[4]

How are the multitudes of countries of immigration categorized among the first two generations? These countries are grouped into two broad divisions – Europe-America and Asia-Africa (with a third category, Israeli born of Israeli-born parents).[5] This ethnic categorization is unique historically among Jewish communities of the world and is constructed as an internal ethnic division only among Jews in the state of Israel. It is a rejection of the historically more complex ethnic division between Sephardi and Ashkenazi Jewries that has a series of cultural linkages.

In the latest Israeli census of 1995 there were, as before, no provisions to obtain the ancestry of respondents directly except for country of origin of the foreign-born and country of origin of the father of the native-born Israeli. Ethnic identifiers are indirectly available for the third generation of Israeli born of Israeli-born parents only through the place of origin of parents among those living with their parents. Among third-generation Israeli Jews not living with their parents, no ethnic origin identifiers are available.[6] Thus, despite the salience of ethnic origin in a multi-ethnic society, nothing beyond foreign birth, or the country of origin of fathers for those who were native-born, is collected, and these are re-categorized into the newly designated ethnic forms created by Israeli society.

One final note relates to the official categorization of the minority populations in Israel who are not Jewish. How does the official statistical bureau deal with the question of non-Jewish populations in Israel? The significant Arab minorities in Israel are citizens of the state but have not been defined or classified by ethnic origin. As constructed in government documents, the Arab-Israeli populations are not Palestinians and are often not designated as Arabs. They are grouped as Moslems, Christians, Druze, and others. The distinction is based on religious, not ethnic/national, divisions. Along with the question of "who is a Jew" (by religion, national identity, self-definition, or religion of the mother), the definition of Arabs in Israel lies centrally in the quagmire of whether Jews constitute a nationality or a religious group or both. The issue of definition is at the core of political and ideological debates about the nationality of the Arab population. The treatment of Arabs as religious groups denies (symbolically) their ethnic national identity and their political relationship to Arabs elsewhere in the region.

This "religious" designation appears on Israeli identity cards and on all formal documents (nationality among Jews does not appear but "religion" does). The category "non-Jews" is regularly used in official publications to contrast with Israelis who are Jewish. There have been some changes in how these ethnic designations are presented in some recent Israeli publications from the Central Bureau of Statistics of Israel. In the late 1990s there are official Israeli publications that have tables and charts that present statistics comparing "Jews" and "Arabs", but there is almost always a reversion to the category Moslems as the "ethnic" subgroup among Arabs. In a politically comic but revealing document of official statistics among Palestinians, data in tabular form are presented to document the Arab population in Israel and refer to them as the "non-Jewish" population of Israel! This was the category used in the first current status report, series no.1, of the Palestinian Bureau of Statistics, 1994, published by the Palestinian National Authority under the signature of Chairman Yassar Arafat, largely copied from the *Statistical Yearbook of Israel.*

The designation of Arabs as "non-Jewish" is consistent with the earliest reference in official documents. The Balfour declaration of 1917, specifying the British commitment toward the establishment of a national homeland for the Jewish people, explicitly notes that the civil and religious rights of the "non-Jewish" communities should be safeguarded. Indeed the "minority" issue in Israel is a religious issue within the government bureaus, and political and economic allocations are through the Ministry of Religious Affairs. The formal designation of Arabs as non-Jews and the subdivision of Jewish Israelis as of Asian-African, of European-American or of Israeli origins is embedded in the political, social and cultural orientation of everyday Israeli life. The official classification reinforces ethnic group labeling and, hence, the ethnic divisions within the society.

Ethnicity in a multicultural context: the complex case of ethnicity in Canada

Israel creates newly designed forms of ethnicity in the political and ideological context of ethnic denial for Jewish-Israelis and religious designation for Arab-Israelis. In contrast, Canadian constructions of ethnicity have been extensive in the attempt to categorize immigrants and their children, as well as to identify the ethnic origins or ancestries among the third and later generations. This parallels what has happened in the United States in the official attempt to identify, categorize, and measure ethnicity through census questions about ethnic ancestry and origins.

When complex and multiple ethnic questions are asked, the results are equally complex. This has become increasingly the case in Canada (and, as we shall see later, in the United States as well), when ethnic self-identification through self-enumeration replaced the classification of ethnicity by enumerators and when multiple responses are encouraged in an open-ended ancestry question. The complexity becomes exacerbated when lists of examples of possible responses are included as part of the census question, since the order of ethnic choices on the list and the specific origins listed influence the responses given. To further complicate matters, the *absence* of multiple choices on race or ethnic questions in the census forces respondents to select a single group when their own identities are more complex.

Changes over time in the formulation and presentation of census questions result in a lack of comparability from one census to the next; hence the difficulty in assessing changes in the ethnic composition of the population. While analysts enjoy the challenge of complexities, bureaucrats do not, and policy-makers are left with ambiguities and discrepancies. It is of little significance that some of these challenges reflect the social reality, since ethnic boundaries need to be clearly defined and policies need to be implemented for designated groups. One consequence of the ambiguities both in the count and in the designated boundaries of racial and ethnic groups in complex multi-ethnic societies is the leeway this allows for institutions and agencies to construct their own definitions of ethnic groups and to interpret the direction of changes over time in group numerical strength.

The measure of ethnic identification has varied over time in Canada as the government has directly confronted the difficulties of measuring ethnic origins generations after immigration has occurred. In the twentieth century, only the first five decennial censuses in Canada (1901–41) used racial origins questions. Questions about "ethnic group" identification or "ethnic and cultural origins" (including what had previously been classified as race) have characterized decennial censuses since then. The 1991 census did not include an explicit race question ("racial" minorities were derived from other ethnic and place of birth data in 1986 and 1991). The 1996 census asked a direct question on the country's "racial" minority populations for the first time. This was the result of legislative requirements regarding employment equity issues, race relations, and racism in Canada (Boyd *et al.* 1998). The question on visible minorities was "Is this person . . ." and the responses were listed as White, Chinese, South Asian, Black, Arab/West Asian, Filipino, Latin American, Japanese, and Korean. These categories are clearly Canada-specific.

Over time, the ethnic origin questions have been modified to eliminate two specifications: (1) paternal ethnic inheritance; and (2) ethnic origin on coming to "this continent". In the 1961 census, the question was *"To what ethnic or cultural group did you or your ancestor (on the male side) belong on coming to this continent?"* In 1991, the census question was *"To which ethnic or cultural group(s) did this person's ancestors belong?"* Canadian censuses shifted away from questions limited to ethnicity based on an "ancestor on the male side" in 1961 and 1971 to "ancestors" in 1981. Changes in the wording of questions have also shifted from identifying respondents' ethnic and cultural group "on first coming to this continent" to the 1991 census question on ancestors. These shifts occurred along with the introduction of self-enumeration in 1971 and the acceptance of multiple responses to the ethnic origin question in 1981 (P. White, *et al.* 1993: 221–30 and appendix A). Unlike the multiple responses accepted in the ethnic and cultural question (four write-in spaces are left for this question), there is only one space for the pre-coded responses to the visible minorities question.

No less important are the changes in the list of possible responses to the single ethnic origin question and to their order on the questionnaire. The list of origins offered as examples in the question has included national origin groups (such as "French" and "English") as well as "Native Indian" or "North American Indian", "Negro" or "Black" and "Jewish". So ethnic origin is classified in the broadest sense to include "race" and religion as well as national origins. The order of origins listed has shifted as well, from an alphabetical list in the 1961 census to a listing of English before French ethnic and cultural origin in 1971 to French before English in 1981 and 1991.

The irony is that, despite the emphasis in Canadian censuses on multiple ways of measuring ethnic origins and identity, an increasingly large number of Canadians define their ethnic origins as "Canadian." In earlier censuses, ethnic identity in terms of "Canadian" or "American" was not considered within the realm of ethnic origin in Canada. Respondents were not encouraged to report these groups as ancestries, and before 1951 such responses were not accepted as valid (P. White *et al.* 1993: 233). In the 1996 Canadian census, "Canadian" was included for the first time on the list of legitimate sample answers to the ethnic origin question. The power of that sample list was such that in 1996 "Canadian" had become the largest ethnic origin group in Canada, accounting for one-third of the ancestry responses: one in five persons (5.3 million) declared "Canadian" as their only ethnic ancestry, and another 3.5 million reported "Canadian" in combination with other origins.

The response to ethnic ancestry in terms of Canadian does not simply reflect major population composition shifts but also is a consequence of the fundamentals of identity politics. In part it reflects newspaper and media campaigns emphasizing "count me Canadian", as well as increases in the population with long-term historical roots in Canada and the very sharp decline in French ethnic origin responses in 1996. This is partly because there are different symbolic meanings of "Canadian" and its French equivalent "Canadien." The latter term is imbued with the flavor of an indigenous group, while the former refers to location within a nation or shared community in a territory governed by the Canadian state (Boyd 1998). Canadien is how descendants of French settlers used to identify themselves in contrast to the English. In a country where English and French language and nationality are part of a continuing social and political debate, the ethnic origins question on the census is not marginal. Increasingly, those responding to an ethnic question on the census are identifying neither as British nor as French but as something else, and increasingly not something of any non-Canadian ethnic or cultural origin.

Nevertheless, the political salience of ethnicity is as profound in Canada as in Israel, although clearly in different ways. As in Israel, ethnic origin issues are embedded in national and local politics and in the social and cultural life of Canadians. Ethnicity as a concept, and ethnic origins as an official measure, are central to the implementation of key federal government programs in Canada. Who you are ethnically and how you are defined ethnically in official records really matters politically (Boyd 1997).

Thus, unlike Israel's denial of the salience of ethnicity in their official records, Canada has responded to ethnic issues and multiculturalism by multiplying the ways in which ethnicity is constructed in their censuses and in official statistics. They have attempted to test and pre-test these questions, with the general population and with the organizations and agencies that serve the interests and needs of ethnic and cultural groups. In turn, the ways in which the census has constructed these categories have influenced the ways in which the people have identified themselves. Ethnicity in Canada involves both government interests and the interests of the multiple governmental organizations that relate to statistical collection agencies and interest groups. There is almost always an implicit threat among powerful agencies to boycott the census if the instrument is not to their liking. In addition to centralized statistical agencies, which have direct input into the construction of ethnic measures in official data systems, there are agencies that deal with multiculturalism and equity in employment that are also concerned with ethnic issues. There are agencies in the federal government of Canada (e.g. Canadian Heritage) whose power derives from numerical counts of groups other than English or French. Another group of players consists of those who are the likely beneficiaries of funding programs that are based on ethnic origin data. Increasing "Canadian" responses imply losses of funding to particular groups at the federal and the local municipal levels. The lobbying of groups for measures of ethnicity that reflect their numerical strength is obvious: principles of survey research and census design often take a back seat to where the real power lies.

Empirically, there is substantial ethnic flux, by which Canadians over time lose one or more of their parental ancestries without acquiring others. Ethnicity is conspicuously multidimensional in its measurement in Canada. Language, race, ancestry, place of birth, and ethnic identity have been investigated separately in the past, with specific questions on religion. By 1991, these questions were combined into one ethnic or cultural origin question. As a result, the variation over time is enormous and the difficulties of tracing changes in ethnic composition over time are considerable. The ethnic and cultural origin questions result in complexities and ambiguities, although the results fit in with the argument that ethnicity involves choices and complexities rarely captured by simple or "objective" questions.

The flux, or the generational and life-course variation dimensions of ethnic identity that result from multiple responses, is not a weakness of the measurement but its strength. The emergence of Canadian as a response in the 1996 census for specific ethnic subgroups suggests that the high volatility between earlier and subsequent censuses is a serious challenge for researchers. Lobbying efforts around the development of the census questionnaire will increase for the Canadian census in 2001, as it has for the 2000 census in the United States. The flux generationally, and the "inconsistencies" over several surveys by the same respondents, are not evidence of error but reflect the detailed measures of ethnicity and ethnic origins. Researchers have concluded that "fine-tuning one ethnic origin question will not necessarily produce levels of validity and reliability that are commonly associated with more fixed traits such as age, and that are usually considered to indicate sound survey research" (Boyd 1997).

The United States: ethnic ancestries, Hispanics and race

The experience of asking questions about ethnic origin in the United States census parallels in many ways the patterns in Canada. The conspicuous differences rest with the continuous separation of race from ethnic categories in the United States and the emphasis on a separate question regarding those of Hispanic origins. Both distinctive features reflect the particular racial history of the United States and the specific connection to Hispanic-origin and Spanish-speaking populations of Mexico, Puerto Rico, Cuba, and others from Central and Latin America.

The 1990 United States census included five ethnic- and race-related questions: direct questions on (1) race; (2) Hispanic origin; and (3) ancestry, plus (4) place of birth of the individual; and (5) current language use. The race and Hispanic questions were asked of all persons, and the ancestry question was asked of a sample. Since 1970, these questions were based on self-enumeration. Information on the racial identification of individuals prior to 1970 was obtained primarily through observation by the enumerator, curtailing self-identification among those of mixed racial parentage.[7] There has been a race question included on all US censuses since the first census in 1790[8], as well as a question on place of birth.

Hispanic-origin self-identification questions have been included since 1970 and the ancestry question was included in 1980 and 1990. Hispanic-origin populations were identified in earlier censuses through indirect measures based on birthplace of persons and parents, mother tongue, and Spanish surname items. However in 1980 and 1990, the question on the place of birth of parents was dropped, having been included since 1870. The ancestry question has been open-ended, requiring persons to write in their responses. Unlike the race or the Hispanic-origin questions, multiple origin answers were permitted for ancestry. Examples of acceptable ancestry were included with a list of twenty-two ethnic origins, along with specific instructions to exclude religious groups as an ancestry. Hence, Jews exist as an ethnic and cultural group in Canada but explicitly do not in the United States. The 1980 census included ancestry for the first time, moving away from limiting ancestry to the first two generations.[9] The proportion that report American or United States as their ancestry, unlike in Canada, remains relatively low.[10]

A comparison of 1980 and 1990 US census ancestry groups, when taking into account whether the group was listed as an example, is most revealing. Both German and English were listed in 1980 and had the same number of persons who selected that group as their ancestry. But German, not English, was listed in 1990. The numbers selecting German ancestry increased by 18 percent; the number selecting English ancestry declined by 34 percent. Similarly, the number of persons selecting Italian and French ancestry was similar in 1980, when both were listed. In 1990, when Italian was listed, the number selecting Italian ancestry increased by 21 percent; the number selecting French ancestry (which was not listed) declined by 20 percent. Similarly, there were very significant increases of those selecting an ancestry when listed in 1990 and not listed in 1980. For example, "French Canadian" was not listed in the US Census as an ancestry in 1980 and 780,000 persons selected that ancestry. In 1990, when listed as an ancestry choice, 2,167,000 selected French Canadian as an ancestry (Passel 1994).

In a similar way, the constructed categories of ethnicity and the form of the question posed is influenced by the changing extent of political identification with a group. Between 1960 and 1990 the population of American Indians increased almost fourfold, to just under 2 million persons. This very high rate of increase in the absence of immigration is simply incompatible with what we know about American Indian birth rates and mortality rates. It is estimated that three-fifths of the growth can be attributed to changes in self-identification. Any analysis of the American Indian population must take into account these identification changes (Sandefur *et al.* 1996).

As in Canada, the special race question in the United States and the forced single response in that category has precluded multiracial identification. Thus, children of mixed-race parents are forced to choose a single racial group on official census forms. When parents select the race category for their children in racially mixed households, the results are interesting and differ among groups of different "racial" origins.

An analysis of the children of mixed-race households (Black and White Americans and Japanese and White Americans) in the United States is revealing. An analysis of US census data shows that in 1990 children in Japanese-White households were about equally as likely to be identified as White or Japanese (43 percent) with about 15 percent identified as "Other." During the decade 1980 to 1990, these bi-variate patterns display an *increase* in the proportion who identify their children as Japanese and a *decrease* in their identification as White or "Other." This finding for Japanese-White families is in sharp contrast to the racial identification of the children of Black-White families. In 1990, almost six out of ten respondents in Black-White families identified their children as Black (58 percent) and only one-fourth identified them as White (25 percent). Thus, the overall proportion of children identified as White is significantly higher in Japanese-White households compared to Black-White households. Moreover, in contrast to Japanese-White families, the proportion of Black-White families that identify their children as Black *decreased* significantly in 1980–1990 from 74 percent to 58 percent, and the proportion identifying their children as White *increased* from 15 percent to 25 percent (Peterson and Goldscheider 1997).

These findings on the children of those who are inter-racially married in the United States point to three conclusions. First, single measures are always inadequate to capture the complexities of racial and ethnic identification. Single forced responses cannot be the basis of identifying an increasing number of persons of mixed-race background, as it cannot for mixed ethnic origins. Second, children of inter-ethnic and/or inter-racial marriages may have an ambiguous relationship to their identities, but it is not predictable which of their identities they (or their parents) will select, at least at the time of the census reporting. Third, the race and ethnic identities derived from single questions and forced categorical responses are not likely to be constant over time. There are social and political contexts that shape the relative importance of one response or another (Perlmann 1997).

Some analytic implications of official ethnic measurement

Clearly the way we measure ethnicity reflects the constraints of our data-gathering techniques and our theoretical perspective. We have tended, especially in census-type studies, to limit our measures to cross-sections and to static views of ethnic differentiation, identifying the best ways to categorize individuals. We have de-emphasized the dynamics of ethnic groups over the life course, and have rarely developed household-based measures of ethnicity. Official censuses tend to favor more "objective" rather than "subjective" criteria (preferring, for example, place of birth data to questions of ethnic self-identification) and agonize over the meaning of multiple responses to our ethnic categories, even as we recognize the potential reality of such responses. The complexities result from the premise that one can have multiple ethnic ancestries and that specific social contexts shape which of these ancestries might be invoked at any given time. Some researchers have suggested that the separation of ethnic self-identity and national origins would lead to better measurement. This would involve separating questions about primary identity among the major ethnic groups in a society from questions about an individual's descent or ancestry. Two questions are proposed: (1) "among the groups listed which do you consider the one closest to your primary identity?" and (2) "thinking about your parents your grandparents and your ancestors, what nationalities or ethnic groups are represented in your family history?" (Hirschman 1993).

If the ethnic data that are collected by the census are limited, what can we do to enhance their value? With all the limitations and variance that we have identified, I would continue to argue for a fuller exploitation of existing official data sources for exploratory analyses of ethnic variation and change. Within the context of the questions asked and the responses obtained, we have an extensive database for characterizing the ethnic composition of neighborhoods, as well as for individual-level identification. While there is always room for improving the formulation of questions that we ask and always good arguments for asking more questions, the major advances in our understanding of ethnic differentiation will come from new forms of analysis of the data that have already been collected.

We have not fully utilized the data that we have already collected, nor maximized the value of large-scale census collections on the questions we have already asked. Indeed, the issue of studying ethnic categories is not only the adequacy of questions to be included but also the inadequate theoretical modeling to assist us in developing measures and constructs from the data we have already collected. Our models of ethnicity tend to be oversimplified and do not always guide us toward the utilization of the extensive rich data that are available. It is clear that ethnic differentiation is not simply the "identification" of individuals, without social or cultural contexts. To disentangle the relative meanings of ethnicity we need to link individual expressions to social contexts, both socioeconomic and cultural. And these, in turn, should be integrated within a life-course analysis at the household, if not at the family, level. We should place more prominently on our research agenda three major interrelated themes in the analysis (i.e., in the modeling) of ethnic differentiation: the importance of community; the role of institutions; and the inclusion of intensity in understanding ethnic distinctiveness.

There is little need to justify the importance of examining the community contexts of ethnic differentiation. By exploiting the hierarchical nature of census information and the details available for small areas, we should be able to construct a series of ethnic measures at the community-neighborhood level. In turn, these measures could be attached to each individual and household. In this way, we could examine, for example, whether persons of Hispanic ancestry living in households where all the other members are also Hispanic, and in areas of high Hispanic density, differ in some ways from Hispanics living in households where all the other members are not Hispanics and/or are in areas of low Hispanic density. Do those who identify themselves as of Irish ancestry, who live in households (and neighborhoods) of high Irish density, differ from those who live in households and neighborhoods of low Irish density? This is a straightforward, hardly innovative suggestion that flows from a conceptualization that links ethnic identity at the individual level to the household and neighborhood levels. Nevertheless, we have not systematically followed through on its implementation at the level of households and at the neighborhood, small area levels.

In addition to ethnic density at the local level, we should also attach other contextual indicators to individuals and to households. These might include local economic market conditions, local policies relevant to ethnic groups, and the presence of local ethnic institutions. This latter point needs special attention, since data on local institutions often come from different data sources than individual-based survey and census data. The presence of ethnic social clubs or ethnic churches within a community may influence the expressions and meanings of ethnic differentiation. Linking these to neighborhood characteristics brings us closer to the community contexts of ethnic groups.

This leads us to re-emphasize the importance of investigating issues of ethnic intensity. The concentration of ethnic groups in jobs, neighborhoods, and in schools are obvious examples of indicators of ethnic intensity. Establishing the inter-ethnic household composition goes a long way toward obtaining the ethnic context of everyday life, as does the analysis of neighborhood composition. Moving to the acceptance of multiple responses to both the ethnic ancestry and the race questions will go far in recognizing the value of these categories (along with their limitations). An interesting variant is to obtain information on the ethnic identification of children whose families are of mixed ethnic origins. The assumption that ethnic intermarriage is the quintessential indicator of assimilation, and that high rates imply the erosion of ethnic communities, assumes further that the children of such intermarriages will not select the ethnic identity of one of the parents. It seems plausible to begin testing that inference directly with the data available. Linking the neighborhood and household ethnic characteristics provides an important basis for assessing how the inter-ethnically married relate to differential ethnic family origins.

Clearly the linkages between individual identity, households, and community factors will bring us closer to measuring the emerging patterns of ethnicity in diverse societies. The ways in which ethnic categories are constructed in official documents can be more fully exploited so that social scientists can escape from the trap of treating ethnic origins as only an individualistic and oversimplified construct, blaming the limitations of census categorization for their own limited perspective.

Comparisons of how ethnic groups are defined in the censuses of Israel, Canada, and the United States reveal the extent to which the contexts of these countries influence, and are influenced by, the social constructions of ethnic categories. Since ethnic identity changes over time in the life course of persons and in the history of states, it is not surprising that there have been adjustments and changes in the census categories. Although there are methodological ways to maximally exploit the available data, only systematic attention to the formulation of and changes to ethnic categories will assure that fundamental errors of assessment are not made.

It is difficult, nevertheless, to conclude that the rich cultural and social experiences of ethnic communities are captured by the type of questions that have been included in censuses. We should not be surprised by critical assessments and skeptical evaluations of census questions when changes occur in the way a census ethnic question is formulated, when we insist on ethnic self-identification, when some ethnic groups are included and others excluded as examples of legitimate responses, and when some questions insist on single responses while others allow for multiple combinations to be filled in by respondents. The consequence of these characteristics of census questions on ethnic origin is not firm, objective, and rigorously valid ethnic categories but new constructions of ethnicity. Census constructions of ethnic groups may best be considered evidence of the *discourse* about ethnicity rather than ethnicity *per se*. Perhaps the construction of these categories are valuable not only as pieces of the ethnic puzzle but also as reflections of the puzzle itself.

NOTES

1 Others have provided insights using different illustrations. See, for example, the studies in Goldscheider 1995 on the USSR, China, Southeast Asia, Africa, Brazil, the United States, and parts of Europe in the early twentieth century; on Canada, the United States, Malaysia, Great Britain, Australia, and the USSR see the articles in Goldmann *et al.*, 1993. See also other chapters in this volume.
2 Oscar Handlin, in his classic saga on American immigration (*The Uprooted*), pointed out that he began to write the history of American immigration only to discover that immigration *was* American history. The background materials on Israel are derived from Goldscheider 1996.

3 One of the government ministries in Israel that deals with immigrants is the Ministry of Immigration and Absorption. There was an attempt to rename the ministry as ministry of "social and economic integration" or of "immigrant integration." The difference in the name is a reflection of the changing goals away from "absorption" and towards "help[ing] immigrants build lives in Israel." More directly, the ministry has had to cope with the very large influx of Russian immigrants in the recent period, and the Russian word for absorption brings to mind thoughts of a science department rather than social affairs. The Minister in 1999 said that the name of the Ministry "really sounds like a lesson in organic chemistry." As reported in the *Jerusalem Post*, March 4, 1999.

4 It is another paradox of Israeli life that the ethnic origin of Israeli Jews follows paternal lineage while definitions of religion (Judaism) follow the religion of the mother.

5 Some classifications are revealing. For example, Jews from South Africa are in the Europe-America category; those from Ethiopia are in the Asian-African category.

6 A recent creative effort to obtain data on the ethnic origins of the third generation has been carried out by a team of researchers headed by Dov Friedlander of the Hebrew University, Jerusalem, in his studies of educational attainment using 1995 matched to 1983 census data. See Friedlander *et al.*, 1998.

7 Enumerators were still allowed in the 1970 census to fill in blanks through observations; that is, whenever an unrecognized racial category was offered, they were instructed to recode. For instance, "Chicano" became "White."

8 See the chapter by Noble in this volume on the race question in early US censuses.

9 On the questions about ethnicity in the United States census, see McKenney and Cresce, 1993; also White and Sassler, 1995.

10 The ancestry question is reviewed in Lieberson and Waters, 1988. See also Petersen, 1980.

REFERENCES

Boyd, Monica 1997, "Offspring-Parent Shifts in Ancestry: Ethnic Bedrock or Ethnic Quicksand?" Center for the Study of Population, Florida State University, WPS 97–138, Working Paper.
  1998, "Canadian 'Eh?', Ethnic Origin Shifts in the Canadian Census," Research paper no. 10, Chair in Ethnic Studies Lecture Series, University of Calgary, March.
Boyd, Monica, Goldman, Gustave and White, Pamela 1998, "Race in the Canadian Census," in Ledo Driedger and Shivalingappa S. Halli (eds.), *Visible Minorities in Canada*, Ottawa: Carleton University Press, pp. xx.
Eisenbach, Zvi 1992, "Marriage and Fertility in the Process of Integration: Intermarriage among Origin Groups in Israel," in Calvin Goldscheider (ed.), *Population and Social Change in Israel*, Boulder, Col.: Westview Press, pp. 131–47.

Friedlander, Dov, Eisenbach, Zvi, Ben-Moshe, Eliahu, *et al.* 1998, *Religion, Ethnicity, Type of Locality and Educational Attainments among Israel's Population: 1950–1980*, Department of Population Studies, Working Paper Series, November.

Goldmann, Gustave *et al.* (eds.) 1993, *Challenges of Measuring an Ethnic World: Science, Politics, and Reality*, Proceedings of the Joint Canada-United States Conference on the Measurement of Ethnicity, April 1–3, 1992, Washington, DC: Bureau of the Census; Ottawa: Statistics Canada.

Goldscheider, Calvin 1996, *Israel's Changing Society: Population, Ethnicity and Development*, Boulder, Col.: Westview Press.

Goldscheider, Calvin (ed.) 1995, *Population Ethnicity and Nation-Building*, Boulder, Col.: Westview Press.

Hirschman, Charles 1993, "How to Measure Ethnicity: An Immodest Proposal," in Gustave Goldmann, *et al.* (eds.), *Challenges of Measuring an Ethnic World: Science Politics, and Reality*, The Joint Canada-United States Conference on the Measurement of Ethnicity, Washington, DC: Bureau of the Census; Ottawa: Statistics Canada, pp. 541–54.

Lieberson, Stanley and Waters, Mary 1988, *From Many Strands: Ethnic Groups in Contemporary America*, New York: Russell Sage Foundation.

McKenney, Nampeo R. and Cresce, Arthur R. 1993, "Measurement of Ethnicity in the United States: Experiences of the U.S. Bureau of the Census," in Gustave Goldmann, *et al.* (eds.), *Challenges of Measuring an Ethnic World: Science Politics, and Reality*, The Joint Canada-United States Conference on the Measurement of Ethnicity, Washington, DC: Bureau of the Census; Ottawa: Statistics Canada, pp. 173–220.

Passel, Jeffrey 1994, "Racial and Ethnic Differentiation in the United States: Comments and Observations," Paper prepared for the workshop on Race and Ethnicity Classification: An assessment of the Federal Standard for Racial and Ethnicity Classification, National Academy of Sciences, Washington, DC, February.

Perlmann, Joel 1997, "Multiracials, Racial Classification and American Intermarriage – The Public's Interest," The Jerome Levy Economics Institute of Bard College, Working paper 195, June.

Petersen, William 1980, "Concepts of Ethnicity," in Stephan Thernstrom (ed.), *The Harvard Encyclopedia of American Ethnic Groups*, Cambridge, Mass.: Harvard University Press, pp. 234–42.

Peterson, Kristen and Goldscheider, Calvin 1997, "Children of Racially Intermarried Couples: How are Mixed Japanese-White Americans and Mixed Black-White Americans Identified?" Paper presented at the Annual Meetings of the Population Association of America, Washington, DC, March 27–29.

Sandefur, Gary, D., Rindfuss, Ronald R., and Cohen, Barney (eds.) 1996, *Changing Numbers, Changing Needs: American Indian Demography and Public Health*, Washington, DC: National Academy Press.

White, Michael and Sassler, Sharon 1995, "Ethnic Definition, Social Mobility and Residential Segregation in the United States," in Calvin Goldscheider (ed.), *Population Ethnicity and Nation-Building*, Boulder, Col.: Westview Press, pp. 267–97.

White, Pamela, Badets, Jane, and Renaud, Viviane 1993, "Measuring Ethnicity in Canadian Censuses," in Gustave Goldmann, *et al.* (eds.), *Challenges of Measuring an Ethnic World: Science Politics, and Reality*, The Joint Canada-United States Conference on the Measurement of Ethnicity, Washington, DC: Bureau of the Census; Ottawa: Statistics Canada, pp. 221–67.

4 Language categories in censuses: backward- or forward-looking?

Dominique Arel

While the concept of the cultural nation cannot be reduced to a single marker of identity, language is often its most potent component. Most nationalist movements in the world view the language of their group as a key marker establishing the group's boundaries. There are well-known exceptions, of course, such as the Irish, who "lost" their language but not their religiously-defined identity, and the Serbs, Croats, and Bosnian Muslims, who shared a common standardized language in Yugoslavia.[1] Moreover, one could cite endless examples of particular individuals who identify with a culturally defined nation without speaking the national language well, or conversely, who do not identify with the nation despite having learned its language as their native tongue.

The point, however, is about nationalist *movements* and how their discourse is shaped by nationalist elites. The Irish have survived the loss, for most practical purposes, of their language, but many nineteenth-century Irish nationalists did not think they would (Connor 1994, 105). The independent Croatian state is engaged in the re-standardization of Croatian, to make it evolve away from Serbian (Durkovic 1999). The Masurians, a minority of Eastern Prussia who spoke a dialectical variety of the Polish spoken in Warsaw staunchly clung to a Prussian/German identity, claiming that their mother tongue did *not* politically matter (Blanke 1999). This did not prevent Polish nationalists from claiming that the Masurians were *theirs*. The examples could be multiplied. In the *politics* of nationalism, language is almost always a point of contention.

This is so for two main reasons. The first is that language, contrary to religion, cannot be dissociated from the state (Kymlicka 1995). The modern state can function as a mostly secular agency, leaving religious practice to the communitarian and individual realm, but it cannot operate without a "high culture" whose core component is a language (Gellner 1983). The adoption of the language of the state by non-native speakers can be historically non-conflictual, as has generally been the case in the United States and France, but this does not make English or French "neutral" languages, or devoid of the emotional component of identity.

The United States represents the prototypical case of an "immigrant" state, where the fact that the language of the early European settlers – the British settlers of New England – became the language of official discourse was never seriously contested by subsequent waves of immigration, although some fear that this could change with the fast-growing Spanish-speaking population in the twenty-first century.[2] France embodies the classic case of a "civic" state built on the notion that state legitimacy is derived from the political "nation," based on the equality of all citizens and a common and indivisible public identity, of which the French language is a pillar. Non-French-speaking groups at the periphery of the French state have either proven incapable (Bretons), or declined (Alsatians) to contest the state hegemony of the French language, while post-war North African immigrants, whose integration is otherwise politically charged, do not contest the sole use of French in public domains.[3] These cases are important, but they hardly constitute the norm. In a modern setting, languages cannot long survive without being supported by the state (in schools, administration, and the media) and, from Belgium to Latvia and Somalia to Quebec, the question of *which* language, or languages, will have official status turns into a political flashpoint time and time again.

The second reason that language so often leads to conflict is that, much more than religion, it is a fluctuating marker. People often add languages to their linguistic repertoire, and might experience a shift in their "private" language (the language they feel most comfortable with) during their lifetime or, more commonly, might have children whose private language differs from their own. Nationalists portray this linguistic assimilation as forced, unnatural, and fundamentally illegitimate, the result of destructive policies by the "imperialist" state. Yet, from a comparative standpoint, linguistic assimilation is a "normal" occurrence: not in the sense that most people assimilate, but in that, in most national groups whose language is socially less prestigious, and therefore less useful for social advancement, there are individuals who choose to assimilate. But the less other markers of identity, such as religion or race, act as a barrier to assimilation, the more language becomes central to nationalist demands. This is partly because "nationally conscious" and active individuals, perceiving an actual or potential "loss" to the socially dominant nation, feel vulnerable in their very existence.

The nationalist claim that a culturally distinct group has legitimate rights to make territorially-defined political demands implies, first and foremost, that the group must be *recognized* as a legitimate entity by the larger state. Recognition can be obtained in constitutional and political documents, but it is also sought in numbers. With official statistics acting

as "technologies of truth production" (Urla 1993), groups who see themselves as cultural nations want to be counted as such – as distinct nations,
with statistics engraving, as it were, their numerical weight in the political
space. The ultimate register of the "truth" is the Census, as it constitutes
the privileged medium of the state which, while targeted at individuals,
bestows group *recognition* and (numerical) *proportion*. The statistical representation of the intimately related concepts of "nationality" (cultural
nation) and "language," however, has been fraught with conflict historically, and this continues to be the case. This is so because there exist two
politically opposed views on how to capture nationality and language,
and how to interpret them. Census-makers, seeking the magic formula
to "objectively" and "scientifically" record these categories, have repeatedly found themselves in the midst of political strife. This chapter will
explore the ways in which language, as the kin concept of nationality, can
prove to be such a controversial dimension of the modern census.

Language and nationality

While decennial censuses became a generalized practice in Europe and
the New World in the first part of the nineteenth century, states did not
then inquire about the language(s) of their inhabitants. Belgium was the
first to introduce the category, in 1846, with Prussia and Switzerland
following in the 1850s. When the International Statistical Congress – a
periodic gathering aimed at establishing international standards of
demographic statistics and, more particularly, of census categories – held
its first session in Brussels, in 1853, the category "spoken language"
(*langue parlée*, in the original French, the official language of deliberations
at the Congress) appeared as one of the proposed items of a standardized
census questionnaire, but did not elicit discussion (Tebarth 1991).

At the Vienna session of the Congress, in 1857, the question of language was raised, but indirectly. What interested statisticians at the time
was the new meaning of "nationality," which was becoming a force in
Europe. Nationality had first acquired the meaning of citizenship in
the French Revolution, with the implicit acknowledgment that the nation, as a *political community*, had a single public culture and thus a
single state-supported language. At a subsequent session, in London in
1860, a French delegate expounded on the theory that the nation was
contained within the "natural frontiers" of the state. The Germans, however, offered an alternative definition of nationality, depicting it as a
cultural community not necessarily coterminous with the boundaries
of the state, a stance grounded in the geopolitical realities of the time.
German-speakers, for instance, were dispersed across dozens of states and

principalities. In the German view, it was culturally-defined nations that were "natural," not state borders (Kleeberg 1915: 28–29).

In Vienna statisticians debated, for the first time, whether this cultural concept of "nationality" could be codified in a census. The author of the main report, the Austrian Czoernig, argued that the boundaries of nationality resulted from the complex interaction of language use, customs, physical characteristics and "spirit," something which nowadays would be called *mentalités* (Labbé 1997: 131). Thus, Czoernig believed that nationality was the property of a group and could not be reduced to the language spoken by an individual (Zeman 1990: 32). This ethnographic approach, however, was rejected as inappropriate for statistics. After briefly being touched upon at the 1860 London session, the issue was revisited in 1872 in St. Petersburg. The rapporteurs, the Russians Semenov and Maksheev, contended that cultural nationality, in the German sense, ought to be recorded by the census at the *individual* level and that language was the most reliable indicator of nationality, since "each perfectly knows the language used since childhood to think and express oneself" (Labbé 1997: 133).

While cognizant of the fact that cultural nationality could be influenced by several factors, the statisticians who convened in St. Petersburg reached a consensus that language was the only valid category which could *statistically* capture cultural nationality. Böckh (1974 [1866]), the leading Prussian expert on the statistical representation of nationality, who, curiously, did not join the Congress before 1876, came to the same conclusion independently. In singling out language as the sole census category, the St. Petersburg session did *not* recommend that cultural nationality appear as a category on its own. Statisticians at the time aimed at objectively recording the nationality of individuals, but shared the belief that a direct question on nationality was likely to confuse a great many respondents not accustomed to thinking in "national" terms, and therefore open the door to invalid *subjective* assessments. Language was deemed the best objective indicator which could possibly be devised, precisely because "each perfectly knows (one's) language." In this view, it would be possible to ascertain the nationality of a respondent, even if the latter was oblivious to his/her national identity. Language was meant to be the great decoder of nationality.[4]

The recommendation of the St. Petersburg session, however, remained vague on how concretely to define the language question on the census. The actual term used in the recommendation was *langue parlée*, defined as "the language spoken in usual interaction" (Kleeberg 1915: 39). Yet no distinction was specified between *private* and *public* interactions (Bohac 1931: 107). The language usually spoken at home can differ from the language usually spoken at work or in informal public exchanges. The ambiguity inherent in the St. Petersburg category was a portent of profound political disagreements looming ahead. The Russians themselves interpreted their own recommendation to mean "native language," a category which had already appeared in urban censuses in the 1860s and which was preserved in the first Imperial census of 1897 (Roth 1991). The Austrians, on the other hand, opted for "language of use" in their first census of 1880. As it turned out, both "native language" and "language of use" proved ambiguous and politically controversial.

When a language question began to appear in several East European censuses in the last two decades of the century (Austria 1880, Hungary 1880, Prussia 1890, Russia 1897), language was indeed used as a proxy for nationality, even though such a direct linkage was officially denied in Austria.[5] After World War I, when the linguistically contested areas of the multinational states of Austro-Hungary, Germany, and Russia became either independent states or part of the Soviet Union, the censuses in these new states broke with the dominant pre-war practice and directly asked about the nationality of their citizens, either in lieu of language (Romania, Poland), in addition to language (Soviet Union), or together with language (Czechoslovakia: "What is your nationality [mother tongue]?").

The prominence of the nationality concept in late nineteenth-century Eastern Europe, and its eventual fixation in census categories in the interwar period, has led to the common practice of classifying "Eastern" nationalisms as special cases, different from their Western counterparts. Western statisticians attending the sessions of the International Statistical Congress did not think that nationality, as a cultural community, applied to their own states (West of Germany, that is, since Germany – and Vienna – was then seen as part of the East). Nationality, in the West, was equated with the state of birth (and eventually, the citizenship) of an individual. The French census consequently distinguished between respondents of French and "other" nationalities (i.e., foreigners), while being totally uninterested in the cultural attributes (language, religion) of these non-nationals (Héran 1998; Blum, this volume).

Even though the first censuses to include a language question were actually from Belgium and Switzerland, the consensus among Westerners was that the linguistic communities in these states were not nationalities, but rather the bi- or tri-lingual manifestations of a single (Belgian and Swiss) nationality. The practice of placing the Eastern cases in a league of their own evolved into Hans Kohn's famous dichotomy of Eastern nationalisms as ethnic and retrograde and Western nationalisms as civic and progressive (Kohn 1944), an approach which has quietly retained much of its appeal in the West. Comparing the political dynamics underlying the language questions in censuses suggests, however, that geographically diverse multinational states have more in common than generally believed, despite the use of distinct terminologies.

Language situations

There are three language "situations" that can be captured by censuses: (a) the language *first* learned by the respondent; (b) the language most commonly used by the respondent at the time of the census; and (c) the knowledge of particular *official* language(s) by the respondent. The language may be the same in the three situations, as with a Russian of Moscow for whom Russian is the only language he ever knew, or it may differ in all three, as with the child of a Vietnamese immigrant in Montreal who may have first learned Vietnamese, but used mostly French at the time of the census and knew English as a third language. The Canadian census is one of the few censuses which attempts to capture all three situations (since 1971). Most censuses with language questions have either one or two, and generally only one of them.

Language fluency

Census questions about the *knowledge* of an official language as a second language, rather than about its use in private or public, or its acquisition as a child, tend not to be politically charged. The politics of language arises from disputes over the use of language in concrete situations and over the relevance of language as a criterion of public identity, but not necessarily over whether an additional language is known. In Quebec, the rise in support for the independence option has been accompanied by a rise in bilingualism among Québécois of French mother tongue, a phenomenon which may appear paradoxical to the outsider but not to a Québécois nationalist, who clearly distinguishes between having French established as the main language of public discourse in Quebec and learning English as the global language.

There are, as always, exceptions to the generally apolitical use of census data on second language. In the Soviet Union, the number of citizens with Estonian as a mother tongue who declared themselves fluent in Russian decreased significantly between 1970 and 1979, a trend which everyone knew was unimaginable (Silver 1986). Many Estonians were, most likely, registering a protest against what they saw as the encroachment of Russian in public institutions of Estonia. Their protest, however, was not necessarily about having to learn Russian – since Russian was obviously a prerequisite for traveling in the Soviet Union – but at having to use it in situations where, in their view, Estonian should have predominated.

More controversial are cases where a respondent names two languages in response to a question about primary language, whether asked in terms of "mother tongue" or "language of use." Census makers, seeking discrete and exhaustive categories for their questions, have generally resisted categorizing hybrid cases. This has been true of racial and ethnic indicators as well, where the possibility of entering multiple identities is extremely recent (Kertzer and Arel, this volume). In the case of language, German and Prussian statisticians, in particular, had long discussions over the statistical fate of those claiming to speak two languages equally, and a bilingual category appeared on a few censuses in Germany and Prussia in the 1850s and 1860s (Böckh 1974 [1866]). Eventually, as elsewhere in Central and Eastern Europe, the assumption was made that, in all cases, one language had to predominate at the individual level, and, consequently a single primary language was assigned to the professed bilinguals.

Census results regarding knowledge of a language have often been criticized as of questionable validity, since people may exaggerate their actual fluency in a language. Even when true, however, the ungrounded claim of fluency (or, in the case of Estonians, in 1979, of unilingualism) in itself constitutes a significant sociological fact (McRae 1997: 99), as long as the results indeed reflect individual assessments and not the whims of state officials (as was clearly the case with the stupendous rise in bilingualism in the Soviet Republic of Uzbekistan in 1979). Validity is increased when fluency in a language is assessed in gradation (e.g. speaks well, with difficulty, not at all) for specific acts (reading, writing, speaking, comprehension), as has been the practice in Basque and Catalan censuses since the 1980s (Urla 1993: 823).

Mother tongue vs. language of use

The most politically controversial census debates over language have almost always pertained to the first two language situations. Nationalists cannot accept that the recording of language use at any given time is necessarily *legitimate*. They sometimes object to the poor wording of particular census questions, but more fundamentally they object to the cold statistical notion that language behavior can be accepted *as is*, whenever the language is reported to be less spoken than it *should* be. This is so because, in the apt formulation of Brubaker (1996: 79), "Nationalism can be understood as a form of remedial political action. It addresses an allegedly deficient or 'pathological' condition and proposes to remedy it."

Assimilating to another language, whenever language acts as one of the main markers of identity for the group, is perceived as pathological and iniquitous by nationalist leaders.

In this view, the correct statistical representation of the nation is one that is backward-looking (Zeman 1990), i.e. one that reflects the language of one's parents or ancestors. The fact that the respondent may not primarily use, or even know, the language of his or her cultural nation is seen as a temporary aberration, caused by the imperialist policies of the central state, and one that will be rectified once the nation acquires autonomous powers (generally portrayed in nationalist rhetoric as the reconquest of the nation's historic sovereignty). As we will see in some detail below, this stance explains why Czech and Flemish nationalists vehemently objected to the language category used on the Imperial Austrian and Belgian censuses, which focused primarily on the language *publicly* used by individuals, rather than on the language at the core of their identity.

The concept of a *private* language, or of a language used by the individual outside of the reach of the state, is much closer to the nationalist conception of language as a *marker* of identity. This makes "mother tongue" (or "native language"), in principle, the category of choice for nationally-minded activists. Yet "mother tongue," as with all identity categories on the census, can actually be interpreted in diametrically opposed ways. The United Nations defines it as "the language usually spoken in the individual's home in his early childhood" (Silver 1986: 88). "Mother tongue," however, can also be interpreted as the language one speaks best as an adult, when the census is conducted, rather than as a child. In the Swiss census, at least since 1950, mother tongue has been defined as "the language in which [the respondent] think[s] and which [s/he] master[s] best" (Lévy 1964: 261), a definition which omits the language of childhood. Finland has also used a definition of mother tongue similar to the Swiss, in its 1940 and 1980 censuses (McRae 1997: 83–84).

By emphasizing the language in which one thinks (*denksprache*, in German), the Swiss and Finnish censuses allow for the possibility that the mother tongue of an individual might change during his or her lifetime. In fact, this was the assumption underlying the use of a "mother tongue" category in Prussia, Hungary, and Imperial Russia, the three hotbeds of nationality politics, along with Austria, in the several decades leading to World War I. The instructions to the 1890 Hungarian censuses stated ambiguously that "mother tongue" is "that language which you recognize as your own and which you enjoy most speaking" (Roth 1991: 142). The 1910 instructions explicitly indicated that "it may happen that the mother tongue of the child differs from that of the mother"

(Van Gennep 1922: 109). In Prussia, mother tongue (*Muttersprache*) was defined as "that language in which one is most fluent from childhood on and in which one thinks and also prays" (Kleeberg 1915: 67). In Imperial Russia, native language (*rodnoi yazyk*) was left undefined for the 1897 Imperial census, but past practice, going back to the urban censuses of the 1860s and the St. Petersburg Congress of 1872, made it clear that census officials supported the notion that mother tongue can change within one's lifetime, and certainly through generations (Roth 1991).

By recording the language actually recognized as the respondent's *own* language at the time of the census, as opposed to some subjective notion of what that language *ought* to be in terms of one's origins, census makers from these Eastern European states staunchly believed that they were acting as scientists seeking *objectivity*. Yet politics was not far removed from their analysis. While Austria, Prussia, Hungary, and Russia recognized the existence of cultural nationalities, contrary to the so-called "nation-states" of Western Europe, it was in their interest to use a counting method allowing for the greater possible number of speakers of the dominant language: that is, German (for Austria and Prussia), Hungarian, and Russian. In all these cases, the language of social advancement tended to correspond to the language of the central state. This created incentives, in urban areas, for people to linguistically assimilate to the dominant language.

The proponents of the "objective" method of recording language tend to be the speakers of the socially dominant language which *benefits* from linguistic assimilation, and the social dominance of a language is often, although not always, linked with the policies of the central state. Who controls the state may have an impact on patterns of linguistic assimilation and therefore be in an advantageous, and nationally secure, position to record these linguistic changes. Nationalists see a direct link between "unjust" state policies (such as using the language of the politically dominant group as the sole official language) and assimilation, believing that a change in the former will cause a change in the latter. In their view, the recording of illegitimate processes is not truly objective, since it in fact reflects unequal power relations. A few examples will help clarify the point.

Austria: the Czech-German dispute

In the Austrian part of the Austro-Hungarian Empire, also known as Cisleithania, an intense battle opposed German-speaking officials to Czech nationalists throughout the four censuses held between 1880 and 1910. The Austrian census used the concept of "language of use" (*Umgangssprache*) instead of "mother tongue," as was becoming the practice elsewhere in Eastern Europe.[6] The Czechs attacked the ambiguity of the concept, since it could very well refer to the language one *had* to speak publicly, rather than one's identity language. The seminal example, recounted time and again in census debates, was that of a Czech servant working in a German-speaking household, who could spend his days speaking German to his employers, and his evenings speaking Czech to his family. By registering German as his language of use, he was providing incorrect information, in the nationalist view, since he was very much still a Czech-speaker whenever he *could* use the language (Kovacs 1928: 326; Zeman 1990: 33). Czech activists were convinced that the Austrian state had consciously devised an overly equivocal concept in order to maximize the number of German-speakers, at the expense of Czechs and other language minorities (Bohac 1931).

The root of the problem lay with the Austrian decision, in the Constitution of 1867, to recognize the legal equality of several ethnic groups (*volkstamme*) in Cisleithania. Ethnic equality meant that languages other than German could to be used in public domains (state offices, schools), whenever at least twenty percent of speakers of a language were concentrated on a given territory. In resorting to *volkstamme*, a term less charged politically than *nationalität*, with its much clearer connotation of political *rights*, the Austrians aimed at depoliticizing language. This proved an illusion. Despite repeated assurances that the category *Umgangssprache* was not meant to record nationality, both Czech and German activists in Bohemia, the Austrian province, or Crowland, where language disputes were the most acute, acted exactly on the opposite premise – i.e. that the language question on the census *was* recording nationality (Brix 1982). In an intellectual environment where language was proclaimed the marker of nationality throughout Eastern Europe, how could it be otherwise?

The subtext of the census controversy in Austria was the fear of linguistic assimilation, both by Czechs and Germans in Bohemia. In the decades before a language indicator was first used in the 1880 census, there had been notable assimilation to the German language in the big cities of the Bohemian hinterland, such as Prague and Brno, as well as in Vienna. As German was the high-status language in Austria, many parents wanted to maximize the career opportunities of their children by having them acquire German rather than "backward" Czech.

By the 1880s, however, the balance had tipped in favor of the Czech language in Prague, and the next censuses recorded an absolute decrease of 15 percent in the German-speaking population of the Bohemian capital, primarily explained by German (lower-class) assimilation to Czech (Cohen 1981: 100). At the same time, the industrialization of the peripheral and compactly German-speaking areas of Bohemia – a region that would later become known as the Sudetenland – attracted Czech workers. The German nationalists wanted to keep their frontier areas monolingually German, while the Czech nationalists wanted the Czech migrants to preserve their Czech language. Much of the census controversies concerned the language identity of respondents near or beyond what Mark Cornwall (1994) called the German-Czech "language border."

Had the Austrian census officials used a more sophisticated language indicator, such as "language used with your siblings or friends" (see below), they would have recorded more precisely a certain amount of linguistic assimilation among Czechs in the Sudetenland, as well as in Lower Silesia, the other linguistically contested border area (with Czech, Polish, and German populations). Yet there is little doubt that much of the *umgangssprache* data reflected actual linguistic assimilation (in both directions, as we saw), not just confusion about what the concept was supposed to mean. The Czech nationalists could not accept that assimilation to German was legitimate, while German nationalists in Bohemia were increasingly anxious about potential Czech linguistic encroachment into "their" territory.

Not surprisingly, in light of the discussion above, the Czechs were not even comfortable with the concept of "mother tongue," since intergenerational linguistic assimilation inevitably leads to a change in the first language of respondents. When independent Czechoslovakia (with a 30 percent German minority) held its first census in 1921, the Czechs used the hybrid category of "nationality (mother tongue)," with the clear message that mother tongue refers to the group that one *descends* from, irrespective of current language behavior. The Romanians, who felt undercounted in the Hungarian census, even though the indicator used was that of "mother tongue,"[7] were even more explicit in their first post-war census of 1927, asking respondents to indicate their "nationality by birth" (*nationalitatea de nastere*), and omitting altogether a question on language. As with the Czechs in Austria, the Romanians of Hungary spoke what was then a low-status language and Romanian nationalists could not accept that Romanians were becoming linguistically, and therefore nationally, Hungarian, a process that was encouraged by the Hungarian state.[8]

The Soviet cooptation of nationalist discourse

With Czechs and Romanians now in control of their nationally-conceived successor states, they were in a position to impose their backward-looking concept of nationality on their censuses. Surprisingly, however, the concept was also introduced into the census of the new Soviet state, even though most officials of the Soviet central state were Russian-speakers and recording nationality was in the interest of the non-Russian-speaking minorities of the state.

In urban censuses of the 1860s and in its sole statewide census of 1897, Imperial Russia had recorded the "mother tongue" of respondents. As elsewhere in Eastern Europe at that time, the Russian census did not inquire directly about (cultural) nationality, yet the language category was widely seen as representative of national affiliation, at least as far as "European" Russia was concerned. In fact, census instructions explicitly indicated that language meant nationality, and census tables often used the label "nationality" in presenting language data (Blum and Gousseff 1997: 56).

The Bolsheviks did not think that national identity would survive social- ism. In the short run, however, they were divided as to how to approach the nationality question. Lenin argued that the psychological wounds of chauvinism (national humiliation) were real and needed to be cured by the Soviet state in order for the national question to fade into irrele- vance. He thought that all cultural nations needed to be given complete equality, which meant, *inter alia*, being able to use their own languages in public domains. Sharing the same mistaken assumptions which un- derlay imperial Austrian policy, assumptions upon which the so-called "Austro-Marxists" built their project of non-territorial cultural auton- omy at the turn of the century, Lenin was convinced that culture and politics could be entirely separated: full cultural autonomy to the na- tionalities would nip nationalism in the bud, once and for all (Connor 1984).

Soviet census officials internalized the Leninist discourse that nationali- ties had been victimized in Imperial Russia and that "Russification" needed to be reversed (Hirsch 1997: 255). The ethnographers consulted in the preparation of the census were actually unsure whether nation- ality could be recorded "subjectively" or "objectively": that is, whether nationality was to be derived from a respondent's own interpretation, or from his or her antecedents, as determined by census-takers. Under pressure from non-Russian elites, particularly the Ukrainians, the cen- sus opted for the latter. Hirch (1997: 260) reports that Ukrainian del- egates to the IVth All-Union Statistical Conference, in February 1926, shortly before the first Soviet census was conducted, were adamant that "resort to the self-consciousness of respondents" be made only in extreme cases. The Ukrainians feared that "nationally ambiguous" Ukrainians – peasants, Russian-speaking workers – might fail to identify as Ukrainian nationals. Their nationality, therefore, had to be presumed from their lan- guage, irrespective of how a respondent *felt* about his or her attachment to a nationality.

In attempting to legitimize itself by asserting the illegitimacy of assimilation to the dominant group (Russian), the early Soviet state thus resorted to the same discourse that prevailed among nationalists of the Austro-Hungarian Empire, and to the same solutions implemented by these nationalists once they reached power: recording *both* the mother tongue and the nationality of citizens. This choice was also prompted by the realisation that in Central Asia, the Caucasus and Siberia, where most vernacular languages were not standardized – lacking an alphabet, common grammar, and literature – language was a poor indicator of ethnic affiliation (Hirsch 1997: 259). Non-Russian literary languages – Arabic, Chagatai, Turki – were in use in pre-Soviet Central Asia, but the Soviets decided that "nations" (Kazakh, Uzbek, etc.) were contained within these broad linguistic communities and that the language of these new nations had to be standardized. Deriving nationality from a language, as had been the practice in nineteenth-century Austria, Prussia, and the European provinces of Imperial Russia, did not appear to be practical. For the non-European parts of the Soviet Union, ethnographers established a list of official nationalities from a composite of ethnic traits, and language became the core marker retrospectively, *after* the state-sponsored standardization of dozens of languages following the first Soviet census.[9]

Recording language and nationality separately, while making it a central tenet of Soviet nationality policy that each nationality necessarily had a distinct language, left open the possibility of assigning a language-based nationality that was distinct from actual language use. A woman of Ukrainian-speaking parents, who spoke Russian at home and struggled in Ukrainian, could declare Ukrainian as her nationality, even though the Ukrainian nationality presupposes knowledge of its key identity marker – the Ukrainian language. In the Imperial Russian census, where nationality was inferred from language, the woman would have been classified as Russian. This disjunction between recorded language and recorded nationality was institutionalized further by two state practices. First, census instructions never clarified what "mother tongue" – the category used for language – aimed at capturing. Soviet scholars argued that many respondents understood it as "the language of their nationality," irrespective of their own fluency in it (Silver 1986: 88). Second, internal passports (identity documents), introduced in 1932, contained a fixed "nationality" category. Children had to adopt the nationality of their parents and could only choose a nationality if they were the offspring of a mixed marriage (Zaslavsky and Luryi 1979).

The Soviet census policy was thus a nationalist's dream come true. According to the figures of the last Soviet census, conducted in 1989,

Ukrainians comprised 72 percent of the population of the Ukrainian Soviet Republic, with 12 percent of these claiming Russian as a mother tongue. Had the Soviet Union used the category of "language of use" instead, as in pre-war Austria, and presumed that language was a proxy for nationality, as was the consensus among European statisticians during the sessions of International Statistical Congress, then the proportion of Ukrainians would have dropped to half of the population. Several surveys conducted in the 1990s have shown that Russian is used as the main home language by about half of Ukrainian citizens (Arel 1995). Obviously, the Austrian category stands no chance of ever being adopted by Ukrainian census authorities.

Belgium: when counting becomes no longer possible

The Belgian case is instructive as an antidote to the belief that Eastern nationalisms are oranges, not to be mixed with the nationalist apples of the West. The outcome of the Belgian census battles was formally different than in inter-war Czechoslovakia or the Soviet Union, since it involved removing the language question altogether from the census, as opposed to supplementing it with a nationality question. Yet the demands by nationalist groups were strikingly similar. In Belgium, as in Bohemia or Ukraine, linguistic assimilation was occurring to the detriment of people (Flemings, Czechs, Ukrainians) who were undergoing nationalist mobilization. In all three cases, the census recording of this assimilation, by whatever indicator, was deemed illegitimate.

In late nineteenth-century Belgium, French was the high status language and the Flemish bourgeoisie were rapidly adopting French as its home language. This meant that pockets of French were developing in the historically homogeneous Flemish-speaking Flanders, in the northern part of Belgium, as well as in Brussels, the Belgian capital, located on the Flemish side of the linguistic border. In the south, all that could be heard was French or a dialectical version of French (Walloon). From 1866 on, Belgian censuses inquired about the *knowledge* of French and Flemish. (German, whose speakers formed about 1 percent of the population, was also included). The results thus provided proportions of bilinguals and unilinguals. The speakers of a given language were calculated by adding unilinguals (of that language) and bilinguals. The catch, however, was that the bilinguals, for all intents and purposes, were only in Flanders, including Brussels. This was because those born in French-speaking homes had no interest in learning low-status Flemish. Bilingualism thus became identified with French expansion in Flanders (Velthonen 1987: 37). Another practice by state statisticians was to focus strictly on the unilinguals, with the number of Dutch unilinguals decreasing and that of French unilinguals increasing, due to language re-identification from Flemish to French.

Upon pressure from Flemish nationalists, a language question was added to the 1910 census, asking respondents about the "language [they use] most frequently." This allowed the Flemings to identify those among the bilinguals who still retained Flemish as their main language. In the long run, however, it did little to stem the linguistic assimilation of Flemings toward French. Assimilation was reversed in the bulk of Flanders, away from Brussels, following a 1932 compromise which established territorial unilingualism in Flanders and Wallonia, except for Brussels which became an officially "bilingual" (but in fact increasingly French) enclave in a unilingual Flanders. The law indicated that districts outside of Brussels, and therefore located in officially unilingual Flanders, could be attached to bilingual Brussels if census figures revealed that they had become majority French-speaking.

Contrary to the rest of Flanders, the pace of assimilation was not reversed in Brussels. The Flemish nationalists were unable to introduce a question about mother tongue on the census, because of resistance from Brussels parents of Flemish background who were keen on adopting high-status French.[10] By linking official status of French to census figures, while resorting to an indicator (language use) that allowed for a language shift, Belgian policymakers unwittingly transformed the next census (delayed because of the war) into a referendum on official language policy in the outskirts of Brussels (Lévy 1960: 138). Scores of Belgians of Flemish descent behaved in a "forward-looking" mode by identifying with French, as the language they *wished* their children would use in public.

When the much delayed results of the 1947 census showed that a great many districts around the official boundaries of Brussels had acquired French majorities, and therefore needed to be detached from unilingual Flanders, the problem had become politically untenable. Whereas, in Eastern Europe, linguistic assimilation was masked by having recourse to the primordial indicator of nationality, the solution in Belgium was to stop inquiring about language and thus freeze once and for all the linguistic boundaries of the state, and therefore of Brussels. This refusal to count masks the continuing assimilation of foreign and Flemish migrants to French in and around Brussels.[11]

Quebec: whither the allophones?

In Canada, a census question had long been asked on people's "mother tongue." The question was not politically controversial because the assimilation of French Canadians in Quebec was extremely limited. Thanks to a very high birth rate, the French Canadians had been able to withstand steady English-speaking inmigration to Quebec and massive outmigration of Francophones to New England, maintaining their share of the Quebec population at about 80 percent until the 1960s. The modernization of Quebec, however, led to a drastic decrease in the birthrate, as elsewhere in the West, below the actual point of population replacement. Quebec now needed international immigrants to maintain its level of population.

Since French was a low-status language in Quebec, with big businesses owned mostly by English-speakers, immigrants had until then assimilated to English, in a proportion greater than four to one. The language project of Québécois nationalists was to reverse the assimilationist trend and encourage immigrants to adopt French instead of English as their main language. The key provision was the controversial school article of the 1977 language law, which declared that children whose parents had not been educated in English in Canada (in practice, all international immigrants) had to attend French school, up to college level.

From a census perspective, the key indicator became the "home language," or the language primarily used at home. This indicator had been added in 1971 to the mother tongue question. Comparing the data from the two indicators enabled demographers to assess the proportion of immigrants assimilating (or experiencing a "language shift") to French and to English. For the past twenty years, each new publication of census data has generated some political upheaval, since Francophone nationalists are concerned by what they see as the very slow progress made in "integrating" (assimilating) "allophones" (people whose mother tongue is neither French nor English, i.e. immigrants) and the continued "predominance" of English. A close analysis of the data, however, shows that among those post-1977 immigrants who have already assimilated to French or English, that is, identify French or English as their main language at home, 70 percent assimilated to French, an extraordinary reversal of the trend prevailing only a generation ago (Norris 1999). Because the actual aggregate numbers remain small, with most post-1977 immigrants still claiming their immigrant language as their main home language, the perception that the trend is very favorable has not registered in French public opinion.[12]

The perception gap, which has major political consequences since it provides additional support to the secessionist party which came within a hair of winning a referendum in 1995, is partly caused by a misleading census question. According to Veltman (1986), the home language question provides the linguistic picture prevailing *a generation ago*. This is so because children of immigrant parents, who still live at home, put down the immigrant language as their home language since they use it with their parents. But surveys show that a great many of these second-generation immigrants already use another language, French or English, among themselves (siblings or friends), and this language will become their "home language" once they move out of their parents' home. Since 1977, most of these second-generation immigrants have adopted French, rather than English, as the language they use the most with others of their generation. This means that the aggregate numbers of those "children of the 1977 law", who have already assimilated to French, is much higher than recorded in the census.[13]

Such numbers, once internalized, would likely diminish the cultural anxiety of Francophone Québécois and most probably erode popular support for independence, as survey research suggests that concern for the fate of the French language in Quebec remains an important variable in explaining the vote for independence (Castonguay 1997: 473). Yet, a recurring theme in contemporary nationalist discourse is that the francization of allophones is proceeding at an alarmingly slow rate. In a sense, the nationalist *backward-looking* inclination is projected onto the immigrant communities, which are perceived to be clinging adamantly to their cultures and languages, at the expense of French. The fear that the island of Montreal will lose a French majority (see note 15) is predicated on the notion that allophone languages will take over, in a context where no language other than French or English can compete for public space. Ironically, the Canadian authorities control the census questionnaire, but they keep using a question which actually undermines their case.

Census, language and territoriality

Nationalist discourse claims historical "ownership" of a territory, the "homeland." The claim is couched in terms of the rights of first settlement by a culturally distinct group: "who came first" in nationalist mythology has sovereign rights on the land (Horowitz 1985). This assumes that the members of the cultural nation have always had cultural (ethnic) markers distinguishing them from other nations, and still have. It is thus imperative for nationalists to draw the ethnic map of their group. In political terms, this becomes a quest to ensure that the territories claimed contain *majorities* of putative members of the nation. The census is the key instrument "proving" that these majorities legitimately exist, and language, the critical variable.

The most acute pitched battles over the census take place in border areas. Populations in these areas may actually speak a mixture of the two border languages, and/or speak a dialectical version of a standardized language claimed by nationalists as being part of "their" language. Establishing, from the outside, their "true" national identity is thus inherently contentious. A classic example was the Teschen area of inter-war Czechoslovakia, along the Polish border. According to the last Austrian census of 1910, the area was trilingual in terms of people's language of use (*umgangssprache*), with a near majority of Poles (48.5 percent), a sizeable minority of Czechs (39.5 percent) and a growing number of Germans (12.0 percent). Eleven years later, when the Czechs conducted their first census, the Czech population in Teschen grew to 65.1 percent. Since this spectacular rise could not be explained by wartime migration, the Poles claimed that the numbers resulted from countless irregularities committed by Czech census-takers (Paul 1998).

Fabrication was certainly part of the process, with many respondents' answers simply dictated by enumerators. Yet, on the whole, the discrepancy had probably more to do with how national identity was conceptualized by the Czechs. In Austrian Teschen, the most prestigious language was German, followed by Polish, and then Czech. Language reidentification was thus proceeding towards German and Polish, and away from Czech. In the 1921 Czech census, as we saw before, the Czech authorities emphasized the language of the *group*, as opposed to the language actually used by the individual, by resorting to the backward-looking indicator of "nationality (mother tongue)." At the same time, the fact that Czech was now the state language may have prodded many to reidentify as Czech, for Czech was now likely to become the language of mobility.

What is clear is that the Czech state wanted to legitimize its hold on an ethnically mixed border area and felt compelled to use a census question that would maximize the Czech presence. This applied particularly to the German-speaking frontier area of Czechoslavkia, where Czechs, for over four decades, had been attempting to make linguistic inroads (Cornwall 1994). The Czechs had been successful in claiming the Sudetenland as part of their state, on historic grounds, at the Versailles Conference. Yet they were determined to make the region increasingly Czech-speaking to solidify their hold on the land since, after all, the cession of the Sudetenland had been a major breach of the "nationalities principle," according to which the borders of the new states of Eastern Europe were supposed to follow ethnic (nationality) patterns of settlement.

Before industrialization in Bohemia, the language communities were, on the whole, compactly separated from each other, with German speakers living along a western–northern ring of border territories (later known as Sudetenland), as well as in major urban centers of the hinterlands, such as Prague, while Czech speakers lived in rural areas. Industries started to develop in the German-speaking territories, provoking a "natural" exodus of Czech peasants to the factories and potentially upsetting the "language border." The Sudetenland Germans expected the newcomers to linguistically assimilate, while the nascent Czech national movement was determined to drive a linguistic wedge all the way to the border in order to legitimate its territorial claim on the whole of Bohemia.

It is precisely this shifting language border which made the census so contested in Austria. Each village or town "tipping over" to the Czech side, in terms of proportion of speakers, was seen, by both sides, as an extremely critical event (Cornwall 1994). This invariably caused political agitation in the months preceding each census, with Czech and German associations relentlessly attempting to make bilingual respondents conscious of the fact that their decision to select Czech (or German) as their *Umgangssprache* could have a tremendous impact on the very existence of their group in their locality or region in the near future. Census preparation acquired the features of an election campaign, where each "vote" was bitterly fought by the contestants, a development completely at odds with the belief in a "scientifically objective" census (Brix 1982). The Belgian case, related above, was of the same nature. The prospect of each Dutch-speaking commune tipping over to French, as made official by the state through the census, was extremely unsettling for the Flemish national movement and turned the census into a referendum.

Language communities can cohabit without regular political storms if there is an expectation that "language borders" will be respected. What this means is that migrants to a language "zone" (district, province) will be expected to assimilate to the dominant language of that area, and that this "natural" process will not be contested politically. As we will see below, this is essentially the Swiss model, with censuses there showing steady assimilation of newcomers to the official language of the canton (German or French) where they settle. When the language border is not recognized as inviolable, as in old Bohemia and pre-1960 Brussels, a national conflict is likely to break out, and the census, no matter which language category is actually used, only exacerbates it.

The pre-war Austrian, Prussian, and Hungarian census statistics on nationality were major factors in the determination, by the Allied Powers, of post-war boundaries in Eastern Europe – except in areas such as the Sudetenland and Bolzano (South Tyrol) where strategic considerations came into play. The Prussian census, to the ire of Polish nationalists, had recognized a "Masurian" language in Masuria, a border area of Eastern Prussia which was claimed by both Poland and Germany after World War I. Poland argued that Masurian was in fact a dialect of Polish, that the

Masurians were therefore of Polish nationality, and that Masuria should thus be attached to post-war Poland. Germany argued that the Masurians were a separate nationality and had historically identified with Prussia, making it a legitimate territory of post-war Germany (Blanke 1999).

Where did the truth lie? As always with census identity statistics, the "truth" was a function of the group's subjectively evolving assessment of itself *within* politically induced categorizations. The Masurians spoke a language which differed from standard Polish and attended German-only schools from the late nineteenth century on. In Gellnerian terms, they were undergoing a transition from a Masurian/Polish low culture (unstandardized speech) to a German high culture; and, indeed, the last Prussian censuses showed a growing linguistic assimilation to German among them. These "facts," however, were deemed illegitimate by Polish nationalists, who portrayed them as resulting from a Prussian state policy of Polish assimilation. Had Masuria been annexed to Poland, as it eventually was in 1945, the Polish census would not have given the Masurians the possibility of officially identifying as anything other than "Polish." The Allied Powers, however, had decided to conduct a plebiscite in Masuria (an option not given to the populations of Teschen and the Sudetenland), asking the Masurians whether they would prefer to join Poland or Germany. Ninety-nine percent chose Germany. This was an extremely rare case where a border population, whose census representation led to diametrically opposed claims, was unambiguously asked about its identity at a defining moment.

The question was unambiguous, as it simply asked which *state* the Masurian population wanted to be a part of, as opposed to how they defined their (cultural) nationality. The Masurians may not have known who they were in terms of a cultural nation, but they knew they did not feel like "Poles," since their massive vote in favor of Germany indicated that they did not feel like a national minority in Germany. A plebiscite was also conducted in Upper Silesia, resulting in the partition of the area between Germany and Poland. It is estimated that 40 percent of people claimed as "Poles" by Poland voted to join Germany (Blanke 1994; Tooley 1997).

Territorial demands based on the "nationality" composition of border territories were rampant in the inter-war period. Before extending their grip into "subracial" Slavic territory, the Nazis systematically made claims on territories inhabited by German-speakers, as in Bohemia (Sudetenland) and Austria. The Soviets made copycat claims for non-Russian Soviet nationalities, such as the Ukrainians and Belorussians of Eastern Poland and the "Moldovans" of Bessarabian Romania. Nazi Germany even resettled historic German communities, such as the Baltic Germans, into territories directly administered by the Reich (Labbé

1998). In none of these cases were the local populations asked about their preferences. The totalitarian states identified nationalities according to existing census data and used them to further their expansionist aims.[14]

Census and linguistic rights

The census is a crucial arena for the politics of representation (Urla 1993). A critical mass may acquire the consciousness of forming a national minority on a given territory and mobilize for the public use of its cultural markers. Political movements speaking in the name of a national minority may acquire sufficient political weight to have an impact on public policy. Language rights are often a key demand for these minorities. They affect several areas of public life; two of the most important of these are the language used in official interactions with the authorities and in state administration, and the language in schools.

States can acknowledge or reject the principle that minority languages be used in official, i.e. state-regulated, domains. France and Turkey, to give two prominent examples, reject the very notion. Turkey recognizes religious minorities, but not linguistic ones. The Kurdish-speaking Muslim Kurds are consequently not considered a minority. Their censuses are thus devoid of language questions. Among the states that acknowledge the notion of a minority language, two principles can be used: the principle of personality, guaranteeing the use of a minority language irrespective of the territory of residence of the speaker; and the principle of territoriality, which restricts language rights to specific territories (McRae 1975). The principle of personality is rarely adopted, partly because of what it entails in terms of administrative costs. The Canadian 1969 Bilingual Act formally embraced it, by guaranteeing federal services in French and English throughout the country (with the practical proviso that a minimum of 5 percent of French or English speakers was required in any given bilingual district). In Quebec, however, the Bilingual Act had a muted impact, since it applies strictly to federal offices, much less pervasive than provincial institutions, and since the federal government eventually decided not to establish bilingual districts. Since 1977 the sole official language of Quebec, and thus of Quebec institutions, has been French.

The principle of territoriality can entail official unilingualism or the recognition of minority rights in a given territory within the state. In the first case, a single language is used in publicly funded schools and public administration in a territory, although other languages can be used officially elsewhere in the state. This is the principle that governs the language policy of Switzerland: at the canton level, or at the lower district level (in the case of linguistically mixed cantons), a single language always predominates. No publicly funded German-language school can operate in French-speaking cantons and vice versa. Cantonal administration functions solely in the language of the canton. Citizens do have the right to use one of the three official Swiss languages in their correspondence with federal authorities, but in their day-to-day formal interactions in their canton of residence, a single language prevails. Swiss who take residence across the linguistic boundary are *expected* to linguistically assimilate. This is probably why the concept of mother tongue in Switzerland is identical with that of one's *current* main language of use. This completely depoliticizes the language question of the census, merely confirming the continuing unilingualism of cantons and districts.

The principle of territoriality, however, need not be identical with territorial unilingualism. Indeed, its dominant interpretation today, by international organizations such as the Council of Europe or the Organization for Security and Cooperation in Europe (OSCE), is one of territorial *multi*lingualism, whereby linguistic minorities on a given territory are granted the right to use their language in public domains. This interpretation necessarily entails the use of official statistics, since a minimum of minority-language speakers is needed to render practical the use of this language in state-regulated areas. (As we saw above, even the principle of personality has to resort to the practicality of minimum thresholds.) Counting the minority can be inherently conflictual, for the reasons discussed earlier. Beyond the question of who constitutes a minority member, however, lies the question of what constitutes an acceptable threshold.

As with everything else in census language politics, there is no consensus as to what the "right" threshold should be. The statisticians debating the nationality question in the sessions of the International Statistical Congress in the nineteenth century thought that the Austrian standard of 20 percent could serve as a model, but the Belgians required a threshold of 30 percent of speakers of a language (in practice, French in Flanders) for that language to be used in interactions between citizens and the state administration, and 50 percent to introduce it as the sole language of internal administration. The Finns, since their independence, have been using a barrier of 10 percent (later reduced to 8 percent) of minority speakers in a given commune. This was intended to protect Swedish rights in predominantly Finnish-speaking communes, but, through migratory patterns, it has had the long-term effect of transforming previously unilingually Swedish communes into bilingual communes, thereby contributing to the steady decline of the use of Swedish throughout Finland (McRae 1997). The Québécois use a 50 percent threshold to allow municipalities to continue using English internally. In its Framework Convention for the Protection of National Minorities and European Charter on Minority Languages, the Council of Europe leaves the determination of the thresholds to the discretion of states.

Irrespective of the actual numerical barrier, linking the right to use one's language in official communication with the state to territorial language group proportions generated by the census can be politically destabilizing. The Belgians learned this the hard way after World War II. A 1932 law had made the annexation of suburban communes to Brussels contingent on these communes obtaining majorities of residents declaring French as their "main" language. Since Flanders was officially unilingual, but Brussels officially bilingual (with, in practice, French acting as the hegemonic language), the continuous expansion of mostly French Brussels was perceived by Flemish nationalists as territorial loss of the homeland. The 1947 results showing several more peripheral communes acquiring French majorities (due, in large part, to the desire of residents of Flemish mother tongue, or of parents with Flemish mother tongue, to adopt French as their public language) created a storm which resulted, as we saw above, in the elimination of the language question from the census.

The use of languages in public domains can have both identity and instrumental purposes. Being able to use one's language at the post office, for example, may be seen as the natural right to use the language of one's "homeland," i.e. the territory with whom the language group identifies. Being able to use one's language as an employee of the post office may be seen in the same light. Others may not care and may use whatever language appears to be convenient in a given situation. Yet whenever the identity-based claims of the public use of languages are politicized, the census inevitably becomes a main area of contention. In some cases, as in Turkey, the battle is over the recognition of minority languages in the first place, which would entail a statistical representation in the census. In other cases, as in late nineteenth-century Austria, the principle of using minority languages in state offices was accepted, but disagreements persisted as to how to record "languages" in the census. In yet other cases, as in Belgium, the principle was ultimately rejected when it became clear that one language was systematically gaining at the expense of another. The language regimes thus became fixed.

Conclusion

Language is a potent force in nationalist politics, since it simultaneously acts as a symbol of identity, a privileged means of social, economic, and political mobility, and a claim to territory. In the modern era, the "mother tongue" can either evoke strong emotions or be discarded in favor of another language deemed better suited to increase one's life chances. A language-based nationalist conflict can occur whenever *both* the primordial pull of language preservation and the instrumental draw of language assimilation divide a speech community, as with the Czechs of Austro-Hungary and the Flemings of Belgium.

Ethnic nationalists claim territories on the basis of ethnic differences which, more often than not, are grounded on a claim to *language* differences. Recording the language of the putative members of the nation can become a crucial tool to assert and legitimize a territorial claim. The census is the prized instrument to "officialize" the territorial distribution of language communities. It is an inherently political instrument, since the choice of particular categories derives from political choices. Identities being the product of subjective assessments, a "neutral" identity category is an oxymoron.

A census language indicator presupposes an agreement as to what the acceptable "language" categories are. The Prussian state claimed that the Masurians spoke a distinct language, a claim that was derided by Polish nationalists. Yet the standardization of any language implies a decision to include some peripheral dialects and not others. Then, the indicator itself has to be chosen, whether "first" language or language of use, situations that can *each* be captured by the concept of "mother tongue," depending on the national context. An "objective" assimilation of "mother tongue" to "language of use" (Czechs of nineteenth-century Austria), or from "mother tongue" to another "mother tongue" (Romanians of nineteenth-century Hungary) can be judged illegitimate by nationalist forces, being interpreted as the result of "repressive" state policies. The "backward-looking" conception of a language-based identity, where the true identity is the one that allegedly prevailed before assimilation, collides with the "forward-looking" conception which can go as far as projecting one's language preference in the future (as with the Brussels Flemings after World War II).

This not to say, however, that language is necessarily the hot button of all censuses. A consensual expectation of linguistic assimilation depoliticizes the language question. This has been the experience of Switzerland, with each census recording the continuous linguistic homogenization of its French and German cantons. This has also been the experience of the United States, where census language data collection (which has changed so many times over the years as to prevent any diachronic study) has had a minor political impact, due to the continued willingness of each new wave of immigrants to assimilate into English. France could be added to this category, except that in this case the societal expectation to assimilate has been accompanied by an *absence* of language questions on the census. When the consensus on the normalcy of language assimilation is shattered, or absent in the first place, the road to the politicization of the language categories of the census is open.

NOTES

I would like to thank Regine Heberlein and Stefany Van Scoyk for their research assistance, as well as Morgane Labbé, the authors of the other chapters in this volume, and the participants in the Conference on Categorizing Citizens for their helpful comments on an earlier version of this chapter.

1 While different alphabets were used in Croatia (Latin) and Serbia (Cyrillic), the distinction was geographical and not ethnic, as Croatian Serbs also used the Latin alphabet. See Garde 1992.

2 The German and Scandinavian languages were maintained in the relative isolation of the Midwest settlements in the nineteenth century, but quickly faded once modernization set in. As for Spanish, Crawford (1992) claims that linguistic assimilation to English, despite appearances, is actually faster than before. An important exception to this rule are the communities who did not migrate to, but were rather incorporated by the US, such as the Spanish-speakers of New Mexico and Puerto Rico. In the latter case, the forceful imposition of English failed and linguistic autonomy was granted in 1949 (Lerner 1999). Kennedy (1996) does not discount the possibility that "a kind of Chicano Quebec" may evolve in the American Southwest.

3 The Alsatians, annexed by Germany between 1870–1919, kept their German language but continued to identify with the French "nation." In the post-war era, German was maintained in the private and communitarian realms, with French as the uncontested state language of Alsace (Capotorti 1991: 53). The growth of the Islamic Maghreb community in France has called in question the symbols of separation of state and religion, but not the supremacy of the French language.

4 On this point, see the writings of the Austrian statistician Ficker (Kleeberg 1915).

5 While not being recognized as a separate state between 1867–1917, since foreign policy was the domain of the Austro-Hungarian state, Hungary nevertheless had complete autonomy on domestic issues, which included the administration of its own census. As a result, the language question differed in Austria and Hungary. Prussia, part of Imperial Germany since 1870, nonetheless maintained separate questions on language, in order to address the issue of growing Polish-speaking minorities.

6 *Umgangssprache* has been variously translated as "language spoken in daily life" (Bohac 1931), "language of common intercourse" (Zeman 1990) and "usual language" (Petersen 1987). While the word refers more to a social or public interaction than a private one, the historical evidence shows a great deal of confusion in how this census concept was popularly understood. In

that regard, the rather vague term "use" expresses the indeterminacy of the concept during the census years in Imperial Austria.

7 The Hungarian state, whose interest was to record language assimilation to Hungarian in order to increase the proportion of Hungarian speakers in the kingdom, used the indicator of "mother tongue," rather than "language of use" in its census, but in a "forward-looking" way. The instructions to the 1910 Hungarian census indicated that "it may happen that the mother tongue of the child differs from that of the mother, especially when the child has acquired a language different from his mother's, either in school, through other social relations, or because his parents have different mother tongues." (Van Gennep 1922: 109).

8 During the Hungarian censuses of 1880–1910, Romania existed as an independent state, but the contested province of Transylvania, historically settled by both Romanians and Hungarians, belonged to Hungary. It became part of Romania, along with a sizeable Hungarian population, after World War I, a decision dictated by the Treaty of Trianon. In practice, assimilation to Hungarian, as recorded in the Hungarian census, was much less significant among Romanians than among Germans, Jews, and Slovaks.

9 Since "national" consciousness was still fairly undeveloped, particularly outside of European Russia, the 1926 census used an indicator (*narodnost'*) whose connotation in Russian is more ethnographic, i.e. reflective of local customs, than national, i.e. implying a consciousness of belonging to a cultural nation. A word with the latter connotation (*natsional'nost'*) was used in subsequent censuses.

10 According to studies made in the 1960s, if Middle Eastern and African migrants are excepted, half of Brussels is of Flemish descent, even though at most 30 percent of them still speak it as their main language (McRae 1986). The general estimates of Dutch speakers in Brussels vary between 10 and 15 percent, excluding the non-citizens.

11 The proportion of French-speakers in Brussels is now estimated to be between 80 to 90 percent of the population (Verdoodt 1997), and perhaps even more if the North African non-citizen immigrants – who comprise up to 30 percent of the population – are included, since the majority of their children are enrolled in French schools (Herremans 1997). In the last four decades, several districts (communes) located outside of Brussels have probably acquired French-speaking majorities. They remain in officially unilingual Flanders.

12 Several Francophone *démolinguistes* (demographers specializing in language statistics) focus on the fact that, at the aggregate level, three of five allophones experiencing a language shift have chosen English. This misleadingly includes the pre-1977 allophones who were schooled in English. A common argument is also that the proportion of Francophones on the Island of Montreal will soon dip below 50 percent of the population, with allophones and anglophones combined becoming more numerous (Norris 1999). This arbitrarily excludes the heavily Francophone municipalities on the South Shore and North Shore of Montreal, and assumes that the Montreal allophones will not mostly shift to French, despite the evidence adduced by census and survey data.

13 While the "home language" question may underestimate the pace of assimilation to French, the "mother tongue" question may underestimate the pace of assimilation of French speakers to English. As demographer Charles Castonguay (1997) argues, since the census instructions indicate that a "mother tongue" is a "first language still understood," a certain proportion of anglicized Francophones do not appear in census statistics. This, however, would largely apply to Canadian Francophones outside of Quebec, where the rates of assimilation are fairly high. In Quebec proper, assimilation of French to English has always been extremely small.

14 During World War II, the Nazi state ceased relying on census nationality data, since they were based on the declaration of respondents, using instead the "objective" "racial" data, garnered and determined by the secret police (Labbé 1998).

REFERENCES

Arel, Dominique 1995, "The Temptation of the Nationalizing State," in Vladimir Tismaneanu (ed.), *Political Culture and Civil Society in Russia and the New States of Eurasia*, Armonk, N.Y.: M. E. Sharpe, pp. 157–88.
Blanke, Richard 1994, "Polish-Speaking Germans Under Polish Rule: Polish Silesia, 1922–1939," *Canadian Review of Studies in Nationalism* 21: 25–32.
1999, "Polish-Speaking Germans? Language and National Identity among the Masurians," Paper presented at the 4th Annual World Convention of the Association for the Study of Nationalities (ASN), New York, April 15–17.
Blum, Alain and Gousseff, Catherine 1997, "Les nationalités dans les recensements russes et soviétiques," in Jean-Louis Rallu, Youssef Courbage and Victor Piché (eds.), *Anciennes et nouvelles minorités*, Paris: National Institute of Demographic Studies (INED), pp. 49–72.
Böckh, Richard 1974 [1866], "Die statistiche Bedeutung der Volksprache als Kennzeichen der Nationalität," in H. Haarmann (ed.), *Sprachenstatistik in Geschichte und Gegenwart*, Hamburg: Helmut Buske Verlag, pp. 41–186.
Boháč, Antonín 1931, " Nationality and the New Czechoslovak Census," *Slavonic Review* 10: 105–15.
Brix, Emile 1982, *Die Umgangssprachen in Altösterreich zwischen Agitation und Assimilation. Die Sprachenstatistik in den zisleithanischen Volkszählungen*, Wien, Köln and Graz: Hermann Böhlaus Nachf.
Brubaker, Rogers 1996, *Nationalism Reframed. Nationhood and the National Question in the New Europe*, Cambridge: Cambridge University Press.
Capotorti, Francesco 1991 [1979], *Study on the Rights of Persons belonging to Ethnic, Religious and Linguistic Minorities*, New York: United Nations.
Castonguay, Charles 1997, "Evolution de l'assimilation linguistique au Québec et au Canada entre 1971 et 1991," *Recherches sociographiques* 38: 469–90.
Cohen, Gary B. 1981, *The Politics of Ethnic Survival: Germans in Prague, 1861–1914*, Princeton: Princeton University Press.
Connor, Walker 1984, *The National Question in Marxist-Leninist Theory and Strategy*, Princeton: Princeton University Press.
1994, *Ethnonationalism. The Quest for Understanding*, Princeton: Princeton University Press.

Cornwall, Mark 1994, "The Struggle on the Czech-German Language Border, 1880–1940," *English Historical Review* 109: 914–51.

Crawford, James 1992, *Hold Your Tongue: Bilingualism and the Politics of English Only*, Reading, Mass.: Addison-Wesley.

Durkovic, Svetlana 1999, "Language Purification and Language of Purification in Croatia," Paper presented at the ASN 4th Annual World Convention, New York, April 15–17.

Garde, Paul 1992, *Vie et mort de la Yougoslavie*, Paris: Fayard.

Gellner, Ernest 1983, *Nations and Nationalism*, Ithaca, N.Y.: Cornell University Press.

Héran, François 1998, "La fausse querelle des catégories "ethniques" dans la statistique publique," http://census.ined.fr, page "Le Débat," 12 November.

Herremans, Maurice-Pierre 1997, "Le fait bruxellois," *Recherches sociologiques* 28: 45–58.

Hirsch, Francine. 1997, "The Soviet Union as a Work-in-Progress: Ethnographers and the Category Nationality in the 1926, 1937, and 1939 Censuses," *Slavic Review* 56: 251–78.

Horowitz, Donald R. 1985, *Ethnic Groups in Conflict*, Berkeley: University of California Press.

Kennedy, David M. 1996, "Can We Still Afford to Be a Nation of Immigrants?" *The Atlantic Monthly* 278 (November): 52–68.

Kleeberg, Rudolf 1915, *Die Nationalitätenstatistik. Ihre Ziele, Methoden und Ergebnisse*, Thüringen: Thomas & Hubert.

Kohn, Hans 1967 [1944], *The Idea of Nationalism. A Study in Its Origin and Background*, 2nd edn, New York: Collier-Macmillan.

Kovacs, Aloÿse 1928, "La connaissance des langues comme contrôle de la statistique des nationalités," *Bulletin de l'Institut International de Statistique* 23: 246–346.

Kymlicka, Will 1995, *Multicultural Citizenship*, Oxford: Oxford University Press.

Labbé, Morgane 1997, "Le projet d'une statistique des nationalités discuté dans les sessions du Congrès International de Statistique," in Hervé Le Bras (ed.), *Démographie et politique*, Dijon: Presses Universitaires de Dijon, pp. 127–42.

1998, " 'Race' et 'Nationalité' dans les recensements du Troisième Reich," *Histoire & Mesure* 13: 195–223.

Lerner, Ben 1999, "Nationalism in Puerto Rico," International Relations Program, Brown University, manuscript.

Lévy, Paul M. G. 1960, *La querelle du recensement*, Bruxelles: Institut belge de science politique.

1964, "Quelques problèmes de statistique linguistique à la lumière de l'expérience belge," *Revue de l'Institut de Sociologie* 37: 251–73.

McRae, Kenneth D. 1975, "The Principle of Territoriality and the Principle of Personality in Multilingual States," *International Journal of the Sociology of Language* 4: 33–54.

1986, *Conflict and Compromise in Multilingual Societies*, Vol. 2: *Belgium*, Waterloo, Canada: Wilfrid Laurier University Press.

1997, *Conflict and Compromise in Multilingual Societies*, Vol. 3: *Finland*, Waterloo, Canada: Wilfrid Laurier University Press.

Norris, Alexander 1999, "English: It's Where You Live," *The Gazette* (Montreal), May 29.

Paul, Ellen 1998, "Czech Teschen Silesia and the Controversial Czechoslovak Census of 1921," *The Polish Review* 63: 161–71.

Petersen, William 1987, "Politics and the measurement of Ethnicity," in William Alonson and Paul Starr (eds.), *The Politics of Numbers*, New York: Russell Sage Foundation, pp. 187–233.

Roth, Brigitte 1991, "Quellenkritische Dokumentation der erfassten Berichtskategorien," in Henning Bauer, Andreas Kappeler, and Brigitte Roth (eds.), *Die Nationalitäten des Russischen Reiches in der Volkszählung von 1897*, Vol. 1, Stuttgart: Franz Steiner Verlag, pp. 135–284.

Silver, Brian D. 1986, "The Ethnic and Language Dimensions in Russian and Soviet Censuses," in Ralph S. Clem (ed.), *Research Guide to the Russian and Soviet Censuses*, Ithaca, N.Y.: Cornell University Press, pp. 70–97.

Tebarth, Hans-Jakob 1991, "Geschichte der Volkszählung," in Henning Bauer, Andreas Kappeler, and Brigitte Roth (eds.), *Die Nationalitäten des Russischen Reiches in der Volkszählung von 1897*, Vol. 1, Stuttgart: Franz Steiner Verlag, pp. 25–87.

Tooley, T. Hunt 1997, *National Identity and Weimar Germany: Upper Silesia and the Eastern Border*, Lincoln: University of Nebraska Press.

Urla, Jacqueline 1993, "Cultural Politics in an Age of Statistics: Numbers, Nations, and the Making of Basque Identity," *American Ethnologist* 20: 818–43.

Van Gennep, Arnold 1992 [1922], *Traité des nationalités*, Paris: Editions du CTHS.

Van Velthonen, Harry 1987, "The Process of Language Shift in Brussels: Historical Background and Mechanisms," in Els Witte and Hugo Baetens Beardsmore (eds.), *The Interdisciplinary Study of Urban Bilingualism in Brussels*, Philadelphia: Multilingual Matters Ltd.

Veltman, Calvin 1986, "The Interpretation of the Language Questions of the Canadian Census," *Canadian Review of Sociology and Anthropology* 23: 412–22.

Verdoodt, Albert F. 1997, "Présentation," *Où va la Belgique?* Special issue of *Recherches sociologiques*, 28: 1–9.

Zaslavsky, Victor and Yuri Luryi 1979, "The Passport System in the USSR," *Soviet Union*, 6: 137–53.

Zeman, Z.A.B. 1990, "The Four Austrian Censuses and Their Political Consequences," in Mark Cornwall (ed.), *The Last Years of Austria-Hungary*, Exeter: University of Exeter Press, pp. 31–39.

5   Resistance to identity categorization in France

Alain Blum

For many years, public statistics in France, especially censuses, did not categorize the population on the basis of ethnicity. From the mid-1980s on, however, there has been a growing debate on immigration, leading to the progressive resurgence of the ethnicity question. The heated debate, challenging values so fundamental to French society, was fueled by the publication of a study on immigrant populations, pressure by various academic circles on the National Institute of Economic Statistics (INSEE in its French acronym) to change its method of counting immigrants, and by the preparation of the 1999 census. The debate poses some fundamental questions: Should we construct statistical categories based on ethnic affiliation to allow for the formulation of public policies directed against discriminatory practices? How do we define ethnic affiliation? How is demography to be used in the construction of such categories? What role should the census play in redefining the identity markers of individuals?

The debate is interesting in that it echoes the arguments voiced in France during the second half of the nineteenth century on the question of including categories in public statistics based on origins, as well as the recurring debate on the statistical identification of immigrants. Glancing at the debate, one might get the impression that it juxtaposes the adherents of a republican ethic versus those who defend an empirical reality; but, as we shall see, the relationship to the older debate is a complex one.

The debate is both interesting and important, as it raises the issue of the political implications of the analytic categories employed by social science, as well as the question of how these categories affect group formation within a given population. It is also exciting because it reveals numerous assumptions in the use of statistical categories and in the relationship between politics, social science, and political science. Moreover, it demonstrates that, in the relationship between research and politics, there are no straightforward political cleavages.

This chapter presents the major issues raised by the debate and traces their references to the nineteenth century. It then provides an examination of its main arguments.

The issues of the current debate

The debate on the introduction of ethnic categories into the statistical picture reappeared on the public scene indirectly, not during a discussion of the methods of identifying populations in the census, but during the immigration count. Pressure from the extreme right resulted in the circulation of numerous imaginary figures, a large degree of terminological confusion, and the questioning of certain works published by INSEE or INED (National Institute of Demographic Studies). Basically, the extreme right used the information on immigrants to demonstrate that the segment of the population descended from North African immigrants would become preponderant in France one day. These projections were not only dangerous, they also completely disregarded the nationality law and mixed marriages. Scenarios were devised that fit the right's arguments on reproduction or immigration and provided a springboard for attacking immigration of any kind through defending the idea of a "pure" French nation.

At the same time, the decision by the government to institute a commission of inquiry on immigration issues (the High Commission on Integration) necessitated precise statistics.[1] The circulation of false figures and alarmist predictions not only generated great confusion, it also stigmatized the contribution of immigration and foreigners to the French population. It was in this context that the central institutions handling the statistical analysis of immigration sought greater precision in the categories of analysis. They did so by clearly distinguishing between the immigrant and the foreigner (Tribalat 1989), studying immigration's contribution to the formation of the French population (Tribalat 1991), and providing precise definitions of census categories, designed to help identify immigrant populations statistically.

And so the terms of the debate evolved. The initial interest in the flow of migration and its quantification gradually gave way to the question of what had become of the immigrants. Thus, the immigrants themselves became the focus of discussion, and there was already a willingness to include immigrant populations in a precise statistical framework. The questions were posed in strong normative terms, and therefore, implicitly, the debate on assimilation and integration echoes old discussions about differences in the behaviour of immigrants and the degree to which this behaviour was similar to or moving towards that of the (native) French.

Demographic differences (especially in connection with reproduction) and inter-marriages were used as indicators, more or less explicitly, in numerous studies (for example INED 1993; Munoz-Perez *et al.* 1984).

Once the focus had shifted to the immigrant population, the question arose as to how to measure it and how to differentiate within the category. The answer seemed to lie with finding the right descriptive marker and formulating ethnic categories for use in statistics. This phase of the debate coincided with the preparation of the 1999 French census and therefore stimulated discussions on the eventual introduction of new questions, in surveys conducted after the census, that would allow for analyses now felt to be necessary.

Thus, in the beginning, the debate did not refer directly to the categories employed in the census, nor to its history. Very soon, however, the incorporation of the discussion into a much larger debate promoted a rethinking of census categories and lent a historic dimension to the questions being posed.

In its initial phase, this new debate was limited to a confrontation between the public space and the world of research. On one side, institutions connected to research or statistics spent their time explaining the methodological framework of their work, the meaning of population projections, and the relationship between statistical and juridical categories. Certain elements within the media responded to these explications by pointing to the contradiction between the statistical view and a certain "common feeling" or intuition that was assumed to exist among immigrants or foreigners.

These discussions took a new turn in 1995, when a violent polemic exploded within the research milieu itself, involving researchers from various institutions and statistical bodies, as well as the media and the political world. This debate was touched off by the publication of a major survey – the first of its kind in France – on the behaviour of immigrant populations (Tribalat 1995). A brief overview of the debate demonstrates the close relationship between politics and statistical production and research, as well as the role of the public debate, which was filtered through the media.

First, it is worth pointing out the various aspects that made this debate important. The case constituted a clear example of the scientific elaboration of a concept and of its statistical measurement in social science. Numerous social actors participated more or less actively in the process. It is now clear that statistical measuring has a history, and that this history reflects the interaction between research, administration, and society as much as it reflects the internal intellectual debates of the disciplines producing the statistics (Desrosières 1993; Alonso and Starr 1987;

Boltanski 1982). Since the mid-1970s, the logic behind the construction and negotiation of social categories has been the object of various studies (in France, Desrosières and Thévenot 1988; de la Gorce 1991; in the United States, Anderson 1988; in Great Britain, Szreter 1996; on the Soviet Union, Blum 1994; Houle 1997)[2]. Curiously, national categories received such attention only somewhat later, following the publication of works on nationalism (Anderson, 1991) or the brutal reappearance of the national question on the public scene. They are now the focus of a new history of multinational empires (Blum *et al.* 1998; Blum and Gousseff 1997; Hirsch 1997).

The shift in research focus towards the national question since the early 1980s, nourished by the political changes in Europe following the collapse of the Berlin Wall and of the USSR, thus transformed the debate on the nature of social categories and their construction into a discussion of the nature of national categories. The latter were understood in analogous fashion, i.e. as a process of construction and of negotiation between different levels of administration and politics, as well as representative groups of population, and as a process of interaction between different milieu: scientific and political in particular. In addition, a growing interest in the study of the colonial experience provided a field of inquiry and interdisciplinary encounter that went beyond the world of the statisticians or sociologists. This development initiated heightened interaction among the demographers, sociologists, and political scientists, in the investigation of the construction of categories.

Another important aspect of the debate is the fact that the various organs producing statistics participated in it as much as the research institutes and the academics. There was thus a clear confrontation between those who elaborate the analytic categories, and provide advice on and help formulate public policy, and those providing the research on social dynamics. For a long time, social categories had been analyzed critically and mostly independently of the institutions that produced them – even if a statistician like Alain Desrosières, who pioneered this type of research, worked within the central statistical institution (Desrosières 1993). The confrontation between these various spheres on the issue of constructing ethnic and national categories pushed the issue into the public debate. It is likely that the most important consequence of this will be the elaboration of new categories.

The debate also involves a confrontation between two traditions surrounding the use of statistics in social science: the "positivist" tradition, which views statistics as an object of reality, without questioning the nature of their source and the meaning of their categories, and the "constructivist", which makes the elaboration of categories and statistical methods the core of its enquiry. That being said, the opposition cannot be understood simply as a confrontation between two entirely distinct approaches, since the latter approach also attempts to be empirical. Nevertheless, these two directions in social science research suggest their own categories of enquiry and statistical analysis.

More generally, this debate leads to a larger discussion on the tools and measurements that can be employed to characterize the individual. Is the individual, at any point in time, a composite of certain fixed characteristics, or is he or she changeable by nature? Is the person the product of a particular life, of a certain path, or of history? Do individuals define themselves on their own, or more in relation to the world around them, and to what extent is their behaviour a product of their environment? As these questions suggest, the discussion raises questions about methods of analysis, i.e. the biography-based study versus the study of the environment in which individuals and groups live. The issue of how to measure diversity, which concerns the entire French population, is thus central, and raises questions about the role of statistics in general, as well as population studies and efforts to construct "tools" or instruments to help orient public policy at both the central and local levels.

Thus, an important aspect of the debate is that it grapples with the issue of the role of statistics in social science. For some, the formulation of public policies linked to particular social questions necessitates a statistical elaboration of these questions. If one wants to fight against discrimination based on "ethnic affiliation, one has to "identify in order to act" (Simon 1993b), and then to count. For others, it is crucial to bear in mind that statistics have symbolic value and that they not only reflect reality, but also construct it. Moreover, some believe that the conception of statistics as the ultimate tool in the formulation of public policy places too much power in the hands of the central government. The debate has therefore sparked a rethinking of the role of the census and, more generally, of statistical surveys of the public. What role do these enquiries play in the formulation and implementation of social policy? How are they useful?

Finally, the media, especially the press, have been a central participant in the debate, and so the academics engaged in the discussions have become a part of the general public debate.

The political nature of the debate reinforces this dimension since the discussions deal, in particular, with the political consequences of the use of certain concepts (ethnicity, nationalism) and categories (e.g. "immigrant"). It is suggested that demography, by its very nature, has direct uses in politics because of its tendency to focus on the question of origins (Le Bras 1998a) and, more generally, on reproduction and the biological aspect of the individual. This explains the link between certain demographic concepts and the ideology of the extreme right. This view further suggests that we cannot understand a certain discipline and its political impact without knowing its history. In the same way, a statistical tool, and a measurement, cannot be properly understood apart from its origins – we have to know the context in which it was constructed. The same applies for institutions (Le Bras 1994). In response to these views, others defend the measure itself, and maintain that its origins should have nothing to do with its interpretation or analysis.

The debate in historical perspective

The debate on the use of ethnic categories in the census and the criteria employed to identify these categories is an old one in Europe. It first became important in the mid-nineteenth century, during the course of international statistics congresses where, for the most part, European statisticians attempted to construct a single, formal framework for state-generated censuses and surveys in all territories.

Two sides emerged during these discussions, one represented by the empires and the other by states, such as France. On one side, Austria-Hungary and Russia considered ethnic (or national) identification to be primordial and an integral part of a tradition that statistics could help characterize with some precision and refine. The drawing up of ethnographic maps of these two empires was viewed as a progressive step that should be embraced by all. The only real question was how to construct a conceptual framework for censuses and ethnographic surveys which would allow for the fullest picture of the ethnographic characteristics of peoples, as they were then recognized in these empires. The opposing view, held by the French, which came to be embraced only after some years of hesitation in the first half of the nineteenth century, rejected any sort of identification of the kind promoted by the empires, especially in censuses. The definitive articulation of this position took place during the 1870s, and, since then, it has remained a constant in the debate.[3]

The public position generally advanced by the French did not question the existence of ethnographic differences, but argued that they applied only to certain states and were therefore not of great interest. From the French perspective, differences between regions did not need to be reflected or recorded statistically. What was important was to defend the unity of the French nation. Representatives of other states, however, emphasized how the term "nationality" had one meaning in France and another in other countries. When the question of Bretons or the Basques was raised, Levasseur, one of the French representatives, talked about dialects, not about the existence or even the possibility of existence of Breton or Basque nationalities.

The basic question revolved around the criteria for identifying resident populations on the basis of those characteristics used to measure one of the major paradigms of nineteenth-century anthropology: race. Migrant populations did not figure in this particular discussion – the focus was on the characterization of the national population. Migration was of interest more in terms of the issue of movement across territories than in connection with ethnographic or racial questions. The polarization that developed in the debate is best understood in the following way: no distinction was made between countries of immigration and other European states, only between empires and nation-states. The ethnographic question was thus primarily a political question, connected to the political management or governing of the state. The cultural approach to the nation, as developed in Central Europe or in Russia, was not considered to be relevant by the French, who favoured an approach centered on the citizen. Race became increasingly looked upon from a biological standpoint, but in a domain of public discourse having nothing to do with statistics or census categorizations.

The stability of French censuses

These old discussions led to the formulation of the basic framework of the census questionnaires, which was largely in place by the end of the nineteenth century. This framework, which is of great importance to our understanding of the current debate, took form, therefore, in a bipolar context and is characterized, to this day, by a remarkable degree of inertia.

In this connection, the French position has been to distinguish ever more clearly between French citizens and foreigners. The former are viewed as constituting a single, unique nation. As for the foreigners, the approach has been to try to fit them into an increasingly clear, juridically precise, national category. For Noiriel (1988, 1991) or Brubaker (1992), the construction of these categories signifies the strengthening of the nation-state, which we see happening during the course of the nineteenth century. In their view, the censuses point to what Noiriel calls "the invention of the national." The citizen and the foreigner became the two principal categories of analysis. Alongside these developments, the consolidation of the concept of the civic state, as well as the 1889 definition of citizenship, according to which nationality was based on *jus solis*, raised important questions that have remained with us since the end of the nineteenth century (Lacroix and Thave 1997; Gousseff 1997; Simon 1998).

Once the religion question was definitively rejected with the 1872 census, efforts centered on clarifying "national membership," particularly on the basis of the distinctions formulated for foreigners recorded in the census (Gousseff 1997). In the first half of the nineteenth century, questions on nationality were either absent or very broad.[4] The first census to include a question on nationality was that of 1851. However, the lists of nationalities published at the time remained imprecise and combined juridical and political concepts.

The nationality question assumed full form by 1872 and has been modified very little since then.[5] Central to the issue are two questions: place of birth and citizenship. The birthplace of persons born in France concerns the commune and the department of birth, and the colony (up until 1946) or country for those born outside of France. The main change to the question on nationality dates to 1891 and was the result of the 1889 law establishing *jus solis*. In 1891 and 1896, there were three possible responses to the question on nationality: "born to French parents", "naturalized French", or "foreigner, of which country". In 1901, the responses were changed to: "born French" (or "of French birth"), "naturalized French" (or French through naturalization, through marriage, since 1946), and "foreigner, of which country" (since 1946, "of which nationality"). These questions have remained basically unchanged to our day, except for the introduction, in 1962, of a supplementary question on the original nationality of naturalized individuals.

Thus, respondents are basically characterized as either French or foreigner, juridically speaking, although "French through naturalization" is a category that does not entirely conform to this characterization. Country of origin is specified, but there is no ethnic dimension for the French. Such a dimension is also absent from the questions on migration, which sometimes ask (1968 and 1975) for the date of arrival of those respondents who came to France in between censuses. The major change in the 1999 census, to which we will return shortly, is the insertion of a question on the date of arrival of respondents born outside of France, regardless of when they came to the country (in 1968 and 1975, the question applied only to those who arrived in between censuses). Thus, to this day, immigration is treated like any migration, internal to the territory, and not like a separate variable, although the question is more precise at times. The changes introduced in 1999 do, however, point towards greater differentiation, i.e. towards a distinction between international and internal migration.

Thus, the nineteenth-century approach appears to be firmly established. Once resident in France, the immigrant is not subject to any differentiation on the basis of his origins. He is simply treated as an individual.

From the beginning of the century down to the decades following World War II, the debate surrounding immigration often had ethnic overtones, as attempts were made to distinguish the "good" immigrant from the "bad," or to distinguish immigrants who could be assimilated from those who could not (Bertaux 1997). Studies by Mauco (1932) and Sauvy (1954) have identified groups that are clearly ethnic in an effort to help formulate specific migration policies. This did not have an impact, however, on census categories, nor on large public surveys.

We are looking at a tradition, therefore, which seeks, first and foremost, to affirm the identity of each respondent. This tradition is a solidly entrenched one, but never extended to the colonial empire, where the issue of citizenship for the indigenous population was faced with contradictory tensions. Thus the census used in the colonies was the only statistical enquiry that included an ethnic dimension.

Colonial ambiguity

The coherence of the French approach to the census diminishes when we turn to the census used in the colonial territories (Blum *et al.* 1998), as was highlighted in 1878 by de Pietra Santa, during the First International Conference on Demography. The categories employed in the colonial census largely used distinctions that were considered ethnic elsewhere in Europe. Algeria is a good example (Kateb 1998a and 1998b). The Algerian census tended increasingly towards the homogenization of the Muslim population into one ethno-religious group starkly differentiated from the "French" population, which itself was viewed as a single group into which other Europeans were gradually absorbed. During the 1830s, in the first few years after the colonization of Algeria, the military administration described the various populations it came into contact with in great detail, enumerating many different ethnic groups (Mzabits, Arabs, Kabyles, etc.). However, the progressive evolution of Algeria into an integral component of France, which did not grant citizenship to indigenous peoples, led to the simple distinction between Muslims and the European population.

During the 1850s, the growing idea of an Algerian "race," representing a fusion of the various European populations inhabiting the colony, began to threaten the French government, which was fearful of secessionist movements. Thus, a 1865 decree provided all Europeans who had lived in Algeria for at least three years the possibility of becoming French, while the 1889 law on nationality extended *jus solis* to any European child born in Algeria. By contrast, a person indigenous to Algeria could become French only with enormous difficulty (Kateb 1998b). In 1870, the Crémieux decree had granted French nationality to all Jews living in Algeria.

The census reflects these contradictions. Since the end of the nineteenth century, the Algerian census has included three main categories: French; French as a result of the Crémieux decree; and indigenous. Kamel Kateb (1998a) observes:

> In 1830, the colonizers found and described a population which it perceived as ethnically unusual, including Turks, Arabs, Kabyls, Mozabits, Koulouhglis, indigenous Jews, and Maurs. A century later, the indigenous population consisted only of Arabs, Kabyls, and Mozabits. And following the promulgation of the organic law on the status of Algeria in 1947, the French administration began to distinguish between Muslim and non-Muslim only. As paradoxical as it may seem, the Colonial administration promoted the Arabization of the once Berber-speaking population, as well as the spread of Muslim law, to the detriment of the customary law of the territory.

The census used in the Overseas *Départements* (Guadeloupe, Martinique, etc.) and *Territoires* (New Caledonia, Polynesia, etc.) resembles that devised for the colonies.[6] Each territory is issued a separate questionnaire, not only because each one has a different administrative status, but also to accommodate political considerations and negotiations specific to each territory. Rallu (1998) has shown how the colonial conception of ethnic questions has produced various responses or approaches reflecting the interplay of diverse forces. In all of the *départements* abroad, the questionnaire used is the same as that for metropolitan France. However, the questionnaires issued to certain *territoires* have gradually changed from census to census in terms of how ethnicity and inter-breeding are measured. These changes are the result of political negotiations. In some cases, questions are introduced and later removed. In others, the census is interested only in the pure "races," and ignores the mixed population (Rallu, 1998). In two cases in Polynesia, in 1996, questions on ethnicity were dropped. In New Caledonia, the multiple declaration is simply not an option, although some have sought it, as also has been the case in Wallis and Futuna. Thus, the categories employed in these censuses are constantly changing, which makes for little continuity between one census and the next.

A history of the debate

Let us now turn to the "technical" origins of the debate. In 1992, after a lengthy discussion and elaboration (which has yet to be studied), INED and INSEE conducted a survey entitled, "Geographic Mobility and Social Integration" (MGIS), dealing with the behaviour of immigrants and their offspring. The two institutions that produced the survey are both public institutions, involved in research, the gathering of statistics, and political activity. The former (INED), is a research center attached to both the Ministry of Social Affairs (now the Ministry of Employment and Solidarity) and the Ministry of Research. INSEE, which is the central statistical institution (Direction de la statistique), comes under the Ministry of the Economy and Finance. Its major tasks include the census, vital registration statistics, and large public surveys, such as those on employment, the family, health, and housing.

The survey was first presented to the public in 1993 (Simon 1993a) and the first results were published in 1995 (Tribalat) in *Faire France*, a publication with a large audience. Another trigger to the debate, and especially to the interaction between the survey and the census question, was the criticism leveled against INSEE by certain academic authorities, suggesting that the census could measure neither the forms nor the effects of immigration (Dupâquier 1997; INSEE 1998).

The main idea behind the MGIS survey was to break with the traditional distinction between foreigners and French citizens employed in French censuses. Instead, new criteria were used which took into account the very process of migration and length of stay in France, and which distinguished between citizens whose parents were born in France and those whose parents were immigrants. The aim was to produce a study of immigration and its future, of immigrants and their descendants, and not of the nationality of the population.

Neither the planning nor the conducting of the survey prompted any particular discussion. An acrimonious debate did, however, ensue with the publication of its first results, the statistical categories used, and the more general way in which the results were presented. In the introduction to the first work to appear on the survey, the author noted that the survey allowed for a departure from the "republican" tradition that ignored ethnic differences and was peculiar to France:

In France, the departure from the distinction foreigner/French is a difficult move for purely ideological reasons: To distinguish the French on the basis of their national or ethnic origins is simply ignominious, a defamation, as it opens the door to discrimination. (Tribalat, 1995a)

The author's position is thus explicitly in opposition to a "republican conception of statistics," although, as we shall see, the debate is not a continuation of the old discussions outlined above. Different concepts were used in each debate. However, references to the past and to the history of statistics gathering do inform certain arguments belonging to this position. It is true that the French census tradition is peculiar,

given the absence of ethnic criteria, which are employed in many different ways in numerous countries. According to the author, this peculiarity
is attributable to an "ideological" refusal, in continuation of nineteenth-
century stances. The approach of the MGIS survey represents a new way
of characterizing individuals, a more objective way which reflects a reality
that can no longer be denied. We are dealing with no less than a rupture,
as is demonstrated by the strong opposition of numerous institutions:
for instance INSEE, which collaborated on the survey, but then, according to Michèle Tribalat, tried to censor it (Tribalat 1995b). This survey
thus provided a way of resisting the "politically correct" attitude that has
dominated social science and statistics gathering to this day. It rejected
the artificial idealization and homogenization of the population of France
in favour of the observation of social reality.

Thus, while the survey was formulated and conducted in order to study
the behaviour of immigrants, it became a means towards the preliminary
exploration of ethnic diversity once published. It therefore broadened the
debate by raising the larger issue of whether and how to deal statistically
with ethnic diversity. Given its position, INSEE was necessarily impli-
cated in the debate, the question being what role it should play in this
line of research, which would eventually require new census questions.

The broadening of the debate was not only self-generated, but also
the result of a growing sensitivity in the political world and among the
media to issues having to do with urban violence, the exclusion of certain groups from schools, and discrimination in the workplace and in
housing. Previously, these issues had been addressed discreetly and on
the basis of geographic dictates, as was done by the Ministry of National
Education when it established the Priority Educational Zones, followed
by the Sensitive Zones, which were defined geographically, not ethnically.
As the debate grew in scope, however, these issues affecting French society were suddenly perceived as conduits to understanding the nature of
ethnic tensions and exclusion.

Once the study was presented to the public, the debate evolved in
various settings and assumed various forms, attesting to the diversity
of participation in a discussion that cut through several public spaces:
research, statistical institutions, political institutions, and the media. The
press devoted much attention to the first publication based on the survey,
focusing on its demonstration of immigrant integration and of a lesser
degree of segregation than had been assumed to exist to date. A first set of
articles soon appeared in a journal symposium (*Revue française des affaires
sociales*, 1997), raising the question, in rather contradictory fashion, of
"the categories pertaining to foreigners of foreign origin." The concepts of
integration (Decouflé 1997), assimilation (Bertaux 1997), and of census

categories used to count foreigners (Gousseff 1997; Lacroix and Thave 1997) were the focus of these first articles. I cautioned against an analysis of immigrants that locked them into a narrow category, as opposed to a demographic approach lending itself to a more complex understanding of the individual. The latter approach takes account of the individual's experience or history, and eschews the idea of a fixed, or unchanging identity (Blum, 1998).

The debate thus spread in different directions. It grew further with the publication of a work that was very critical of the survey (Le Bras 1998a and 1998b) and, especially, of the relationship between social science research and political stances based on the categories employed in the survey.[7] Some time later, during a day-long session entitled "Statistics without Conscience Spells Ruin...," the labour unions of INSEE cautioned against the use of ethnic categories in the census. The session's title aptly conveys the complexity of the issues emerging from the growing debate, which now clearly extended to the census question and the possible consequences of an ethnically-based analysis of public statistics.

At the start, there were five main criticisms leveled against the ethnic approach that was presented in *Faire France* (especially in: Bertaux 1997; Blum 1998; Rallu 1998; Héran 1998; and Richard 1999b). I will summarize these, before discussing the responses to these criticisms.

The first criticism centered on the expression "Français de souche" (French by root, or indigenous French), which is used to describe persons born in France to parents also born in France. The commonly used expression came into question for several reasons. There was concern about how the term, heretofore used mostly by the extreme right, might be used politically if it were endowed with a scientific legitimacy. The very origins of the term as a racial description also came under scrutiny, as did the possibility of defining the population, given mixed marriages and other connected processes of differentiation. Finally, a contradiction was noted in the term itself, which links a juridical concept to a natural one. If one is "French", this means one is of the French nationality as understood by the courts; "de souche" refers to a biological fact. Indeed, we have seen that, since the nineteenth-century, the conception of "French" became a juridical one, and not a socio-cultural one; or, more precisely, the socio-cultural conception was reduced to the juridical one.

The second criticism revolved around the way that the ethnic category had been devised and defined. Several authors pointed out that it was defined differently for different groups, depending on the origins of the respondents. Nationalities (in the sense of citizens from another country) were used for those respondents born in Europe (thus French, Spanish, Portuguese, but not Catalan, Basque, or Breton), and only a small number of ethnic, or non-national categories were employed to describe members of the North African and Turkish populations (Berbers, Arabs, Kurds). The sub-Saharan Africans fell into several categories (Fulani, Mands). According to the critics, such use of the ethnic category stemmed from colonial practice. Finally, the use of a mother tongue as a criterion in the construction of these categories was called into question. On a more general level, the criticism regarding ethnic categories expressed a concern about subjecting weak perceptions of group affiliation to statistical analysis. Echoing views expressed in nineteenth-century works on racial anthropology, this latter argument cautioned against rushing to analyze something that was only just coming into being and, by so doing, making it a reality (Blum 1998; Todd 1994, for his earlier reflections on the subject).

A third area of disagreement centered on the contradiction between the willingness to analyze the process of migration on the one hand, and, on the other, the use of ethnic categories which focussed the study on the origins of the respondent, rather than his or her biography or experiences. The issue was not whether there should be questions on place of birth, parents' place of birth (or parents' original nationality), or mother tongue. Such questions had already appeared in numerous surveys going back many years, including those conducted by INSEE (Héran, 1998). The point had to do with making these questions the center of the analysis and, in particular, with their "conceptualization" as ethnic categories. This shift has fundamental implications. Ethnicity cannot be defined by a criterion like origin, whether it is defined by place of birth or ascendancy, since it results from a combination of multiple criteria, having equally to do with origin, place of residence, social networks, migratory path, etc.

The debate was transformed into a polemic that grew more public and more passionate in connection with the fourth body of criticism. The issue here had to do with the political use of such analyses, and led some to denounce the link between certain demographers and the political milieu of the extreme right. Social science's interest in the concrete conditions behind the transmission of concepts and ideas led to an exploration of the political uses of demography (Le Bras 1998a; Richard 1999). This produced an analysis of the various networks of people who bridged demography as a scientific discipline and demography for political use. The study was based on an examination of traditional French political circles, for whom birth and reproduction are pivotal issues (Le Bras 1981 and 1991). In this milieu, population growth through reproduction is encouraged, while immigration is often forgotten or rejected. It was this type of analysis that led to legal action, as was indicated earlier. INED, which launched the suit, felt that its credibility had been called into question because of an alleged proximity to the extreme right, although this charge was never stated outright by the author.

Finally, criticism also revolved around the census and the population registers in connection with the issue of privacy and how the information gathered by these means would eventually be used. French society today is very uncomfortable with the creation of files on individuals. This wariness is attributable, in part, to the power wielded by CNIL (Commission on Computerization and Freedom), which is responsible for handling such files, and also because of disturbing historical recollections triggered by the discovery of a file on French Jews, compiled by the Vichy régime during World War II. This file, and its relation to the census and the SNS (National Statistical Service), were under study during the course of the debate and had just been the object of an official government report (Rémond 1996), following a lengthy polemic revolving largely around the question of its preservation. It is not surprising that INSEE unions' one-day session on ethnic statistics also dealt not only with the issue of the use of ethnic categories in present-day public statistics, but also with the work of SNS and the census in connection with French Jews in World War II.

Response to criticisms

The responses to the criticisms outlined above were based, generally speaking, on an argument which had little to do with the initial publications on the survey, but which has since become dominant in the debate: the need to fight discrimination based on people's origins and to devise methods of instituting real policies against such practices. For several years, there has been a growing awareness of and reflection on the discrimination problem and other social issues, including urban violence, access to employment, and the management of social policy. The institutional need for better information on immigrants, supported by the High Council on Integration, has often given support to demands for a better knowledge of immigrant populations according to their origins. The basic issues raised on this side of the debate (Simon 1998) had to do with the difficulties that immigrants encountered in their search for employment and housing, as well as with the criteria that police used in identity checks, which are often based on physical appearance, family name, etc.

The debate on discrimination, which has grown to unprecedented levels in the past ten years, is not only about immigrants and issues relating to immigration. It is also about discrimination between the sexes, especially in politics, generating a discussion of quotas versus other, voluntary methods of prompting real equality. However, these two threads of the same debate have barely intersected. They are handled differently and deal with issues that hardly concern them both: access to employment and housing, academic performance, and urban violence as a consequence of discrimination are issues important to the discussion on the introduction of ethnic categories in public statistics, while the debate on gender equality focuses on the question of access to politics.

Another argument on this side of the debate is that there is a need for the use of explicit tools to help in the formulation of policies. Proponents argue that policies are often introduced which take ethnicity into account surreptitiously, but do not explicitly admit to doing so, or explain how. A clearer picture of the ethnic situation would help produce policies that were open and comprehensible without reference to complicated, convoluted explanations, which have a tendency to deform reality and can be dangerous to boot.

Another line of response to the criticisms discussed above is a formal denial of any link to the extreme right. The emphasis placed by some of the participants in the debate on the relationship between certain circles in the demographic world and the National Front, or on the question of how demography could easily be used to justify some extremist arguments, was seen by certain researchers as an attack on them personally or on their institution, even though they were far removed from extremist politics.

This latter response is connected to the difficult issue of the political uses of statistical categories and the responsibility of the institution or researcher involved in the future use and possible implications of these categories, especially in the hands of the extreme right. For some, there is a responsibility, but others are more concerned with what they perceive as an unjustified and slanderous questioning of the motives behind research conducted in connection with, or under the auspices of formal, established relationships. A good example is that of INED and how it originated. The institution, originally called the Alexis Carrel Foundation, was established by Vichy, and its founder was known for his extremist and eugenist positions. The researchers currently affiliated with INED have nothing to do with its dubious beginnings. Why, then, should INED's origins be used in arguing about the dangers presented by certain works emanating from this institution?

Finally, the experience of other countries with regard to the use of ethnic statistics is often cited as a positive argument. Examples from the Anglo-Saxon world figure prominently in this discussion, and are used to demonstrate the absence of any particular political stance in connection with the use of ethnic statistics (Simon 1997). The peculiar French practice is thus denounced as a means by which a strong ethnic reality is left hidden. According to this argument, the use of racial and ethnic categories in the British, American, and Canadian censuses legitimates the statistical enquiry into ethnicity.

Ambiguities

Let us now turn to an examination of the various levels and ambiguities in the debate. The development of an open debate on the internet, through a discussion group, has promoted broader participation and offered new emphases, which helps us to distinguish between different levels of arguments.[8]

We must first distinguish between what might be considered as falling within the scope of public statistics and that which has more to do with specific research, conducted by research teams. The statistics, or large surveys conducted by public institutions which largely monopolize the study of these questions, quickly become points of references, contradicted by no one.

One of the reasons for the confusion in the discussions has to do with the fact that research and public statistics do not share the same imperatives. It seems clear that a general census of the population should in no way include measures and personal files relating to "linguistic," or "religious" groups, or to categories such as "French with at least two French grand-parents" etc. . . . since these kinds of categories take hold in the collective imagination (sometimes strengthening the ideological categories present in public opinion). More importantly, public statistics, particularly the census, constitute an official database compiled by means of obligatory response to an official agent. (Tripier 1999)

Another important aspect to consider in examining the debate relates to the evolution of social science thinking in our time, including important changes in the characterization of the individual. In an earlier article (Blum 1998), I observed how

the naturalism [primordialism] expressed in these two works (Tribalat 1995 and Todd 1994) . . . is striking in more than one way. This attitude, which gained in importance during the second half of the nineteenth century, slowly but surely took hold of researchers, leading to an approach that ignored the individual, as well as his daily activities and life experiences. Moreover, this line of thinking did not recognize the importance of multiple paths in the individual's behaviour. Its statistical component rested on the construction of sharply defined categories that were supposed to a be a faithful reflection of reality . . . One current that is apparent in social science and history today distances itself from this kind of determinism [Lepetit 1995]. A new approach is being constructed, which attributes a much greater complexity to the individual, taking into account experiences and interactions that can no longer be understood solely in terms of the opposition, or the relationship between large groups or classes . . . .

It is obvious that the biographical dimension of migration necessitates a research approach that goes beyond place of birth and mother tongue in attempting to understand the individual. These markers are part of an individual's make-up, but they interact with other, dynamic factors. It would be impossible to take this complexity into account were one to introduce a definition of ethnicity based only on these markers.

The question arises, therefore, as to whether there exist in demography concepts which favour the latter approach. Several works suggest that there are. The calling into question of the traditional tools of demography by numerous researchers interested in approaches which take into consideration the individual's experiences further suggests that profound changes that break with past methods are not only possible, but probable (Courgeau and Lelièvre 1996).

Furthermore, even if it is well known and accepted that an individual's self-perception is closely connected to the conditions prevailing at any given moment in time, to the context in which the question is asked, and to the individual's position when questioned, asking people to define themselves is still a worthwhile exercise. The complexity of identity warrants great caution. It is taking caution quite far, however, when one seeks to define identity externally, without asking people what they think. There is thus a significant difference between the Anglo-Saxon approach, where each person states what he or she thinks he or she is, or would like to be, and the positivist approach, which considers ethnic identity to be an external characteristic. Implicit here is the difference between "ethnic categories" and "ethnic characteristics." By constructing statistical categories on the basis of a few simple variables, the researcher creates static categories independent of, or separate from, actual cultural experience.

On a more general level, the central issue is how best to measure diversity in social science:

No less important is the question of which theoretical and methodological tools are the most effective for grasping and describing the complexity and richness of a society in motion. It is at this general level that the basic questions arise since, if there is one thing that is understood in social sciences – and has been for the past few years – it is that the essence of the historical process lies in diversification. Historians and sociologists, anthropologists and economists all know that society is changing constantly. At every moment, it is being transformed by the incessant activity of all of its members. At every moment, France is profoundly different from what it had been in the past and from what it will be in the future for no other reason than because each person is constantly confronted by new situations which compel him to adjust his perceptions, his beliefs, his views, and . . . his memories . . . The challenge facing research is thus to find a way of grasping diversity and complexity in motion. Every person has a past. I would even say that every person can imagine himself in numerous pasts and with numerous roots, as sociologists and anthropologists know very well. The interesting thing, therefore, is to understand how these multiple origins and memories, and the constant adjustment of perceptions, operate and manifest themselves over time. In present terms, understanding difference means understanding the dynamics of a society. (Gribaudi 1998)

Finally, one has to consider the political dimension of these issues. We have already looked at this angle in terms of the political debate. Here, I would like to discuss the relationship between a political, institutional system and the analytical categories used. An ethnic category is also meaningful, in terms of being a socio-political actor, if it plays a role as such in the socio-political relations characterizing the life of a given society. When a community is represented as it is, or behaves as a lobby, it is a real entity and acts as an intermediary between the various social and institutional levels, or components present in society. By contrast, when a community does not play a role on its own, a researcher should not seek to invent it.

The first level of analysis is the social, followed by statistical observation and the reification of the analytical categories. The question arises: is statistical observation a necessary and effective tool in the fight against segregation and discrimination?

The complexity of the discussion is connected to the fact that there are three levels to the debate, each interacting with the other: the political, the sociological, and the statistical. In addition, there is often confusion among these levels. The political dimension has to do with the relationship between the individual and the political institution, which is tied to the particular political models of given states, as they have evolved over time. The sociological dimension of the debate revolves around the issue of ethnicity in France, whether ethnic reasoning or thinking is present, and to what extent ethnicity plays a role in interactions between individuals at the professional and social levels. The question thus is: can we study and actually observe an eventual ethnicization of French society? This question is inherently a sociological one. There are a few works that deal with it, in the context of more micro-social than macro-statistical studies, and these demonstrate the complexity of any eventual ethnic-based thinking (Simon 1998; Simon and Tapia 1998). The central question in the debate examined here is more about whether we can study behaviors related to ethnic configurations, or discrimination based on ethnic criteria, through an approach that combines research among immigrants on the one hand, and statistics generated through censuses, or large public surveys, on the other. The statistical approach constructs and reifies without necessarily grasping complex and changing realities.

It is worth noting the predominance of immigration and related issues in the debate on the use of ethnic categories. The question arises not about refining the description of the French population, on the basis of cultural diversity observed in regions, or of networks of people defining themselves on the basis of some regional origin, but only about refining the description of the immigrant population. This makes it difficult to draw in other pertinent discussions, despite numerous references to the American, Canadian, and British experiences, since in these countries ethnicity is largely disassociated from the question of migration. It also accounts for the centrality of integration and assimilation to the debate, both of which are constantly linked to ethnicity, while multiculturalism receives relatively little attention. This explains the fact that almost all of the participants in the debate invoke the republican model, regardless of their position.

The construction of reality

It is still too early to say what effect the debate will have on statistical practice in France and on the perception of which characteristics are most effective or most appropriate for describing a given population. There is no doubt, however, that the introduction of ethnic statistics, which is being discussed largely in public institutions, remains a possibility. A recent report on discrimination observed: "We must first measure discrimination, before we can combat it. This means that we must revise our statistical tools in such a way as to take into account *ethnic or national characteristics*, while, at the same time, *taking precautions against possible ill uses of the data*" (Bernard 1999)[9]. The debate, however, has been conducted in an atmosphere of growing suspicion regarding the creation of various files containing precise markers identifying individuals or groups. It is worth observing that the same arguments are found in the United States, as in the decision of some states (California, Washington, and Texas) "to ban the collection of racial demographic information and data on ethnic inequality" (Jenkins 1999).

It is also apparent that hazy and poorly constructed concepts have made steady inroads into various discussions. Thus, a historical magazine (*L'Histoire*, 1995, n. 195, p. 39) aimed especially at teachers included a "dictionary of terms connected to immigration," which provided precise definitions for such terms as "Français de souche" (indigenous French), "integration," and "assimilation." As shown by Le Bras (1998a), the same magazine reproduced figures on polygamy which were based on a statistical error without employing or issuing any caution. It shows how large public surveys conducted by public institutions can be accepted uncritically by the media. If new terms or concepts are introduced in such a survey, they quickly begin to be considered as "scientific" and to be widely used.

Is this to say that such a statistical approach was needed before public policies based on ethnic distinctions could be implemented? And is it not unrealistic to claim that, without this kind of statistical approach, ethnic categories would not take shape? There are certainly no straightforward answers to these questions, but two examples from public policy can help throw some light on these issues.

The first example is a violence prevention policy, implemented by a Parisian public transport organization (RATP), which oversees urban transportation in the Paris area. Michel Wieviorka (1999) offered the following observations: faced with increasing violence in the transport sector, RATP adopted a mediation policy aimed at communicating with or reaching out to the perpetrators of violent acts, through intermediaries who are close to them. These intermediaries, referred to as "big brothers" and "agents of social prevention and mediation," are recruited in neighbourhoods populated largely by immigrants. From the start, the "big brother" initiative was conceived by RATP in explicitly ethnic terms, since a large number of the young "trouble-makers" are of immigrant background (from sub-Saharan Africa and the Maghreb). Given this profile, it was decided to recruit young men of similar immigrant stock, who might be perceived as authority figures by troubled youths from cultures where elder brothers are indeed viewed in this way (Wieviorka, 1999).

The second policy is connected to national education, which is faced with both problems of academic difficulties and problems of violence in schools. The creation of the Priority Educational Zones (ZEP) and the Sensitive Zones, which define geographic sectors where the educational establishments wield substantially enhanced financial resources and enjoy the services of a larger number of personnel, does not seem to have been handled, for the most part, from an ethnic angle. Although there is a connection between these zones and those sectors heavily populated by immigrants, the negotiating points that were developed from the local level all the way up to the national are tied, first and foremost, to difficulties associated with resources and support, rather than to mechanical criteria related to the proportion of this or that population in a particular area. The educational zone policy employs a spatial approach based on social analysis and practice, rather than one which categorizes the population on the basis of origins. Wieviorka's work on violence explains how ethnic criteria were used to formulate a policy to combat violence in urban transportation settings. Interestingly, however, there is no discussion of such criteria in the discussion of the problem of violence in schools. The descriptions of school incidents sent to the authorities refer only to the social background of the students involved, not to their ethnic origins.

This does not mean that the criteria employed in granting ZEP status take no account at all of the characteristics of the population or of the schools under review. The enquiries that are made to establish the statistical criteria needed in considering whether to grant ZEP status take social composition (the PCS) and nationality into consideration, on the basis of files put together by students' parents. In addition, the perception of these special educational zones is rather strongly linked to an ethnic vision, a vision of what could be "the two priorities – the two urgent tasks of the ZEP policy (and of the network of priority schools): social and ethnic mixing, and the quality of human resources and staff" (G. Chauveau and R. Chauveau 1995; G. Chauveau 1999). This approach, favoured by Chauveau, shows clearly what is at stake in a differential policy which is aware of the relationship between immigration and academic failure.

That being said, it is undoubtedly the case that the decision to grant ZEP arises from a negotiation process. Moreover, it is a political decision that takes into account the balance of power between rectorates, teachers, unions, and ministries. Negotiations are thus highly exclusive, and are based on interactions between local collectivities and the central administration, rather than on the establishment of precise criteria. Such criteria are used more after the fact, so to speak, when analyzing the importance of sectors, and not so much during the negotiation phase. Tensions and grievances, such as those expressed in 1998 in the department Seine-St-Denis, result in prompt negotiations and in the granting of ZEP status independent of predefined criteria.

Conclusion

The debate discussed in this article was spawned by the publication of one particular survey. Its relevance, however, goes beyond this survey. As it evolved, the debate unmasked the underlying tensions that existed in the complex relationship between the issue of representing a society in ethnic terms and social science in France.

The complexity of the debate stems, in part, from its link to polemics that have affected French society since the mid-nineteenth century. These polemics juxtaposed a republican ethic with national affirmation, the latter term being understood very much from an East-Central European perspective. The current debate often refers to the older arguments, which sometimes obscures the fact that the discussion has since undergone a profound transformation.

The transformation can be seen at various levels of the debate: by integrating advances in social science in the use of statistics, the current debate distinguishes, albeit not always quite clearly, between the construction of a statistical category on the one hand, and an understanding of particular phenomena, such as segregation or racism, on the other. By virtue of its universal and formative nature, the statistical category is constructed not simply for the purposes of analysis, but also has strong institutional links. The construction and naming of statistical categories are not neutral exercises. Furthermore, these categories freeze situations that are in motion, or in flux, by attaching individuals to a single affiliation, thus making it difficult to understand the phenomenon of multiple identity.

The use of statistics as a "universal" tool in the formulation of policy is also at issue. If the fight against discrimination in the workplace and in the housing sector rests on a careful study of variables of an overtly ethnic type, it is far from certain that a simplified and very incomplete approach, based on a "recording" of ethnicity, is the direction to take. In addition, the absence of this tradition in France has led researchers to attempt to define such categories without taking account of how individuals define themselves. This makes the exercise even more artificial.

Above all, there is no absolute in the representation of identity, and a social science approach cannot deduce the universal character of certain concepts and expressions from particular experiences. Moreover, one cannot ignore the various influences affecting the construction of categories, from social and institutional imperatives to public activity and political pressures. The existence of numerous alternative approaches to the study of the ethnicization process suggests that a return to the analytical framework developed in the nineteenth century would obscure the complexity of identity. There is certainly a political demand for an understanding of ethnicity, but this need not necessarily translate into the formulation and use of statistical categories. The goal should rather be to develop multiple forms of analyses, at different levels, which will not bind the individual exclusively or perpetually to a particular ethnic group.

There is no doubt that the strong pressure on INSEE or other public institutions to take ethnicity into account could lead to a change in current practice. However, the diversity of opinion makes the introduction of census variables of a North American type doubtful. Many arguments support this observation. It is important to bear in mind that the fight against discrimination currently underway is often linked to a firm opposition to identifying individuals through categories that could be used to ascribe identity based on ethnicity. On the other hand, in the absence of a long-standing perception of these types of categories, it appears that it is practically impossible to propose categories expressing a generally accepted identity. We can, therefore, assume that even if political and social pressure is strong, the responses will be numerous and complex. It is unlikely that they will converge towards any generally accepted categorization scheme, such as would appear on a French census.

NOTES

1 When dealing with important social questions, the tendency in France is to set up an independent structure which serves as intermediary between society and the body politic: the High Commission on Population and the Family, Ethics Committee, the High Commission on Integration, as well as the National Commission on Computerization and Freedom, the National Committee on Statistical Information, etc. The composition of these structures is supposed to reflect a balance between representatives of various social groups. They are politically "neutral" spaces, designed for confrontation and negotiation between social partners (unions are often represented in these bodies), judicial authorities (members of the State Council, etc.), and researchers.

2 The influence of Michel Foucault on more general categories connected to public activity is apparent, even though it is not always explicitly acknowledged.

3 For an analysis of the debates that took place in the 1850s to 1870s, particularly during the International Statistical Congresses of 1857 and 1872, see Labbé 1997.

4 Contrary to the usage in Eastern Europe, where "nationality" referred to an ethnocultural affiliation within a larger civic affiliation, "nationality" in France specifically referred to a civic affiliation. For example, a French resident from Germany without French citizenship was categorized as someone of "German nationality," and thus as a "foreigner." A Breton-speaking French citizen, however, was categorized as someone of French nationality, with no official category available to express a Breton cultural identity. In Austria, by contrast, a Czech-speaker of Bohemia was categorized as both of Czech nationality and of Austrian citizenship, since "nationality" was officially considered to be a different concept than "citizenship."

5 See http://census.ined.fr, a website that reproduces most of the French census forms.

6 The Overseas French territories have two different administrative status: they are either *Départements (DOM: Départements d'Outre-Mer)*, or *Territoires (TOM: Territoires d'Outre-Mer)*. The first ones have the same administrative status as all the other *Départements. Territoires* have a more autonomous status.

7 The author of this work was even sued by his institution, which chose to respond to his assertions through legal action in July 1998. The press thus began to pay greater attention to the debate. Hervé Le Bras has been accused of defaming his institute. The complaint was withdrawn in April 1999 by a new director of INED. The roots of this episode, which are discussed more fully below, lie with Hervé Le Bras' political analysis of relations between the extreme right and demography.

8 The debate, "Démographie et catégories ethniques," is archived at http:// census.ined.fr.
9 The italicized terms are taken from a report by Jean Michel Belorgey, "Lutter contre les discriminations," prepared for Martine Aubry, Ministry of Employment and Solidarity.

REFERENCES

Alonso, William and Starr, Paul (eds.) 1987, *The Politics of Numbers*, New York: Sage.
Anderson, Benedict 1991, *Imagined Communities*, London: Verso.
Anderson, Margo J. 1988, *The American Census, A Social History*, New Haven: Yale University Press.
Bernard, Philippe 1999, "Un rapport préconise une 'autorité indépendante' contre les discriminations," *Le Monde* (7 April): 10.
Bertaux, Sandrine 1997, "Le concept démographique d'assimilation: un label scientifique pour le discours sur l'intégration?" *Revue française des affaires sociales*, 2: 37–52.
Blum, Alain 1994, *Vivre, naître et mourir en URSS*, Paris: Plon.
    1998, "Comment décrire les immigrés? A propos de quelques recherches sur l'immigration," *Population* 3: 569–88.
Blum, Alain and Gousseff, Catherine 1997, "Les nationalités dans les recensements russes et soviétiques," in Jean-Louis Rallu, Youssef Courbage, and Victor Piché (eds.), *Anciennes et nouvelles minorités*, Paris: National Institute of Demographic Studies (INED); London: John Libbey, pp. 49–72.
Blum, Alain, Desrosières, Alain, Gousseff, Catherine, and Magaud, Jacques (eds.) 1998, "Compter l'autre," *Histoire & Mesure* 13 (thematic issue).
Boltanski, Luc 1982, *Les cadres, la formation d'un groupe social*, Paris: Editions de Minuit.
Brubaker, Rogers 1992, *Citizenship and Nationhood in France and Germany*, Cambridge, Mass.: Harvard University Press.
Chauveau, Gérard and Rogovas-Chauveau, Eliane 1995, *A l'école des banlieues*, Paris: ESF éditeur.
Chauveau, Gérard 1999, "Les ZEP, effets pervers de l'action positive," *Plein droit* 41–42: 56–59.
Courgeau, Daniel and Lelièvre, Eva 1996, "Changement de paradigme en démographie," *Population* 3: 645–54.
Decouflé, André-Clément 1997, "L'intégration: quelques idées simples," *Revue française des affaires sociales* 2: 29–36.
De la Gorce, Gilles 1991, "L'individu et la sociologie–soixante ans d'étude de la mobilité sociale," *Revue de synthèse* 2: 237–63.
Desrosières, Alain 1993, *La politique des grands nombres, Histoire de la raison statistique*, Paris: La Découverte.
Desrosières, Alain and Thévenot, Laurent 1988, *Les catégories socioprofessionnelles*, Paris: La Découverte.
Dupâquier, Jacques 1997, "Les chiffres de l'immigration: mythes et réalités," *Revue des sciences morales et politiques* 1: 71–99.

Gousseff, Catherine 1997, "L'élaboration des catégories nationales dans les re-censements: décalages entre législation et outils de mesure," *Revue française des affaires sociales* 2: 53–70.

Gribaudi, Maurizio 1998, "Penser la diversité comme processus," 14 November, Available at http://census.ined.fr.

Héran, François 1998, "Ethnique ta statistique?" in *"Statistique sans conscience n'est que ruine..."* Actes du colloque, Paris: CGT/CFDT INSEE, pp. 28–35.

Hirsch, Francine 1997, "The Soviet Union as a Work-in-Progress: Ethnographers and the Category Nationality in the 1926, 1937, and 1939 Censuses," *Slavic Review* 56: 251–78.

Houle, René 1997, "Russes et non Russes dans la direction des institutions poli-tiques et économiques en URSS, Une étude des recensements, 1926–1979," *Cahiers du Monde russe* 38: 347–66.

INED 1993, *Vingt-deuxième rapport sur la situation démographique de la France*, Paris.

INSEE 1998, "Droit de réponse du directeur de l'INSEE à Jacques Dupâquier," *Revue des sciences morales et politiques* 2: 131–38.

Jenkins, Alan 1999, "See No Evil," *The Nation* (28 June): 15–19.

Kateb, Kamel 1998a, "La gestion statistique des population dans l'empire colo-nial français, Le cas de l'Algérie, 1830–1960," *Histoire & Mesure* 13: 77–112.

1998b, *Histoire statistique des populations algériennes pendant la colonisation française (1830–1962)*, Ph.D. dissertation, Ecole des Hautes Etudes en Sciences Sociales.

Labbé, Morgane 1997, "Le projet d'une statistique des nationalités discuté dans les sessions du Congrès International de Statistique (1853–1876)," in Francis Ronsin, Hervé Le Bras and Elisabeth Zucker-Rouvillois (eds.), *Démographie et Politique*, Dijon: Editions Universitaires de Dijon, pp. 127–42.

Lacroix, Janine et Suzane Thave 1997, "Les immigrés dans les recensements: décalages entre législation et outils de mesure," *Revue française des affaires sociales* 2: 71–100.

Le Bras, Hervé 1981, "L'histoire secrète de la fécondité," *Le Débat* 8: 76–101.

1991, *Marianne et les lapins – l'obsession démographiques*, Paris: Olivier Orban.

1994, *Le sol et le sang*, Paris: Editions de l'Aube.

1998a, *Le Démon des origines, Démographie et extrême-droite*, Paris: Editions de l'Aube.

1998b, "Les Français de souche existent-ils?", *Quaderni* 22: 36.

Lepetit, Bernard 1995, *Les formes de l'expérience: une autre histoire sociale*, Paris: Albin Michel.

Mauco, Georges 1932, *Les étrangers en France, leur rôle dans l'activité économique*, Paris: Armand Colin.

Muñoz-Pérez, Francisco and Tribalat, Michèle 1984, "Mariages d'étrangers et mariages mixtes en France," *Population* 3: 427–62.

Noiriel, Gérard 1988, *Le creuset français: Histoire de l'immigration, XIX–XXème siècle*, Paris: Seuil; translated as *The French Melting Pot, Immigration, Citizenship, and National Identity*, Minneapolis: University of Minnesota Press, 1996.

1991, *La tyrannie du national: le droit d'asile en Europe, 1793–1993*. Paris: Calmann-Lévy.

Rallu, Jean-Louis 1998, "Les catégories statistiques utilisées dans les Dom-Tom depuis le début de la présence française," *Population* 3: 589–608.

Rémond, René 1996, *Le «fichier juif», Rapport de la commission présidée par René Rémond au Premier ministre*, Paris: Plon.

Revue française des affaires sociales 1997, "Insertion, intégration: concepts et pratiques," special issue.

Richard, Jean-Luc 1999, *Dynamiques démographiques et socio-économiques de l'intégration des jeunes générations d'origine immigrée en France, Etude à caractère longitudinal (1975–1990) réalisée à partir de l'échantillon démographique permanent*, Ph.D. dissertation, Institut d'Etudes Politiques, Paris.

1999, "Qu'est-ce qu'un Français?" *Les dossiers de Pour la Science (French edition of Scientific American)* 24: 22–27.

Sauvy, Alfred 1954, *Théorie générale de la population, Tome II: Biologie sociale*, Paris: Presses Universitaires de France.

Simon, Patrick 1993a, "Chronique de l'immigration," *Population* 1: 125–81.

1993b, "Nommer pour agir," *Le Monde*, 28 April.

1997, "La statistique des origines–"race" et ethnicité dans les recensements aux Etats-Unis, Canada et Grande Bretagne," *Sociétés Contemporaines* 26: 11–44.

1998, "Nationalité et origine dans la statistique française: les catégories ambiguës," *Population* 3: 541–68.

Simon, Patrick and Tapia, Claude 1998 *Le Belleville des Juifs tunisiens*, Collection Monde 104, Paris: Autrement.

"Statistique des différences ethnographiques de la population d'un État, comprenant leur influence sur le bien-être, les mœurs et la civilisation de la nation)," in E. Engel (eds.), *Compte rendu général des travaux du Congrès international de statistique dans ses séances tenues à Bruxelles, 1852, Paris, 1855, Vienne, 1857 et Londres, 1860*, Berlin and St-Petersburg, 1863, p. 156.

Szreter, Simon 1996, *Fertility, class and gender in Britain, 1860–1940*, Cambridge: Cambridge University Press.

Todd, Emmanuel 1994, *Le destin des immigrés: assimilation et ségrégation dans les démocraties occidentales*, Paris: Seuil.

Tribalat, Michèle 1989, "Immigrés, étrangers, Français: l'imbroglio statistique," *Population & sociétés* 241: 1–4.

1995a, *Faire France*, Paris: La découverte.

1995b, "Censure à l'INSEE," *L'Histoire* 193: 39.

Tribalat, Michèle (ed.) 1991, *Cent ans d'immigration, Etrangers d'hier, Français d'aujourd'hui*, Travaux et documents, 131, Paris: INED/Presses Universitaires de France.

Tripier, Maryse 1999, "De l'usage de statistiques 'ethniques' ", *Hommes et migrations* 1219: 27–32.

Wieviorka, Michel 1999, *Violence en France*, Paris: Seuil.

A large bibliography of articles published about this polemic is available on http://census.ined.fr.

6 On counting, categorizing, and violence in Burundi and Rwanda

Peter Uvin

There are few countries in the world where the acts of categorizing and counting people have been as omnipresent, crucial, and steeped in violent stakes as in Burundi and Rwanda. There are also few countries where social constructivist expectations regarding identity and category seem to be so well verified, and are actually being invoked (although without the scientific jargon) by local people themselves – alongside deeply essentialist interpretations. This article analyzes the techniques, functions, and stakes of population measurements and categorizations in both countries dating from the arrival of the colonial powers at the beginning of this century to the recent decades of independence, development, and violence.

This chapter focuses on two types of acts that are crucial to the exercise of power in Burundi and Rwanda. Part 1 deals with *counting* the administered: the process, during the colonial period and after, of calculating just how many people there actually were in each country. Although this seems the easiest and most value-neutral of all activities, the following pages will demonstrate that this is far from the case; these pages will also make clear to what extent even this simple act is linked to dynamics of power and resistance in the region.

In part 2, I discuss the much more complicated and sensitive matter of *categorizing* the population into relevant groups and then measuring these groups. In the case of Burundi and Rwanda, the foremost category is of course the ethnic distinction between Hutu and Tutsi, which will be discussed at length. After Independence in 1962, however, another player rode into town – the development game, itself in need of data to lend the appearance of apolitical and universalistic objectivity. Categorizing the poor and the underdeveloped was a way of accomplishing this, as will be discussed in part 3. Again, this enterprise was closely linked to processes of legitimization and domination, albeit in new guises.

The conclusion seeks to draw together some empirical and theoretical lessons emerging from this analysis, coming back to some of the issues outlined in the introduction to this volume.

Counting the administered

The colonial state

The business of counting began immediately upon the arrival of the first adventurers/ethnographers and intensified when the colonial enterprise began soon thereafter. Note that until Independence, most data were collected for the territory of Ruanda-Urundi, an integrated administrative entity first under German and then Belgian rule.

At the end of the nineteenth century, the German captain Bethe estimated Rwanda's population at 2 million; in the first decade of this century, both German scientists like Hans Meyer and Czekanowski and colonial administrators made further estimates, some of which were wildly off the mark, and others that proved later to have been quite accurate. During the period of German colonization, however, the official estimates were systematically too high (Louis 1963: 108). Hans Meyer, for example, estimated Ruanda-Urundi's population in 1913 to be 5 million, while Fuchs thought it was 4 million – both vast over-estimates. In the same period, Thodl thought Rwanda's population to be 3 million in contrast with his colleague Czekanowski's estimate of 1.5 to 1.7 million (Louis 1963: 108; Niyibizi 1986: 269; Barandereka and Berciu 1988: 52). All used similar methodologies of small-scale measurements – or even impressions – extrapolated throughout the area, the differences being largely accounted for by the fact that Meyer's fieldwork had been carried out in the most densely settled central area of Rwanda where the Germans had set up garrison.

The Belgians took over Ruanda-Urundi from the Germans in 1916 and, between 1919 and 1925, set up the area as a mandate from the League of Nations (Lemarchand 1970: 63). From then until the end of the colonial period, the Belgian authorities produced yearly detailed data on the populations they administered (Louis 1963: 109; Barandereka and Berciu 1988: 53; *Rapports annuels sur l'administration belge du Ruanda et de l'Urundi, 1921 – 1961*); this was part of their obligations as Trustees of the area under the League of Nations and later the United Nations. For forty years, four categories were used, reflecting racial divisions considered scientifically evident and administratively relevant at the time (note the similarity to South Africa's racial categories, which were developed around the same time).

The first category, Europeans, was very precise; in practice, it was operationalized as "whites" (thus including a few North Americans). The total number was below 1,000 until the late 1930s, and grew rapidly during World War II when many Greeks immigrated into the territory; after the war, it dropped at first and then rose rapidly each year to reach almost 8,900 by Independence. The group was subdivided according to profession – again precise up to the last number – with the largest category, almost half, being those without profession, i.e., mainly spouses. In 1961, of those with a profession, 919 were missionaries, 638 civil servants, 898 employees of parastatal enterprises, and approximately 200 were traders (*Rapport annuel* 1961: Annex 1).

The second category, "mulattos," referred to the children of white men with black women. Their number remained low during the first decades – 24 in 1921; 79 in 1935 – but began rising quickly after the arrival of many whites during the war: 267 by 1947 and 367 by 1957. This category was certainly greatly underestimated, as it comprised only the minority of *recognized* children from mixed unions (Gahama 1993: 295). From 1950 onward, a new sub-category was added of "mulattos from Asians and indigenous women" – 891 were counted that year.

The third category, "Asians and other coloreds," referred to Indians, Chinese, and others, mostly traders. There were a few hundred of them during the first decades of Belgian colonization; their numbers, too, were precise up to the last digit. They constituted a small group of Muslim, Swahili-speaking traders, mainly living in one neighborhood in Bujumbura. By the last years of colonization, they numbered between 2,000 and 3,000.

The fourth category, "blacks," was divided in two: a small group of "blacks not submitted to customary chiefs" on the one hand, and the mass of "indigenous" blacks on the other. It is in this category that the figures become rapidly more unreliable – little more than "guesstimates." The first category of immigrant laborers was measured not by the single digit anymore, but by the hundred, in rounded-off figures; it grew rapidly from 5,500 in 1921 to 59,000 in 1947, as the colonizers imported people from the Kivu region to assist in public works and police tasks.[1] However, it is the subcategory of indigenous blacks – in other words, the native population – that was largely unmeasured, although yearly attempts were made to get a grasp on these figures.

The need to count the indigenous population was directly related to the development of taxation as a means to finance the colonial enterprise. Later, it also fulfilled the political function of demonstrating to the League of Nations and then to the UN the good effects of Belgian trusteeship and mandate (Thibon 1987: 75): increasing population figures demonstrated that the natives were not starving and were thus doing fine. A final reason for the attention devoted to the counting of the population resided in the widely held belief that the territory of Ruanda-Urundi was vastly overpopulated – a belief that constituted the basis of many of

Belgium's policies in the region, and which evidently required statistical documentation (Louis 1963: 108).

Over the decades, different methods were employed for measuring the total size of the population, each encountering its own problems in terms of cost, methodological weakness, and political resistance. The first endeavor, under German colonial rule, was a partial headcount census in Rwanda: colonial officials used askaris (African soldiers) and policemen to count each person in several districts; the resulting total – two million – was probably fairly accurate. Further attempts at headcounts were soon abandoned due to lack of communication, infrastructure, and personnel. Headcount censuses were not attempted again until the 1970s, under post-independence rule.

At the same time, first in Burundi and later in Rwanda, local chiefs were asked to count the huts in their areas of authority (Louis 1963: 108). The problem with these censuses was that the chief's collaboration was not assured (Thibon 1987: 76; Nyrop *et al.* 1974: 11; Government of Belgium 1925: 32); moreover, many local people sought to hide themselves or their children. The reason for this dissimulation was that the population feared that this counting exercise was related to taxation – an impression not diminished by the fact that many local chiefs did indeed combine the two (Government of Belgium 1925: 32; the same report also observed that many local chiefs overestimated the number of adult men so as to increase their tax capacity). Yet this did not stop the Belgian Ministry of the Colonies from exclaiming: "the inquiries are made extremely difficult by the distrust, ignorance, and sometimes stupidity of the locals. The latter simply cannot grasp that any other goal than taxation would underlie these researches." (*Rapport annuel* 1926: 47)

Although the exercises occurred yearly and general figures were printed in each report to the League of Nations, the Belgian Ministry of the Colonies recognized the deficient nature of the resulting data. Every year, the report promised that a headcount census would soon be undertaken – but every year this proved too costly, the locals were not sufficiently reliable, and other priorities were too urgent. However, during most years, small-scale detailed headcounts were done, allowing the estimation of death and birth rates in limited areas. At the same time, a major exercise in cartography was underway, too; in 1926, no fewer than 6 cartographers were employed by the colonial administration, out of a total of 101 employees (*Rapport annuel* 1926).

From the mid-1930s onward, the colonial government improved its capacity to count the people, focusing on adult males – not surprisingly, as these were the unit of taxation. The method here was extrapolation from partial registration data: all adult males were obliged to register with their chiefs; they needed written permission and new registration whenever they traveled to another village (*Rapport annuel* 1933: 65), a policy continued until today. From 1935 onward, using statistical co-efficients derived from the before-mentioned micro-level studies, total population estimates were produced derived from these adult male data. Apart from the period during World War II, these estimates were up-dated yearly, showing a steady and entirely predictable progression, with Burundi always slightly larger than Rwanda. In other words, for decades these data were wrong, for Rwanda's population, as we now know, was always significantly larger than Burundi's.

In the 1950s, two methods were used: yearly sample surveys (*sondages*) of less than 10 percent of the population, with extrapolation of the re-sults to the entire territory (1953–57); and administrative censuses based on the collection of data at the level of the *sous-chefferies*, the territorial divisions at which civil registration data were kept (1958–62). The lat-ter system would continue to be the basis for population estimates after Independence.

The independent state

Following independence, counting the population became even more important: with major international support, the quantity and quality of population data increased rapidly. By the 1950s, both Burundi and Rwanda had more or less well-functioning civil registration systems. Orig-inally, these systems had been managed by the Catholic Church, but af-ter independence they were brought totally under the control of the state (Niyibizi 1986: 269). In 1971 in Rwanda and in 1980 in Burundi, the registration of all births and deaths was made mandatory, and all citizens were required to keep up-to-date record cards at the commune offices (Niyibizi 1986: 274–5; Barandereka and Berciu 1988: 56; Coale and Van De Walle 1968: 169; Lorimer 1961: 128–29). Until the late 1970s, all data on Rwanda's and Burundi's population came from yearly "admin-istrative censuses" based on compilations of these civil registrations; their quality is widely considered high, better than most in Africa at the time (Niyibizi 1986: 274–5). There was nevertheless significant "leakage," with people not declaring births and deaths, registration being incorrect, or papers getting lost (Barandereka and Berciu 1988: 53). Yearly reports, for example, would for a long time continue to show erratic variations in total population figures as well as suspicious findings on fertility and mortality.

The other predominant method employed during this time was the sample survey. Such surveys had first been used in the 1930s in

Ruanda-Urundi, but they were very weak (Barandereka and Berciu 1988: 53). In 1952, a major, well-designed sample survey was carried out in Ruanda-Urundi – only the second conducted in sub-Saharan Africa at the time (Lorimer 1961: 139). In Rwanda, in 1970, another similar, but more sophisticated, survey was carried out, while Burundi did the same in 1965 and 1970–71 (Barandereka and Berciu 1988: 56). All of these surveys provided reasonably good data on marital status, migration, fertility, and so forth (Niyibizi 1986: 275; Lorimer 1961: 142).

It was only in 1978, 16 years after Independence, that the first full national "door-to-door" survey was conducted in Rwanda: for 24 hours, no citizen was allowed to leave home, and throughout the country, a whole army of teachers and bureaucrats, accompanied by military personnel, went from house to house collecting data on 36 variables. In Burundi, the first such census took place in 1979 and a second one in 1990; Rwanda had a second census in 1991, during the civil war. Smaller regional surveys were conducted in three provinces in Rwanda in 1990. The results of all this activity (national census, regional censuses, civil registry data) are considered extremely reliable – precise up to the last person – except for the ethnicity category, which is widely considered to have been fixed for Rwandan Tutsi at just below the 10 percent mark; in Burundi, there was no ethnicity question.

No matter how reliable these data and the process through which they were gathered (including the international involvement) may seem, they contain major omissions and capacities for manipulation. A brief analysis of the visibility of mass violence in population statistics makes this clear. As is widely known, Burundi and Rwanda have had tumultuous and violent post-independence histories. Among the many instances of mass violence, a few episodes stand out. In Rwanda in early 1962, for example, more than 2,000 Rwandan Tutsi were killed and in late 1963, at least 10,000 more were massacred. During this time, between 140,000 and 250,000 Tutsi fled the country – 40 to 70 percent of the then Tutsi population (Watson 1991). Almost none returned.[2] In Burundi, the Tutsi-controlled army, called in to end a Hutu rebellion in a southern province in late 1972, killed between 100,000 and 150,000 Hutu, with 150,000 more fleeing (Kay 1987; Watson 1993).

Yet, as I have shown in detail elsewhere (Uvin 1994), both Rwandan and Burundian population statistics manage to hide these instances of mass violence. The Rwandan figures give no indication whatsoever of the death and flight of hundreds of thousands of people (around 10 percent of the country's early-1960s population). With annual population increments at the time in the range of 60,000 people, incidents such as the killing of up to 10,000 in 1963 and the fleeing of at least 100,000 in

1960–61 should be clearly visible. Instead, all sets of Rwandan population data indicate that population increases continued exactly on trend. In the case of Burundi, population data do indicate a dip in annual population increases at the beginning of the 1970s. Yet this dip appears as a slow, decade-long, gradual trend, first downward and then upward again. In reality, hundreds of thousands of people (more than 10 percent of the country's then population) either died or fled Burundi in May and June of 1972 – but none before and few after.

Both the governments of Rwanda and Burundi have always refused to acknowledge the massive killings within their boundaries, executed largely by their military apparatus. Hence, it comes as no surprise that they would also seek to cover up these events in their population data. The more interesting question is how they managed to do so. Take the case of Burundi. It had a small, partial census in 1970–71. The selective genocide that killed more than 100,000 Hutu took place in 1972, and the complete census that was to be executed that very year with the UN Fund for Population Assistance (UNFPA) was predictably dropped.[3] The government then waited for seven more years before executing a high-quality headcount census with UN support. This new census, in all likelihood, produced a reasonably accurate picture of the 1979 population; in order to make that figure compatible with older data, a ten-year-long decline in population growth was invented (and then reproduced by the United Nations) – and the selective genocide had disappeared with a sleight of the statistical hand.

Observations

Three observations emerge from this overview. One is the lack of rupture in the counting enterprise of Burundi's and Rwanda's population, a quest which continues with undiminished, if not increased, intensity after independence.

The second trend is a continued increase in the quality of the data: from the first guesstimates to the headcount censuses in 1978–79, a great trajectory had been traversed. This improvement in data quality seems especially pronounced after independence, when sophisticated censuses were carried out with international support and under international auspices. However, as objective and accurate as the current data may seem, they are still characterized by dramatic gaps and uncertainties.

Third, even the simple act of counting, so seemingly neutral and objective (as opposed to the much more blatantly political and subjective act of categorizing), is deeply political. The guiding force, the rationale, behind the counting is deeply political, both seeking to control the population (for taxes, communal works, etc.) and to strengthen the rulers' claim to legitimacy by projecting knowledge, objectivity, and scientific grounding. Little has changed in that respect between the colonial and the postcolonial period. In addition, controlling censuses allows governments to manipulate data in order to gain political advantage – in this case, to wipe out evidence of state-sponsored violence. Even nowadays, with sophisticated and expensive methodologies and with international collaboration, population data can be constructed in such a way as to dissimulate massive state-sponsored violence. The capacity to wipe out partial genocide in one's population data – and to acquire United Nations' complicity in this – is surely symptomatic of the functioning of power.

Categorizing the administered

Since the early colonial period, ethnographers and colonial administrators have speculated about the nature of the social categories in Burundi and Rwanda. By the end of the nineteenth century, the three ethnic groups were already being distinguished by adventurers, missionaries, and administrators alike. The explanation of their origins and social roles that became dominant was that the Tutsi were Hamitic peoples, i.e. of a different – partly white, and certainly superior – race than the Hutu, who were traditional Negroid Bantus (Chrétien 1993).

However, all of this scientific certitude did not make the actual measurement any easier, for the usual indicators of racial difference[4] – a separate and distinct history, culture, geographical origin or area, religion, language, or color of skin – did not exist in the case of the Hutu and the Tutsi, who belonged to the same clans, lived side by side in the same territory under the same king, believed in the same God, and largely shared the same day-to-day cultural practices. There were only two possibilities open to colonial officials: use of self-identification, in which one would accept people's own self-description; or use of a more "objective," scientific method of measuring physical differences, with Tutsi defined as taller, with finer noses and facial structures or different blood composition.

During the early years, due to lack of funding, self-identification was the primary method used. The first figures on the proportion of Hutu and Tutsi were collected during the years 1910 to 1919, when hut-to-hut inquiries were made by colonial policemen, and local chiefs and people were asked to state their "race." There is a strong suspicion that the *enquêteurs*, being largely Tutsi, deliberately under-counted the number of Tutsi so as to keep the privileged class as small as possible. The results of these first measurements suggested that up to 95 percent of the population was Hutu, 4 percent were Tutsi, and less than 1 percent Twa.

In the 1930s, the Belgians introduced identification cards with ethnic notations.[5] The method used was self-identification, and the proportions this time were 84, 15, and 1 percent respectively (Des Forges 1999: 37). In the earliest years, there existed a brisk trade in identity cards (IDs), whereby those who could manage to do so bought Tutsi IDs in hopes of gaining greater power. These cards remained in use until the 1994 genocide, greatly facilitating its execution. They have now been abandoned.

After World War II, the scientific enterprise of categorizing Hutu and Tutsi moved into full gear, and more objective, scientific methods were employed. The most famous examples are Pierre Gourou's agronomic maps, Jean Hiernaux's anthropometric data (1954), and Jacques Maquet's ethnicity surveys (1961). The latter two did extensive fieldwork dealing with the question of the distinctions between, and origins of, the Hutu and the Tutsi. They followed very different methods, with Hiernaux measuring people's height, nose size, and skull circumference, among others, and Maquet working solely through interviews. Hiernaux's data clearly demonstrated major distinctions between the physical characteristics of Tutsi and Hutu; Maquet demonstrated major, and fully internalized, social differences. Both have been subject to strong criticism focused on their sampling methods: Hiernaux measured only people who were selected by the colonial authorities and missionaries, and, it is believed, these people were selected on the basis of their closeness to the ideal type as seen by the Belgians (Chrétien 1993: 321; Gahama 1983: 277). Maquet interviewed only people in the core region of the Rwandan monarchy who were referred to him by missionaries and Tutsi clergy, and thus failed to grasp much of the nature of social relations in the country (Grosse 1996).

Note, however, that during this period, the various partial censuses made by the Belgian authorities did not include information on ethnicity, the only categories being those of men, women, girls, and boys. Each annual report, however, *did* mention the existence of three "races"[6] in Burundi and Rwanda, and the proportions of 90 percent Hutu, 9 percent Tutsi, and less than 1 percent Twa.

Only once during the 1950s did the Belgian government publish data on ethnicity based on questionnaires administered to samples of the population. Thus the 1957 report provides detailed province by province data on the proportion of Hutu, Tutsi, and Twa (*Rapport annuel* 1957: 303). In this report, the proportions changed again, this time to 84 percent Hutu, 15 percent Tutsi and 1 percent Twa.

After independence, data on the ethnic/racial categories became the subject of intense passion and political importance. The nature of these debates, however, varied dramatically between Burundi and Rwanda.

Hence, in order to understand the political importance of ethnic categories, it will be necessary to present a brief history of political trends from the early 1960s onward. But before I do so, I wish to analyze the nature of these racial distinctions and the racist ideology behind them.

On the origins of ethnic categories

There exists considerable disagreement as to the origin of these categories – a disagreement that to some extent mirrors the distinction between constructivist and essentialist approaches to ethnicity. Many people believe that the ethnic categories are little more than constructions of the colonizer; reference is often made to the Belgians exporting their Flemish-Walloon divisions to Africa, mistaking and essentializing economic distinctions for ethnic ones. This has been the position of a significant part of the Tutsi elite in Burundi in the past and in Rwanda now; it is backed up by a number of scholars. Others argue that the ethnic categories are deeply grounded historically and locally, preceding colonization; this is the position adopted by many Hutu and backed up by many other scholars. In its extreme form, it constituted the basis of the genocidal ideology.

It seems most probable that images of fundamental distinctions between Hutu and Tutsi (accompanied by actual socio-economic differences) already existed when the colonizers "discovered" Rwanda and Burundi. Although the first ethnographers, missionaries, and colonial administrators profoundly misinterpreted much of what they saw, they did not invent these images *ex nihilo* (Lemarchand 1970: 45; Feltz 1995: 286–88). This is not to say that these images necessarily bear a close resemblance to reality: for the case of Rwanda, it has been suggested that they reflected the ideology of an expanding Tutsi kingdom, seeking to add historical legitimization to its recent conquests and centralization of power (Chrétien1995: 85). As elsewhere, this ideology was in flux, "the outcome of a contest between various forces" (Mamdani 1996: 22). It seems likely that, when the first Germans came, the then Rwandan king was more than happy to make them believe in the long-standing and accepted nature of his rule; and indeed, the Germans, by conquering new territories in the north, greatly helped the king extend his power (Prunier 1995).

The colonial authorities rigidified this ideology both through the use of racialized images, describing Hutu and Tutsi as two distinct races with greatly differing intellectual and moral capacities, and through the institution of indirect rule, which forcefully implemented these images (Elias and Helbig 1991). Both the administrative authorities and the Catholic

Church accepted these images of the Tutsi as naturally superior and born to rule, and of the Hutu as the opposite in all respects (Franche 1995).[7] For decades, Tutsi men were treated as the natural rulers of society and given almost exclusive rights to so-called customary power and privilege, while almost all Hutu people were excluded from these opportunities. It is no wonder that both sides came to believe in these images, projecting them back to time immemorial. At the same time, the Tutsi "native authorities" implemented, under Belgian orders, forceful and constraining policies, including taxation, forced labor, forced cultivation, and forced migration (Braeckman 1994: 30). By the time Rwanda gained independence, a century of myths and associated practice had created the ideology that was to underlie the post-independence instability. These profound, divisive images were largely shared by all Rwandans (Prunier 1995: 9, 37).

Under these conditions, it is not surprising that the struggle for independence became also an ethnic struggle – a fight not only against the (remote) Belgians but also against the (much closer) local Tutsi acolytes (Mamdani 1996). While not all Tutsi were wealthy and powerful under colonial rule, it is clear that almost no Hutu were; it is equally clear that the majority of the Hutu suffered greatly from the increased demands (including onerous taxation and forced labor) placed upon them during colonial rule. In that respect, Burundi and Rwanda followed the same continent-wide processes described by Mamdani (1996: 24):

> [T]he form of rule shaped the form of revolt against it. Indirect rule at once reinforced ethnically bound institutions of control [far beyond their real customary reach – PU] and led to their explosion from within. Ethnicity thus came to be simultaneously the form of control over natives and the form of revolt against it. ... The anti-colonial struggle was first and foremost a struggle against the hierarchy of the local state, the tribally organized Native Authority, which enforced the colonial order as customary.

In this respect, it is fascinating to look at the terms in which, from 1955 onward, the nascent political debate in Rwanda was cast, and the images that were developed in the first political texts from that time and are still referred to today. The 1957 Hutu Manifesto, written by a small group of Hutu intellectuals including Rwanda's first president Kayibanda, is without doubt the most important of them: it was to be the founding document of "Hutu consciousness" and of the independent state. Its central passage states that "the problem is basically that of the monopoly of one race, the Tutsi ... which condemns the desperate Hutu to be for ever subaltern workers." In return, the circle of notables around the king wrote that there could never be fraternity between the Hutu and the Tutsi, for the Tutsi had conquered the Hutu and the latter would always be

subservient. Hence, from completely opposite perspectives, these people followed identical images. In Burundi, the differentiation between
Hutu and Tutsi was equally clear but slightly less negative, for the royal
elite were considered to be neither Hutu nor Tutsi (but Ganwa) and had
managed to keep more of its legitimacy intact.

In conclusion, the ethnic categories were not invented *ex nihilo* by the
Belgians, nor by the Germans who preceded them; people knew themselves as Hutu and Tutsi before colonial officials classified them as such.
This does not mean these distinctions were "real," in the sense of being
direct and neutral representations of a fixed reality "out there." These
ethnic categories were in all likelihood the products of a kingdom in full
expansion, seeking to develop an ideology that justified its power; they
were a moving, contested field – but they did exist, and were profoundly
ingrained in the social fabric of Rwanda and Burundi.

The colonizers added at least two elements to these categories: a puta-
tively scientific, deeply racist, and prejudicial interpretation of the origin
and nature of these differences; and a concomitant practice of indirect rule
in which major social, political, and economic advantages were awarded
almost exclusively to one group. Notwithstanding the appeal of drawing
parallels between the Belgians' domestic situation of division between
two large "ethnic" blocs and their behavior in Africa, there was nothing
particularly Belgian about all this; it by and large reflected the ideologies and practices that were common at the time among all colonizers.
As elsewhere, too, these practices modified the nature of the social relations between the two groups and laid the basis for the politics of the
post-independence period.

It seems that what caused this social and political impact was not the
act of categorizing and measuring as such – for the categories *did* overlap
with pre-existing ones (although certainly not every individual was cor-
rectly categorized) – but rather the colonial policy of indirect rule and
the racist ideology that was associated with it. It was these factors that
crystallized the categories and set them against each other. Admittedly,
this distinction is rather theoretical, for, in practice, the naming of the
categories employed in the census can hardly be dissociated from the use
of these same categories in daily political and intellectual practice during
the colonial period. Census categories are not invented in isolation of, or
outside of, social discourses and political constellations of power; they are
created, employed, and modified within those dynamics, and form part
and parcel of them. That said, one of the intellectual projects of this book
is to understand the specific role of censuses in the creation of identity.
It seems then, that, contrary to much of the recent literature that treats
statistics as constitutive of social reality (for example Urla 1993: 820) – in

old methodological terms, as an independent variable – they are rather reflective or, at the most, intermediary variables.

It has been argued in other contexts that, even where the social categories pre-dated any census, the colonial project of categorization and enumeration did something more than simply reference them; the project also "unyoked social groups from the complex and localized group-structures and agrarian practices in which they had previously been embedded" (Appadurai 1993: 327, writing about India). Discussing caste distinctions in India, for example, Appadurai argues that, while castes certainly existed before the arrival of the colonizers, so did other, alternative, relevant distinctions: caste distinctions were part of a much broader, locally variable, and socially embedded set of relations and practices, which were eroded as the colonizers chose to neglect them in their fixation on caste. Thus, in India as in Burundi and Rwanda, it can be argued that the colonial fixation of dividing the population into a few essentialized groups solidified and simplified what used to be more fluid, complex, socially embedded categories. Once formally defined, the new categories allowed no further escape from the boxes they created (literally, through the IDs), and reduced the margin for maneuver in social, political, and economic life.

In this respect, returning to the case of Burundi and Rwanda, many anthropologists have argued that, before colonization, there was mobility between the groups: Hutu who became wealthy and amassed cattle would eventually become Tutsi, and vice versa for Tutsi who became impoverished (Gravel 1968: 23, 25). Another prevalent argument has been that both Hutu and Tutsi were part of the same lineages and clans, and that these attachments meant as much, if not more, to people than the ethnic ones. If any of these assertions are correct, one could argue that the act of categorizing itself *did* reduce social fluidity and close off social mobility and thus "named into existence" (Kertzer and Arel in this volume) new identities. Censuses and associated instruments of measurement and classification would then constitute not "the liberation of an essential cultural identity that was always there, but the bringing into being of new forms of subjectivity" (Urla 1993: 836).

The argument sounds cogent and it would please me to be able to affirm it. However, all I can truly observe is that there exists a total lack of agreement among Burundians, Rwandans, and outside specialists of the region on the character of precolonial social relations. Profound disagreement exists on the nature of the distinction between Hutu, Tutsi, and Twa. Are they distinct ethnic groups, even races, as some contend, displaying major physical differences and historical origins? Or are they socio-economic groups, akin to castes, or even classes, in which whoever managed to acquire a sizable herd of cattle could become Tutsi?[8] Another important issue that divides the specialists is the nature of the precolonial political system. Were these kingdoms highly centralized and inegalitarian, as many accounts suggest, or was the power of the king more theoretical than real outside the region immediately surrounding the capital? What were the levels of mutual control, exchange, and obligation between Tutsi and Hutu? What was the role of lineages, which included both Tutsi and Hutu, in the social and political system? What possibilities for upward mobility were open to Hutu?[9] Finally, a third debate, ensuing from the previous two, relates to the impact of colonization. Did colonization create ethnicity *ex nihilo*, turning socio-economic stratification into essentialized ethnicity? Or did it simply codify an already highly unequal and differentiated relationship between Tutsi and Hutu? Or was it even a liberating force, which, through the provision of education and the organization of elections, allowed the Hutu masses to free themselves from oppression?

There exist no consensual scientific answers to any of these questions. This is partly due to the difficulties of recreating the histories of oral societies, as well as to the distortions introduced by the eurocentric and often blatantly racist accounts by the first colonizers, missionaries, and ethnographers. However, the main obstacle to reaching consensus on these issues is the fact that they have acquired extreme contemporary political importance (Erny 1994; Guichaoua 1995). Radically divergent interpretations of history provide the basis upon which collective identities are built and act as powerful justifications for current behavior. All we can say for sure, then, is the colonial policy of indirect rule and the racist ideology that was associated with it, rather than the act of categorizing itself, explains the nature of ethnic identities in Burundi and Rwanda.

This argument is strengthened by the frequency with which people's self-identification does not coincide with the officially available categories. In Burundi since 1966, and in Rwanda since late 1994, the official state policy is that ethnic categories do not exist, have never "objectively" existed, but were artificial creations of the colonizers, manipulations of the previous governments. Yet, for the last decades, there has not existed a single Burundian who did not know where he/she stood on the ethnic divide; in families of mixed parents, the dividing line sometimes runs internally, with some children identifying as Hutu and some as Tutsi. The reason for this lies to a large extent in the fact that, rhetoric notwithstanding, a small Tutsi elite monopolized almost all positions and resulting benefits of state power. Another example can be found in the neighboring Kivu region in Zaire, where hundreds of thousands of Rwandans have lived for decades. Although composed of both Hutu and Tutsi and having ties to Rwanda, they were widely known and treated in Zaire as one ethnic group, the Banyarwanda, *and considered themselves as such.* They displayed a high degree of solidarity against attempts by the Mobutu regime to strip them of their assets and citizenship. It is only recently – and especially since 1994, when up to two million refugees fled Rwanda, including most of the genocidal apparatus – that this community has broken up in bitter opposition between Hutu and Tutsi. The reason for this resides in the export of the genocidal ideology and behavior by the refugees, and the games played by local politicians against a background of land scarcity and regional animosity – a complex matter, far beyond the scope of this article. What all these dynamics demonstrate is that actual policies of discrimination and exclusion weigh much more than the specific ethnic categorizations put in place by the state.[10] The social life of the ethnic categories is determined much more by real-life social processes than by the naming exercises of the powers that be.

Nature of the postcolonial state

Between 1958 and 1962, a small group of Catholic-educated Hutu over-threw the monarchy in Rwanda. This so-called "social revolution" took place with the acquiescence, if not connivance, of the departing coloniz-ers who, during the last years before independence in 1962, in the name of a suddenly discovered attachment to representative structures, as well as out of fear of the more radical (leftist, anti-colonial) Tutsi elite, had switched their favor to the Hutu.

The process took place in three stages (already hinted at during our dis-cussion of violence and population data in Rwanda). In late 1959, local-ized anti-Tutsi violence and small pogroms took place in some provinces: hundreds were killed, and many Tutsi fled the country. In 1960 and 1961, legislative elections led to a massive victory of Parmehutu, a rad-ically anti-Tutsi party, and the subsequent overthrow of the monarchy. More Tutsi, including the previous powerholders, fled the country. From 1961 to 1964, some of these Tutsi refugees attempted to return militarily, launching guerrilla assaults from Burundi and Uganda. These assaults were stopped quite easily, but led to organized mass killings of inno-cent Tutsi civilians within the country, foreshadowing events thirty years later. Rwanda would have two presidents in thirty years, both employing a strong anti-Tutsi ideology and associated discriminatory practice as the basis for their rule.

In Burundi, the monarchy survived the colonial period with more so-cial strength than in Rwanda and, as a result, a royalist and bi-ethnic party, Uprona (Union pour le Progrès National, led by a prince, Louis

Rwagasore) won elections both before and after independence. However, Rwagasore was soon killed by the opposition, and his party fell apart as a result of internal conflict. Competition for state power developed between three groups: the Tutsi-Banyaruguru (who were closely associated with the royal court); the Tutsi-Hima (cattle-herding Tutsi of significantly lower social prestige); and a small emerging Hutu elite. The stakes were high. In Burundi, as in Rwanda and most of newly independent Africa, the state was the main source of enrichment and power in society, conferring great opportunities to those who controlled it. Moreover, following the events in Rwanda, state control became the sole vehicle for elite Tutsi to retain their privileges, while, conversely, it was the sole means of rapid social advancement for those Hutu who felt excluded.

After a *coup d'état* by Micombero in 1966, it was the Tutsi-Hima – the group that controlled most of the army – who monopolized power. To do so, they excluded from political competition most other Tutsi and Hutu. From 1966 to 1993, political and, by extension, economic power in Burundi was tightly held by three military regimes (Micombero 1966–82, Bagaza 1982–87, and Buyoya 1987–93), that used their military might to maintain privileges. All three presidents were Tutsi-Hima from the same village in the Bururi region and born within two miles of one another; Buyoya is the nephew of Micombero. Almost all positions of importance in Burundi were monopolized by the Tutsi minority, including the higher levels of the single party (which continued under the name Uprona but became an instrument of the power elite seeking to use the symbols of the royal past to legitimize itself), the full command structure of the army, the police and security forces, and the judicial system (even in 1994, after years of "opening up," only 13 out of 241 magistrates were Hutu). Only at the end of the 1980s was there a noticeable increase in the representation of Hutu in the formal economy and public sector.

In summary, ethnic divisions played a crucial role in the fierce competition for state power in both countries. In both countries, small groups captured state power with backing from the army. Yet, the social composition of that state class was very different, if not opposite – Hutu in Rwanda and Tutsi in Burundi. Their social bases being very dissimilar, these groups employed different strategies for maintaining power, thus setting into motion differing dynamics of conflict.

The two regimes Rwanda has known since independence were not averse to the use of repression. The Kayibanda regime (1962–73) chased out or killed most former Tutsi powerholders and politicians, even the most moderate ones, as well as many opposition Hutu politicians who did not join Parmehutu. The second republic under General Habyarimana (1973–94) was a military dictatorship. It killed many powerholders of the first republic (including Kayibanda), and its internal security kept a tight lid on opposition and dissension for almost two decades. The legal system was independent only in name, and impunity was the norm. Regular popular elections were a farce in which Habyarimana was always re-elected with more than 98 percent of the vote. Any critical press was produced at the risk of the journalist's life.

The main strength of these regimes, however, lay not in their oppression, but in their capacity to legitimize themselves. One strand of legitimization, widely used in Africa, consisted of the de-politicizing argument that the sole objective of the state is the pursuit of economic development for the masses. In Rwanda, the international community actively bought into that argument, making the country one of the world's foremost aid recipients (Uvin 1998, chapter 2). The second approach consisted of an ethnic, "social revolution" discourse, largely tailored for domestic consumption. This discourse was based on the notion that Rwanda belonged to the Hutu, its true inhabitants, who had been subjugated brutally for centuries by the foreign exploiters, the Tutsi, and that in 1959, the Hutu had wrested power away from their former masters and installed a true democracy, representing the majority of the people. This notion that the government is the legitimate representative of the majority Hutu – and thus by definition democratic – as well as the sole defense against the evil attempts by the Tutsi race to enslave the people again, constituted the powerful core of the legitimization of the ruling clique's hold on power.

This "social revolution" ideology constituted both a reversal and a continuation of long-standing psychocultural images. It was a continuation to the extent that it persisted in its depiction of the innate and profound differences between "the Hutu" and "the Tutsi" as homogeneous, mutually exclusive categories. It was a reversal in that the moral and social privilege associated with the Tutsi – the natural-born rulers, the chosen people – was turned on its head, with the Tutsi now in the role of alien, inferior outsiders to be contained. As one observer remarked, unlike the French Revolution, in Rwanda the distinctions between people were "inversé et non renversé" ("inverted but not overthrown")(Erny 1994: 59; Chrétien 1995: 88; Braeckman 1994: 51).

This ideology was accompanied by an institutionalized structure of discrimination, especially in areas that allowed for vertical mobility, such as modern education, state jobs, and politics. Under the Habyarimana regime, "there would be not a single Tutsi burgomaster or prefect, there was only one Tutsi officer in the whole army, there were two Tutsi members of parliament out of seventy and there was only one Tutsi minister out of a cabinet of between 25 and 35 members. The army was of course the tightest." (Physicians for Human Rights 1994) The system of ethnic identity papers introduced by the Belgians in 1935 was maintained. The return of the Tutsi refugees was categorically denied, with the argument that there was no more space in Rwanda (Adelman and Suhrke 1996: 12). A quota system was installed that limited access to higher education and state jobs by Tutsi to a number supposedly equal to their proportion of the population. Not unexpectedly, ethnicity remained a category in all post-independence censuses, providing consistently unchanged results; it was widely suspected that the numbers had been set in advance by the government!

This quota system was usually only partly implemented. Most authors agree that in the public sector – but not at the highest levels, and not at all in the army – Tutsi remained represented beyond the allocated 9 percent. Moreover, in sectors of society less tightly controlled by the state – commerce and enterprise, NGOs, and development projects – they were in all likelihood present beyond that proportion (Schürings 1995: 496; Guichaoua 1995: 34). Oft-repeated data "prove" that the predominance of Tutsi in secondary school decreased, but that they remained over-represented throughout (Funga 1991; Munyakazi 1993 – note that these data are of course subject to much debate). These quota systems and ethnic IDs, then, served more to keep the distinctions alive and to allow for social control by the state, than to implement actual discriminatory policies. They were part of the institutional structure of Hutu power – administrative reminders of the fact that the Tutsi were different from everyone else, and that the state was watching out for the interests of the majority Hutu.

In Burundi, the ruling elite represented a much narrower social base than in Rwanda, requiring the regime to employ a much higher dose of repression. The defining events took place in 1972, although purges had occurred earlier, most notably in 1965. The fully Tutsi-controlled army, called in to end a Hutu rebellion in a southern province, went on a two-month rampage, killing 100,000 to 150,000 Hutu, comprising almost all educated Hutu in the country: teachers, nurses, administrators, etc. This created sufficient fear to suppress Hutu unrest for two decades. For years to come, many Hutu parents would not send their children to school for fear of making them targets for future pogroms. These events constitute the defining moments in independent Burundi's history: they crystallized Hutu and Tutsi identities, and created a climate of permanent mutual fear.

In 1988, 1991, and 1992 violence broke out again. In each case, acting on false rumors and a widespread dislike of corrupt local (Tutsi) administrators, Hutu farmers killed local Tutsi; the army then intervened to restore order, killing significantly more people in retaliation. The power base of the small Tutsi ruling clique thus rested on fear and repression, and the military played a key role in this.

Burundi's successive regimes also attempted to use two legitimization strategies to solidify their hold on power. First, they too employed the discourse of development to justify the state's (omni)presence, with less success than in Rwanda – although in the mid-to late-1980s, with the 1972 events long past, the international community seemed willing to believe the development myth.

The second strategy was the exact inverse of Rwanda's (and more in line with general African practice): the denial of ethnicity. The official ideology was that there were in Burundi no ethnic groups, but only Burundians, equal before the law. The mass murder of 1972, if ever discussed, was euphemistically referred to as "events" that resulted from the actions of unspecified "extremists." None of the Burundian censuses after independence, nor any other of the counting exercises we will discuss below, ever inquired into ethnicity; as a matter of fact, even measuring the height of women – an often-used indicator for the measurement of nutritional status – was impossible in Burundi, for it could be mis-interpreted as providing indication of Tutsi-ness! More generally, the existence of differences in ethnicity was explained as an artificial creation of the colonial state, bent on dividing the people to enhance its rule. For decades, then, the official Tutsi position in Burundi – and an important counter-discourse in Rwanda – has been from the very social constructivist stance that the act of categorizing by the colonizer created the identities.

In conclusion, notwithstanding their very different manifestations, in both countries ethnic categories are instruments of domination. In Rwanda, they do so by acting as administrative reminders of the "stranger-ness" of the Tutsi and thus legitimizing the control over the state by the powers-that-be; in Burundi, they do so by camouflaging unequal power and a regime of mass exclusion (by their denial). The dynamics that led to both these outcomes emerged under the colonial period, during which categories were rigidified and invested with racist meaning as well as socio-economic differentiation.

Separating out the role of censuses, and the acts of categorizing embedded in them, in these acts of domination is not easy: censuses are by and large instances, public objectifications, of broader discriminatory policies and attitudes. Sometimes, however, censuses can be used directly for the purpose of committing violence. The case of the Rwandan genocide is a dramatic instance thereof. The identification cards (IDs), instituted by the Belgian colonizer in the 1930s and continued by the post-independence governments, definitely facilitated the execution of the genocide. As these IDs were mandatory and indicated ethnicity, any armed group at roadblocks could easily identify Tutsi and kill them

(Des Forges 1999: 92). More generally, given Rwanda's policy of mandatory registration of the population (all people must be registered at birth,
must ask for permission to travel, and must register immediately whenever
they change residence), the population registers were widely used by civil
servants to prepare lists of all Tutsi in their communes. And at least one
source argues that in February 1994, a census was ordered in Kigali: the
coded notations put on people's residences on that occasion were used by
the genocidal militia to hunt Tutsi down and kill them two months later.
I have not been able to find confirmation of this report; it may belong
to the category of rumors, so pervasive in the region. In September 1996,
the UNHCR suspended its operations in the refugee camps around Goma
because the refugees were boycotting a census. According to Reuters
(1996), "aid workers said the Hutu refugees feared census-takers would
mark them with ink [this does indeed happen: refugees' thumbs are
marked with indelible ink so they will not be double-counted – PU] so
they could be detected by Rwandan government troops of the Tutsi-led
army and mistreated if they were forced back into Rwanda."

To feed the development beast

Building on the domestic and international acceptability of the development discourse and associated practice, a whole range of new actors entered Burundi and Rwanda: bilateral and multilateral development assistance agencies, development non-governmental organizations (NGOs),
development experts, and academics hired by the aid system. They soon
began to produce their own censuses and surveys, providing significantly
larger quantities of data on Rwanda's population and its characteristics
than ever before. In light of Rwanda's poverty, remoteness, and lack
of strategic value, it is astonishing to contemplate the vast quantity of
data that have been produced about the country and, to a lesser extent,
Burundi. The reasons for this include Rwanda's popularity within the
development world, the smallness of both countries and the existence of
a dense network of roads (allowing people to return to a decent hotel in
the capital or a secondary city after a good day's measuring), the density
of the population, and the docility of the people, enabling easy and good
data collection. Having done it myself, I can attest that there was nothing
easier than measuring a few Burundians' lives for the day: once one had
the required permission from the Ministry of the Interior or the governor,
the people were willing to participate, and were in close walking distance
with cheap and helpful translators. Farmers living close to the capital
might be asked to answer questionnaires five to ten times a year.

   As a result, there exists a vast quantity of data on those aspects of
people's lives that are of interest to the development enterprise.[11] The

field of health, including demography, is an arena of massive data production. Foremost are data on fertility: attitudes toward, knowledge of, and use of contraception; desired family size, age of marriage, and all other variables related to the main obsession of the international system concerning Burundi and Rwanda – over-population. These are followed, far behind, by data on nutrition, stunting and wasting, and health service use. Thousands of more or less participatory community surveys, school surveys, hospital and administrative surveys, annual reports, large sample and small sample studies, exist with data on these variables. In 1983, with support from the UN World Fertility Survey team, Rwanda's newly created National Population Office executed a national fertility survey – basically the only thing it accomplished during most of its first decade of existence, for there was no government commitment to the implementation of a family planning policy. Nutritional surveys were carried out at all levels of detail, size of the sample, geographical coverage, and methodological complexity (they are also almost never comparable: Grosse, *et al.* 1995) At the top of the pyramid are the demographic and health surveys, focusing on fertility and health behavior, of 1983 and 1992, funded by the UNFPA and USAID respectively. These were the latest in professional technology, whereby the best and the brightest (usually foreigners), using the latest in sampling techniques and computerized calculations, produced hundreds of pages of exhaustive data on hundreds of variables. These censuses belong to a new type: designed, paid for, and executed by the foreign aid system, measuring the variables the development system is interested in. Their data give rise to lengthy debates.

From the mid-1980s onward, the field exploded with the emergence of AIDS as a subject of measurement.[12] The reasons for this include the fact that Rwanda had one of the world's highest HIV-positive populations, and thus it was much easier to get samples there – sometimes in the thousands. Together with other public health matters and family planning, the data collection enterprise has become heavily dominated by clinical and public health specialists – reflecting a broad trend toward the medicalization of development observed in the 1990s.

Agriculture is the second major obsession of the development system. There exist tens of thousands of surveys and measurements of Rwanda's agriculture and the people living off it: literally every foreign aid project, every student in economics or agriculture, every administrator in both countries seems to feel an urgent need to produce detailed tables on farm sizes, number of plots, crops produced, etc. The most advanced classifying and counting exercises were the National Agricultural Surveys of 1984 and 1991, funded by the UN Food and Agriculture Organization (FAO) and USAID respectively, and involving high levels of foreign expertise. Both of these amounted to full-blown, nation-wide censuses, for which each farmer was visited, and his/her fields, crops, employees, farm implements, etc., were measured. The surveys were extremely reliable and superior to previous data collected by the Rwandan Ministry of Agriculture alone.

Note that this system is strictly and typically apolitical, as the entire development aid system sees its mandate as respectful of sovereignty and limited to purely technical matters. None of these censuses asks questions about ethnicity; certain categories (such as adult height) can be dropped if they are politically sensitive; and, as we saw above, if at times governments have no time to collaborate with the international aid community because they are too busy killing their populations, the expert system will patiently wait until that problem has disappeared. Within a few weeks after the end of the genocide, the demographers, nutritionists, economists, epidemiologists, agronomists, and other experts were back in Rwanda, and the production of data resumed as before.

All of this measuring and counting is closely related to the legitimization of those with power, in both the state and the aid system. For the aid system, the categorizing and measuring serve to justify its existence, and the value-neutral, objective, technically grounded nature of the hierarchical position its practitioners occupy; it also serves to organize, control, and frame ("encadrer," the term used in French development jargon to refer to the activities of the extension system) the poor. In so doing, it creates the subject of the underdeveloped mass of generic farmers – clients for the development enterprise – in need of its advice, money, and benevolence. As Urla (1993: 891) writes, "as part of a modern regime of truth that equates knowledge with measurement, statistics occupy a place of authority in contemporary modes of social description; they are technologies of truth production." By measuring over and over again the state of under-nutrition, over-fertility, low productivity, and high morbidity, the truth of under-development, and the need for assistance, is verified. In the process, the dreams, passions, knowledge, feelings, and identities of Rwandans and Burundians are evacuated, their humanity reduced to producers and consumers.

Conclusion

Synthesizing the history of censuses in Burundi and Rwanda, one is struck by the sheer effort and energy devoted to the classifying and counting enterprise. From the very beginning, this enterprise consumed much of the interest and time of the authorities, whether administrative, religious, or scientific (even though these distinctions were at the time much less clear than now). As time passed, the techniques employed became increasingly sophisticated and costly. For the last decades, the number of censuses, and the area of human activity they cover, are astonishing, especially if the resources used for this purposes are compared to the resources available to the societies and people who are being measured. Counting and measuring African populations surely is big business, for both governments and the development enterprise. The age of statistics has truly dawned on Burundi and Rwanda, where it oddly coexists with extreme poverty and genocidal violence.

And yet, one cannot overlook the extent of ignorance and contentiousness underlying these scientific appearances. There is still no certainty whatsoever about population trends until the 1950s (Thibon 1987 and Chrétien 1987); even afterward, as our discussion on violence and population data shows, major gaps and omissions still exist (Nyrop *et al.* 1974). The proportion of Hutu and Tutsi is until this day subject to virulent debate, as are the nature and origin of the categories themselves.

There is a double, or maybe triple dynamic taking place here. At one level, there is the enterprise of the powers-that-be – missionaries and colonial administrators first, the independent government and the development enterprise later – to count and categorize in order to control, to extend power, but also to obtain legitimacy. Whether concretely motivated by the desire to increase taxation, control population movements, or target development projects and policies, the measuring and the counting are always part of a larger project of the extension and strengthening of power. Censuses measure what those with power consider important to be measured: the categories reflect first and foremost the demands and ideologies of power. Data allow for control through better knowledge; they also allow for legitimacy through the projection of objectivity and truth.[13]

No matter how imperfect and contested the measuring has been, it is not without effects of its own – and these comprise the second level of analysis. The acts of categorizing and measuring become part of society's struggles, both directly – for they set the size of various groups' claims on scarce resources – and indirectly – for they contribute to crystallizing people's identities. This second level, then, is about political and social processes, which, in the case of Rwanda and Burundi, have been extremely divisive and violent. Note, however, that it is hard in this respect to tease out the specific role of the acts of categorization and measurement themselves; to what extent are they independent variables, with a causal force separate from the policies being pursued in conjunction with them, or from any pre-existing identities? In the case of Rwanda and Burundi, this is especially difficult to answer empirically, as the information on the other relevant factors is highly contested. All we can say is that categorization interacts with, and cannot be understood in isolation from, other processes that create identity, such as indirect rule and discrimination, racist ideologies, and the occurrence of past violence. The development of categories and data by the colonizer did not create ethnic divisions, nor did the official attempts to wipe out categories, as in Burundi after independence, abolish these identities.

In short, census categories neither exist by themselves nor create identities by themselves. They are tangible hangers on which to attach intangible processes of power and control: self-identification and group sentiment; dignity and exclusion; opportunism; and science and legitimization. They are stakes in social struggles, podiums for the political theater, but not the active agents. Human beings are the agents, and the outcomes of their political fights are determined by their interests, attitudes, and access to scarce resources.

At times, the counting and categorizing exercises are abused for political purposes. Such is the case, for example, when governments seek to use population data to hide state-sponsored violence; when genocidal forces use population registers (and possibly census results) to target people for killing; when ethnic proportions are fixed in advance, or denied altogether. In this case, the relation between census and politics is direct, as opposed to the indirect one, via identity, which is the subject of most of this book.

At the third level, we find people and their resistance to categorization and control. From farmers and artisans dissimulating their taxable assets to traders selling on black markets, to parents not declaring their children at birth; from farmers answering whatever they think will please the census-takers, to wealthy people buying IDs of the other ethnic group (first Hutu buying Tutsi IDs during colonization and the opposite afterwards), people are in a constant process of manipulating the measurements and categories to which they are subjected. It is unclear whether this should be called resistance rather than opportunism (as when wealthy people buy IDs of favored ethnic groups), or simple manipulation and evasion in order to obtain small advantages. Society is not a product malleable only from above: strategies ranging from accommodation to resistance confront the dictates of power and control.

NOTES

1 Note the theoretical nature of the distinction, with borders being totally porous, and trade, family, and economic relations entailing a constant move of people across borders.
2 The Rwanda Patriotic Front, which invaded Rwanda in 1990, was composed mainly of these refugees and their descendants.
3 This methodological complicity is not limited to the UN. In the late 1970s, the French department of development cooperation, in collaboration with a whole

slew of major French research institutions, organized a series of colloquia on African demography, eventually published in English in two volumes in 1985 and 1988. The articles devoted to Burundi and Rwanda never mention the occurrences of violence and their demographic incidences, or even the contested nature of ethnicity. For example, this is how the Burundian case study describes the preparation of the 1979 census: "the project of holding a general population census was first made in 1970. . . . A UNFPA mission was sent to Burundi to evaluate the needs in population and other data and elaborate a project of assistance. Unfortunately, a variety of reasons caused the project to be interrupted. In 1977, a new request was made by the Government of Burundi to the UNFPA" (Barandereka and Berciu 1988: 5).

4 At a time in pre-World War II Europe when the concept of "race" was often defined culturally, and not merely biologically, in the sense that "ethnicity" has been defined since the war.

5 The ID practice was an extension of the one in Belgium itself, and indeed in much of Western Europe, where every citizen until this day carries one at all times. In Belgium, however, IDs do not mention ethnicity (as attested by language), for to do so would be seen as very divisive.

6 Note that the specific term "race" is used from the very first report on the colonial administration by the Belgian government (1921: 10); the term continued to be used by the post-independence government of Rwanda, and was widely popularly used until very recently.

7 Alex de Waal 1994 argues that the Belgians deliberately reclassified many Hutu chiefs as Tutsi so as to maintain the purity of their belief.

8 For some contributions to this debate, see Chrétien 1985; Lemarchand 1966; Prunier 1995; Vidal 1974.

9 For some contributions to this debate, see Maquet 1961; Newbury 1988; Prunier 1995; Lemarchand 1970; de Heusch 1994; de Lame 1996; Franche 1995; Willame 1995.

10 One way to think through this is to develop a counter-factual scenario. Assume that, at independence, the Muslims, or Swahili-speakers, or fishermen, would have violently conquered power in Burundi and Rwanda, imposing their religion, language, or profession on the country. Would the Hutu versus Tutsi distinction be as salient as it is today?

11 Or to foreigners more generally. From late 1994 onwards, plans for a gorilla census in Rwanda were underway; in 1996, one was undertaken in Rwanda by the Diane Fossey Foundation (Verrengia 1996).

12 A database search on "Rwanda and population" yielded 700 titles, three quarters of which were devoted to AIDS. The databases used were Sociofile, PAIS, EconLit, International Political Science abstracts, and PopLine.

13 Note that the audience of this exercise has always been international as much as (if not more than) domestic: the League of Nations, public opinion in Belgium, or the international community of states were more important audiences in all this than Burundians and Rwandans themselves.

REFERENCES

Adelman, Howard and Suhrke, Astri 1996, *Early Warning and Conflict Management, The International Response to Conflict and Genocide: Lessons from the*

Rwanda Experience, Copenhagen: Joint Evaluation of Emergency Assistance to Rwanda, Vol. 2, March.

Appadurai, Arjun 1993, "Number in the Colonial Imagination," in Carol A. Breckenridge and Peter van de Veer (eds.), *Orientalism and the Postcolonial Predicament, Perspectives on South Asia*, Philadelphia: University of Pennsylvania Press, pp. 314–39.

Barandereka, Sylvestre and Berciu, Aurel 1988, "Burundi," in Groupe de Démographie Africaine (ed.), *Population Size in African Countries: An Evaluation*, Vol. 2, Paris: IDP-INED-INSEE-MINCOOP-ORSTOM, pp. 49–70.

Braeckman, Colette 1994, *Génocide au Rwanda*, Paris: Fayard.

Chrétien, Jean-Pierre 1985, "Hutu et Tutsi au Rwanda et au Burundi," in Jean-Loup Amselle and Edgar M'Bokolo (eds.), *Au coeur de l'ethnie, Ethnies, tribalisme et Etat en Afrique*, Paris: La Découverte, pp. 129–65.

1987, "Démographie et écologie en Afrique orientale à la fin du XIX siècle: une crise exceptionnelle," *Cahiers d'Etudes Africaines* 27: 43–59.

1993, *Burundi, L'histoire retrouvée. 25 ans de métier d'historien en Afrique*, Paris: Karthala.

Chrétien, Jean-Pierre (dir.) 1995, *Rwanda, Les médias du genocide*, Paris: Karthala.

Coale, Ansley J. and Van De Walle, Etienne 1968, "Appendix: Notes on Areas for which Estimates Were Made but not Subject to a Detailed Study," in William Brass, Ansley Coale, Paul Demeny et al. (eds.), *The Demography of Tropical Africa*, Princeton: Princeton University Press, pp. 168–82.

de Heusch, Luc 1994, "Anthropologie d'un génocide: le Rwanda," *Les Temps Modernes* 49: 1–19.

de Lame, Danielle 1996, *Une colline entre mille ou le calme avant la tempête, Transformations et blocages du Rwanda rural*, Tervure: Musée Royal de l'Afrique Centrale.

Des Forges, Alison 1999, *Leave None to Tell the Story, Genocide in Rwanda*, New York: Human Rights Watch; Paris: Fédération Internationale des Ligues des Droits de l'Homme.

De Waal, Alex 1994, "Genocide in Rwanda," *Anthropology Today* 10: 1–2.

Elias, M., and Helbig, D. 1991, "Deux mille collines pour les petits et les grands, Radioscopie des stéréotypes hutu et tutsi au Rwanda et au Burundi," *Politique Africaine* 42: 65–73.

Erny, Pierre 1994, *Rwanda 1994*, Paris: L'Harmattan.

Feltz, Gaëtan 1995, "Ethnicité, Etat-nation et démocratisation au Rwanda et au Burundi," in Manassé Esoavelomandroso and Gaëtan Feltz (eds.), *Démocratie et développement, Mirrage ou espoir raisonnable?*, Paris: Karthala, pp. 277–97.

Franche, Dominique 1995, "Généalogie du génocide rwandais, Hutu et Tutsi: Gaulois et Francs?" *Les temps Modernes* 50: 1–58.

Funga, François 1991, "Pouvoir, ethnies et regions," *Dialogue*, no. 149: 21–35.

Gahama, Joseph 1983, *Le Burundi sous administration belge*, Paris: Karthala.

Gravel, Pierre B. 1968, *Remera, A Community in Eastern Ruanda*, The Hague/Paris: Mouton.

Grosse, Scott, Krasovec, K, Rwamasirabo, S, and Sibomana, J. B. E 1995, *Evaluating Trends in Children's Nutritional Status in Rwanda*, East Lansing: Department of Agricultural Economics, Michigan State University.

Grosse, Scott 1996, "Re: Critical Rwandology (2)," message on Rwandanet (rwandanet@msstate.edu), 20 June.

Guichaoua, André 1995, "Un lourd passé, un présent dramatique, un avenir des plus sombres," in André Guichaou (ed.), *Les crises politiques au Burundi et au Rwanda (1993–1994)*, Paris: Karthala; Lille: Université des Sciences et Technologies de Lille, pp. 19–51.

Hiernaux, Jean 1954, *Les caractères physiques des populations du Ruanda et de l'Urundi*, Brussels: Institut Royal des Sciences Naturelles de Belgique.

Kay, R. 1987, *Burundi since the Genocide*, London: Minority Rights Group.

Lemarchand, René 1966, "Power and Stratification in Rwanda: A Reconsideration," *Cahiers d'Etudes Africaines* 6, 4 (1966), 592–610.

Lemarchand, René 1970, *Burundi and Rwanda*, New York: Praeger.

Lorimer, Frank 1961, *Demographic Information on Tropical Africa*, Boston: Boston University Press.

Louis, Roger 1963, *Ruanda-Urundi 1884–1919*, Oxford: Clarendon Press.

Mamdani, Mahmood 1996, *Citizen and Subject, Contemporary Africa and the Legacy of Late Colonialism*, Princeton: Princeton University Press.

Maquet, Jacques 1961, *The Premise of Inequality in Rwanda: A Study of Political Relations in a Central African Kingdom*, London: Oxford University Press.

Munyakazi, L. 1993, "La question ethnique: un problème mal pose," *Dialogue* 170: 9–11.

Newbury, Catharine 1988, *The Cohesion of Oppression, Clientship and Ethnicity in Rwanda 1860–1960*, New York: Columbia University Press.

Niyibizi, Silas 1986, "Rwanda," in Groupe de Démographie Africaine (ed.), *Population Size in African Countries: An Evaluation*, Vol. 1, Paris: IDP-INED-INSEE-MINCOOP-ORSTOM, pp. 267–80.

Nyrop, Richard F., Lyle E. Brennenman *et al.* 1974, *Rwanda, A Country Study*, Washington, DC: The American University, Foreign Area Studies.

Physicians for Human Rights 1994, *Rwanda 1994, A Report of the Genocide*, London: Physicians for Human Rights.

Prunier, Gérard 1995, *The Rwanda Crisis: History of a Genocide*, New York: Columbia University Press.

Ransdell, Eric 1994, "The Wounds of War," *US News and World Report* 117 (28 November): 74–75.

Rapport annuel sur l'administration belge du Ruanda et de l'Urundi, 1921 to 1961, Brussels: Gouvernement belge, Ministère des Colonies. (A report was published every year between 1921 and 1961.)

Reuters 1996, "UN Refugee Agency Suspends Operations in Camps," 2 September.

Schürings, Hildegard 1995, "La coopération de la République fédérale d'Allemagne avec le Burundi et le Rwanda," in André Guichaoua (ed.), *Les crises politiques au Burundi et au Rwanda (1993–1994)*, Paris: Karthala; Lille: Université des Sciences et Technologies de Lille, pp. 487–501.

Seltzer, William 1998, "Population Statistics, the Holocaust, and the Nuremberg Trials," *Population and Development Review* 24: 511–52.

Thibon, Christian 1987, "Un siècle de croissance démographique au Burundi (1850–1950)," *Cahiers d'Etudes Africaines* 27: 61–81.

Urla, Jacqueline 1993, "Cultural Politics in an Age of Statistics: Numbers, Nations, and the Making of Basque Identity," *American Ethnologist* 20: 818–43.

Uvin, Peter 1994, "Violence and UN Population Data," *Nature* 372: 495–96.

1998, *Aiding Violence, The Development Enterprise in Rwanda*, West Hartford, Conn.: Kumarian Press.

Verrengia, Joseph B. 1996, "Gorilla Census to Begin as Civil War in Rwanda Subsides," *Denver Rocky Mountain News*, 18 August.

Vidal, Claudine 1974, "Economie de la société féodale rwandaise," *Cahiers d'Etudes Africaines* 14: 52–74.

Watson, Catherine 1991, *Exile from Rwanda*, Washington, DC: US Committee for Refugees.

1993, *Transition in Burundi*, Washington, DC: US Committee for Refugees.

Willame, Jean-Claude 1995, *Aux sources de l'hécatombe rwandaise*, Paris: Karthala.

7   Identity counts: the Soviet legacy
and the census in Uzbekistan

David Abramson

> Nations... are not out there to be counted; they are a function of
> social, political, and economic processes.
>
> David Laitin

Identity matters in so far as perceived ties and interactions between people, appearance, speech, place of residence, and behavior are all observ-
able and classifiable differences. How social difference is constructed and
the meanings attributed to those constructions are the basis for abstract,
often overlapping and contradictory systems of classification such as kinship, language, race, ethnicity, and religion. As the chapters in this volume
show, the names of these abstract systems are incorporated into the language of censuses whose manifest function is to count the state's citizens
for a range of purposes including taxation, electoral districting, military
conscription, affirmative action programs, and the selection of official
languages. These studies also demonstrate that the census is a highly
politicized project whose particular forms of interrogation and categorization are subject to contestation and manipulation. The census claims
to represent collectivities in the form of social identity and, thereby, sets
the terms for this very politicking.

My objective for this chapter is to show that in the case of Uzbekistan,
such political possibilities were and are predicated on national difference.
Soviet nationality policies, aided by such official state practices as census-
taking and the application of census results in reinforcing citizenship and
territoriality, have given birth to a political culture organized along the
lines of national difference.[1] This is not to say that post-Soviet "cultures"
are nationally based. Rather, the sovereign national-territorial states into
which the USSR divided in 1991 are now unavoidable social realities
with which the citizens of these new states must contend. The particular
dynamics of these social realities and the politics they enable vary from
one state to the next.

As Silver (1986: 73) points out, the question "Nationality" on each
of seven Soviet censuses was not framed as a question, but presented

as a presumable category of information about a person which the respondent was not allowed to leave blank. Similar to the way the 1897 Russian imperial census did not provide the option of "non-believer" or of expressing one's degree of faith in response to the religion "question," the Soviet censuses did not give respondents the possibility of not belonging to any nationality, or of belonging to more than one (ibid.: 79). This provokes us to ask: What is the subjective dimension behind such an objective question? While Soviet census designers regarded the open question about nationality to be subjective in nature, that claim of subjectivity was spurious or, at best, deceptive. How people respond to an official survey may be contingent on how they imagine the state and perceive its role in their lives, and on the significance of national identity for such documents versus its expression in other forums. Furthermore, as Slezkine tells us, while there was a lack of consensus over the origins, fates, political and economic usefulness, and characteristics of nations and nationalities, "everyone seemed to assume that, for better or worse, humanity consisted of more or less stable *Sprachnationen* [or language-based nation] cemented by a common past" (1994: 416). This was the unquestioned and therefore presumed objective reality.

If "a study of the census category *nationality* offers a point of entry from which to address larger questions about the making of the USSR" (Hirsch 1997: 252), then a study of the politics of census categorization in post-Soviet Uzbekistan can offer a point of entry from which to theorize the ongoing process of identity construction. I argue that the presentation of nationality as an objective category, while framed as a subjective "question" on the Soviet censuses, actually masked an ongoing state project to seize and maintain control of abstract systems for classifying social life and representing social reality. The classification of citizens as national "subjects" was and continues to be one such system. The interesting paradox of such a system is that people had to be convinced of the objective reality of national identity; yet that "hard" reality could only be convincing when framed in subjective terms – as an individual's "natural" response to a census query. I am not arguing here that in responding to the nationality question on the Soviet census each individual magically came to believe her own personal role in a collective national trajectory; rather, the census design reflected and even reinforced the expedience of belonging to a nationality and the political maneuvering over how to define that sense of belonging constituted new social selves.

It is important to emphasize here that this is neither an argument for conspiracy-type theories nor is it a claim that the state is a monolithic structure or actor. Rather, I follow Gupta (1995) in conceptualizing the modern state, minimally, as a translocal institution whose impact on its citizens' lives is refracted through bureaucracy and through representations of the state itself such as public ceremonies, the media, etc. As Hirsch (1997) demonstrates, the Soviet state was by no means a monolithic or unified force in designing a census to create national identities; rather, it was constituted by ethnic Russian and non-Russian academics, bureaucrats, and other state officials engaged over time in an ongoing discussion over how to categorize Soviet citizens and to what advantage. Hirsch's article provides an excellent foundation for the theoretical discussion of the forces behind census design and implementation and, ultimately, the diverse and contesting powers and interests constituting the Soviet state. Building on that foundation, we should now consider more in-depth and on-the-ground approaches to identity formation, in addition to the contributions of ethnographers and bureaucrats to this process.

Censuses are somewhat like opinion polls in that they create public opinion, except that in the case of the census, its results also shape public constructions of the state. Bourdieu suggests that public opinion is created when the same set of questions are imposed on "distinct individuals who in many cases have never asked themselves the questions they are being called upon to answer" (in Colas 1997: xxix). Furthermore, Colas argues, the opinion poll (and, I would add, the census) is "a universalizing process of abstraction that metamorphoses ethical questions into political ones, fabricating a reality that doesn't exist and which in turn legitimates the existing order, for is not what characterizes power relations the fact that they dissimulate themselves and is not this dissimulation precisely what gives them their 'power' in the first place?" (ibid.: xxix). Soviet censuses, as I shall show, contributed to the designation of nationalities, thereby glossing over the intense political wrangling that occurred over what to count from one census to the next.

This chapter focuses on Uzbekistan, one of fifteen newly independent nation-states to rise up from the ashes of the former Soviet Union, as a case study for thinking about the role of the census in how states categorize citizens. As an anthropologist who studies nation-state formation, national identity, and changing notions of community in Uzbekistan, I find the role of the state in categorizing citizens through the census to be an intriguing and challenging test of the colonial model. Uzbekistan, unlike Russia, Georgia, and the Baltic states of Estonia, Latvia, and Lithuania, had never been a sovereign state prior to 1991. In this way, along with the four other Central Asian republics of Kazakhstan, Kyrgyzstan, Tajikistan, and Turkmenistan, Uzbekistan's national sovereignty – a direct legacy of its Soviet past and relationship to Moscow – resonates with the histories of numerous states around the world that were created within the political and administrative frameworks of colonial systems. Consequently, we cannot reach an understanding of how these "peoples" have come to imagine themselves without also understanding the process of Soviet state-building.

Despite its limitations, the colonial model is useful in considering the Soviet Union/Russia's relation to Central Asia. The remarkable degree of external guidance in the reclassification of identities, the political expedience for many Central Asians of defining and then adhering to those reconfigured identities, and the consequent impact on how people subjectively perceive themselves all make the construction of Uzbek identity a particularly interesting study in the politics of national identity formation. Furthermore, the sheer number of "non-indigenes," or recently arrived settlers, and trained indigenous cadres living in Central Asia prior to and at the time of independence in 1991 was vastly higher than in most European colonies in Africa and Asia (Shahrani 1994: 142).

For almost as long as Russia has ruled over Central Asia (predating the Soviet Union by about half a century), there have been nationalist-type movements in one form or another there. Yet it was not until early Soviet attempts to reconcile the nationality problem with a larger socialist and internationalist agenda that republics like Uzbekistan were able to emerge, with the complicity of the new Soviet government in Moscow and the local elites. That complicity involved the establishment of politically acceptable territorial entities and their legitimation through state projects such as the census. The nationality category used in the census contributed to the legitimation of Soviet-engineered identities in the way that it framed social experience, emphasizing spoken language and territory and downplaying or ignoring religious affiliations and literary traditions.

Central Asia and the Soviet census: counting nations, discounting states

When the Russian imperial state conquered Central Asia in the second half of the nineteenth century, there were three territorial states – the Kokand and Khivan khanates, and the Emirate of Bukhara. There were no ethno-national distinctions among the populations of these three polities. Rather, people made other kinds of social distinctions – religious, rural-urban, and nomadic-sedentary – as well as using local cultural categories to distinguish between wealth, social status, region, and language (or dialect). Turkic and Persian were the two main categories of local languages.[2] Nearly everyone spoke variants of these languages and many were able to communicate in both.

The 1897 first and last all-Russia census asked people to declare their religion and language, yet analysts of the time regarded the language

question as a surrogate (perhaps even a synonym) for the Russian concept of peoplehood (*narodnost'*), or nationality (*natsional'nost'*). In the
1897 Russian census, nationality was not a category, but religion and
language were (Khalid 1998: 202–3). Analysts of later censuses tended
to view language, not religion, as the surrogate for nationality in comparing that census with later Soviet ones when nationality and language
were always asked (Silver 1986: 72–73). Yet, twenty years prior to the
formation of the Soviet Union, language use had already become the
most tangible criterion for determining who belonged to which people or
national group.

It was not until the 1920s that some of the social distinctions indigenous
to Central Asia, as mentioned above, were reclassified in ethno-national
terms as Uzbek, Tajik, etc. The reasons for this were many, but, as events
played themselves out from the 1920s into the early 1930s, Uzbekism
turned out to be the most expedient heir to existing movements and discourses of pan-Islamism, pan-Turkism, and regionalism, to the power of
urban elites, and, most importantly, to the stewardship of Soviet nationality policy in Central Asia.

While early Soviet-period academics and bureaucrats eventually settled on "Uzbek" as the ethnonym of choice for carving a new republic
out of Central Asia, the concept of *natsional'nost'* was by no means created *ex nihilo*, nor was Central Asia a blank slate onto which new identities
could be written.[3] As Hirsch notes, "Questions about terminology were
not simply theoretical or epistemological. The decision to use a particular
term could manipulate census results and shift the configuration of the
multinational state." (1997: 261) Baldauf attributes the inclusion of particular features under the label of Uzbekism (as opposed to a number of
other possible labels) to "a change of concepts which is not paralleled by
a change of words" (1991: 92). Baldauf goes on to say: "Uzbek being the
name of the new nation, the concept of nation remained to be re-defined
according to the Russian example" (ibid.: 92). In order to secure this reconfiguration, Central Asians had to be counted and recounted until the
numbers gave increasing meaning to the categories. Censuses were the
means to accomplishing this end. Meanwhile, the wrangling over how,
what, and whom to count provided numerous opportunities for people
to position and reposition themselves (and others) at all levels of the
state bureaucracy and throughout the society at large until state mechanisms (by the end of the 1930s) could more or less fix those positions
to individuals.[4] For example, the Soviet internal, or domestic, passport
policy was first implemented in 1934 in urban areas and gradually spread
to the rest of the country. Unlike the nationality category on the census,
passport nationalities were fixed once they were determined according

to the nationality of one's parents. Since this was a new law, the issue of how one's parents' nationality (or nationalities) was determined is a thorny one.

The struggle over nationality terminology was prompted largely by Soviet state efforts to incorporate a culturally different and internally diverse region into the greater union. In 1924, just seven years after the Russian revolution, the territories of five Central Asian republics were mapped out, and the Soviet state, partly with the help of policies and practices based on early census data, categorized these territories' corresponding peoples as national with their own distinct cultures and languages. Not all territories were treated equally, but rather they were hierarchized into four categories: union republics (15); autonomous republics (20); autonomous regions, or *oblast'*, (8); and autonomous area, or *okrug*. (10).[5] Furthermore, there continued to be officially designated nationalities throughout the Soviet Union (e.g., Poles, Germans, Gypsies, Arabs, and Uighurs) with no eponymous territory.

What was the relationship between Soviet nationality policy and the census? Throughout Soviet rule, but especially during the first two decades, the nationality question on the census was designed, if somewhat indirectly, to re-educate the masses to think that the hierarchical, national, territorial-administrative structure of the Soviet Union reflected the society's natural ethnic composition. This system of territorial-administrative units was based on and reflected a theory of national consciousness that postulated a hierarchy in which the most developed peoples also had the highest awareness of who they really were *qua* people. The terms *natsional'nost'* and *narodnost'*, and in later decades ethnic grouping and ethnos, were all appropriated and used to designate particular levels of collective consciousness. Consequently, while Uzbekistan had never been a sovereign state, its inception as a Soviet socialist republic in 1925 endowed it with a legitimacy that allowed its "citizens" to begin to imagine it as a state; and in 1991 Uzbekistan became independent without any significant, active nationalist movement or ideology.

Sabol notes that one purpose of Soviet nationalities policy was to create model republics out of backward peoples for the purposes of demonstrating socialism's modernizing potential. "Another reason the Bolsheviks insisted on national delimitation," Sabol writes, "was that social and economic differentiation between the various Central Asian peoples rendered, in their minds, impossible the successful implementation of uniform regional policies, such as taxation and education, and others that required mass support." (1995: 236) The idea of nationality or national identity became, on the one hand, an internalized and enthralling (or disciplining) social apparatus and, on the other hand, the very material with which national state citizens learned to (re)imagine their own subjectivity. Yet, the glaring paradox of the Soviet system was that it was a system which, in theory, privileged an international socialism over all forms of national and sub-national identity, but in fact incubated new nationalities (Brubaker 1994).

The paradox of the Soviet system was also its linchpin in that the ambiguity of nations within an anti-national state allowed for greater, if more complex, flexibility in the ideological reconfiguration and control of identity. It also created the necessary cultural tension that allowed Soviet national elites to burgeon, participate in, remain loyal to, and thereby legitimize a system based on difference (Slezkine 1994). This was especially true for Central Asians, whose colonial predicament was rooted in their being stuck between the mutually tempering loyalties to nation and to Soviet international society. The fact that each Soviet citizen had no option but to belong to a nationality was, for some modernizing elites, as troublesome as it was a source of pride. On the one hand, it allowed members of Asian nationalities to claim to be on a civilizational par with other modern European nations; on the other hand, it virtually precluded possibilities for developing social bonds based on other shared aspects of culture such as religion and literary traditions. For others, being a national in an international society was like having one's cake and eating it too, in so far as local political actors could mobilize their co-nationals for state-sponsored (or private financial) projects and, simultaneously, reap rewards for successful service to the Soviet state.

Thus, we might consider that national territories became the standardizing form for the Soviet Union that numbers became for British India. Appadurai writes:

It is important to note here that numbers permitted comparison between kinds of places and people that were otherwise different, that they were concise ways of conveying large bodies of information, and that they served as a short-form for capturing and appropriating otherwise recalcitrant features of the social and human landscape. (1996: 120)

Appadurai points out that the role of numbers was widespread in colonial Indian bureaucratic practices. Initially, there was a numbered valuation of property for tax purposes and then numbers were used more generally to count people as colonial subjects in various capacities. Appadurai argues that it also acquired a momentum of its own and served individuals' needs to mask or distort accountability or project it elsewhere. This misappropriation of colonially produced knowledge by state officials and subjects alike subverted colonial disciplining measures, yet on the whole simultaneously produced new and unanticipated forms of knowledge. Urla (1993), in her study of the role of statistics in the making of Basque identity, argues that numbers, statistics, and the knowledge they generate, far from falling under the control of specialists, scientists, and bureaucrats, were claimed by the population at large. The state has no monopoly on these forms of knowledge, nor should they be associated solely with state projects. But in the process of standardizing and popularizing this technology, few are in a position to challenge the technology itself.

The claim to be able to "identify" (i.e., classify and name) objectively any state subject or citizen, individual, or group is a universally political act. The difficulty lies in making that claim believable. This is the problem that lay behind the Soviet debates over how to ask about identity in the early censuses. Not only did census designers have to work out what nationality meant and how necessary it was to convey that meaning to respondents, but they also had to decide how to present it on the form – e.g., as multiple choice or fill-in-the-blank. In the end, Soviet census-takers were instructed to ask – indeed, require – self-identification from as early as 1926.[6] In order to understand the logic behind this decision to let the respondent state his own national identity, let us take a brief comparative detour into research on colonial rule and the use of numbers in other parts of the world.

In his study of the census in colonial India, Cohn (1987) argues that British systems of classification and counting gave rise to a specific kind of consciousness of Indianness among its Indian subjects. This objectification was novel in the ways that it allowed the inhabitants of the subcontinent to conceptualize themselves as distinct from an equally and oppositionally constructed non-Indianness. Nameable self-identities are not givens. Similarly, neither are essential identities (Who am I? I am X). Identity is a constructed thing, and it is constructed over time and with a shifting awareness of values and meaning attached to certain categories, some of which are more meaningful than others. However, as Anderson (1991: 166–68) suggests with regard to censuses, maps, and museums, if nationality is a term scholars, elites, and bureaucrats in Uzbekistan use to characterize social difference in a population, nations are often what those groups of the population will become, on paper and, perhaps gradually over time, in people's minds as well. In other words, there is a complex objective-to-subjective shift that occurs – a change in knowledge and self-perception that social scientists sometimes call internalization.

As European states in general became more involved in administering their colonies, it became increasingly important for them to develop ever more sophisticated ways of classifying and counting subject populations. For example, Hirschman (1987) documents how, initially, identity categories in the Malaysian census under British rule arbitrarily mixed notions of race, region or language, and religion. This rather haphazard attempt at classification reflected a divide between colonizer and colonized, in which the important issue was distinguishing between groups according to economic privilege and power. Soviet census designers, drawing on Stalin's definition of nation as a "historically evolved, stable community of language, territory, economic life, and psychological makeup manifested in a community of culture" (Stalin 1934: 8), instructed respondents to declare their own national identity. Thus, the shift from the state's objectification of social identity to the popular subjectification of it and the development (or at least promotion) of national consciousness was actually introduced earlier in Central Asia than in places like British colonial Malaysia.

Anthropologists and other scholars have begun making important scholarly contributions to the study of census categorization under colonial regimes and their legacies for postcolonial states (e.g., Anderson 1991; Appadurai 1996; Cohn 1987; Hirschman 1987). The theoretical foundation for these studies is that systems of classification (and enumeration) are not logically grounded in pre-existing forms of social organization, but are instead culturally constructed through the political negotiation of shifting individual and group interests and commitments. As Appadurai (1996) argues, it is not merely the categories themselves that constitute the legacy of the colonial past, but the enumerative practices that enable colonial, postcolonial, and other kinds of subjects and citizenries to imagine themselves with collective identities; as members of specific groups and communities; and with specific kinds of relationships to specific Others.[7] Since the focus on numbers often distracts attention from the need to question what is being counted and why, it is important to bring attention to the fact that the authority of numbers is contingent on these systems of classification. Furthermore, numbers, or numeration, have a parapolitical aspect; and censuses, by making use of numbers in conjunction with systems of classification, are a parapolitical technology: they regroup and represent certain forms of perceived social difference in order to accomplish specific political goals. The census is certainly one instrument in this process and, as a parapolitical technology, is designed to domesticate primordial (or naturalized) sentiments such as collective identities.[8]

How did the project of counting citizens discipline Soviet citizens in the way they responded to state projects? Instituting self-identification in the Soviet census, one might argue, involves citizens in the state in ways that assigning identities for official purposes does not. That involvement and apparent emphasis on individual choice probably masked, and certainly legitimated, the categories used in the census. It changed, in a subtle way, the ethos of ethnicity from one of ascription to one of self-determination, inculcating more and more people into this way of thinking. For example, in the Central Asian republics it took seven years, from the time of the October revolution until the national delimitation (*natsional'noe razmezhevaniie*) of 1924, before the government officially accepted the term "Uzbek" to denote a nation and "Uzbekistan" a national republic. It took at least another four years for local scholars, intellectuals, and political leaders to agree whether "Uzbek" signified the relatively few descendants of the nomadic Uzbek tribe that had conquered the settled regions of Central Asia five hundred years earlier or a broader grouping of people, both urban and rural, who spoke a range of mutually intelligible Turkic dialects.[9] The latter, more inclusive signification won out, but it was not a simple matter for the vast majority of the population to learn to use a term denoting nationality in its properly official way.

In the Soviet Union, there was always a census question on nationality in one form or another that required an open-ended response (as opposed to the multiple choice format in the United States census). As recently as 1989, 823 "ethnonyms" were initially recorded on the forms. Census tabulators would then use a recoding method to reduce these to 128 official "nationalities." For example, if a person responded *Kokandlik* (from Kokand) or *Naiman* (a tribal affiliation) to the question "*natsional'nost*'", the census-taker (or analyst in Moscow) would reclassify the answer as "Uzbek" using a numbered code. The fact that there were as many as 128 official categories in 1989 was the result of scholarly and bureaucratic struggles in coping with the great linguistic and "cultural" diversity of the Soviet Union's population of nearly 300 million. However, what is particularly curious is that while the number of official ethnonyms in the final Soviet census had decreased since earlier censuses, the number of non-registered names had increased. In the 1926 census 530 so-called smaller identities were aggregated into 194 larger ones; in the 1937 census 769 were aggregated into 168; and in the 1989 census 823 were aggregated into 128 (Tishkov 1997: 15). A look at a sampling of individual responses to the nationality question for the seven Soviet censuses before those responses were recodified into official and acceptable categories could explain why the number of ethnonyms in the original responses increased so substantially while the number of official categories decreased between the 1926 and 1989 censuses. Interestingly, the number of ethnonyms that were reclassified as "Uzbek" actually declined slightly between 1939 and 1989. This, in conjunction with the fact that about half of the ethnonyms in responses were different between the two censuses, suggests a framework for a considerable amount of ethnographic research, in addition to archival research, on local usage of ethnonyms.

As people came to accept the nationality category as given (at the very least in the sense that they perceived that everyone else was playing by the same rules) and learned to play accordingly, they both became trapped by the rules and also changed the rules in the process. Nevertheless, the way people responded to censuses and other official forms was not necessarily the same as the way they responded in other day-to-day situations. An excellent example of this can be found in Baldauf's work on the politics of selecting a term for what later became "the Uzbeks." Baldauf, quoting and commenting on Magidovich's ethnographic work in Uzbekistan, is worth quoting here:

"Even as early as 1923, when the census was carried out, in the towns of Turkestan the term 'Sart' occurred only rarely, and the local population fell back on it, to my understanding, only conforming to the view of the Russian census-takers." I think, with this statement Magidovich refers to a crucial point: The foreigners' inclination to use what I would call allochthonous misnomers meets with a certain inclination on the part of the indigenous population in Central Asia to adopt misnomers or even to create some themselves....

In the 1920 census, whose materials were published in 1923, the "Uzbek-Sart issue" was several times pointed out. The *Sarty* had in a large part of the region been recorded separately, but finally they were grouped with the *Uzbeki*. The accompanying commentary stated that there was reason to doubt whether the two were really clearly distinct units (1991: 81).[10]

Not only does this passage provide a perfect example of the way certain ethnonyms were reclassified as proper ones; it also supports, via the census, Bourdieu's point (made above) about the inherently problematic nature of the opinion poll. As my own fieldwork experiences have demonstrated repeatedly, people employ officially sanctioned terms of identity only in certain situations, and they employ more fluid expressions of identity in other situations (Abramson 1998). For example, in addition to drawing distinctions between different cities and regions, people in Uzbekistan would also identify with the neighborhood (*mahalla*) they are from or with their extended family. The cultural logic behind strategies of reserving and drawing on a range of social distinctions that are often overlapping or contradictory is largely economically and politically motivated. In a society where access to even basic resources was and is increasingly dependent on social networks, it makes sense to maintain a variety of sub-national community ties. For example, the term "clan" is and should be used in this context, but only in its broadest possible

sense – socio-economic networks of people based primarily, but not exclusively, on kin ties secured through marriage and birth. Usage can vary
between state-sponsored events, bureaucracy, interactions with foreigners, and familial settings, to name a few. Thus, a survey of responses to
the open-ended census question about nationality would suggest, at the
very least, that people's sense of what and who they are diverges from
how they are represented collectively by the state. It could also shed light
on a series of valuable questions about the relationship between collective
identities and cultural constructions of the state.

Uzbek identity and the Tajik question

Struggles over ethnic minority status within the republic of Uzbekistan
have played an integral part in the formation of Uzbek national identity.
In this section I use the case of the Tajik minority nationality in Soviet and
post-Soviet Uzbekistan to show how numbers and what is being counted
acquire the power to represent reality.

In addition to the seven Soviet censuses there were also a number of
less comprehensive urban censuses and ethnographic surveys. For our
purposes, the 1920 urban census is particularly interesting because of
what it reveals about number and nationality in relation to the 1926
census. The fact that the national delimitation of 1924 – by which the
fledgling Soviet government divided Central Asia into, initially, the three
union republics of Kazakhstan, Turkmenistan, and Uzbekistan, and the
two autonomous republics of Kirgizia and Tajikistan – occurred between
these two censuses is what makes this comparison revealing.

The Tajik-speaking population lived throughout the region, but was
concentrated especially in the cities of Samarkand and Bukhara. According to Masov (1991), the nationality question in the 1920 urban-only
census yielded counts of 44,758 Tajiks and 3,301 Uzbeks in Samarkand.
The 1926 full census, just six years later, revealed there to be 10,716 Tajiks
and 43,364 Uzbeks living in Samarkand. Similar reversals occurred in the
largely Tajik-speaking city of Bukhara. What explains this dramatic shift
in numbers? Masov argues that the change is a result of "not physical,
but documentational genocide" (1991: 78) and points to several factors
which may have persuaded thousands of "actual" Tajiks to declare themselves officially Uzbek. These factors ranged from directly coercive measures, such as threats to resettle "Tajiks" to the Tajikistan Autonomous
Republic (ibid.: 80), to the determination that only Uzbeks have the right
to work within the borders of the newly formed republic of Uzbekistan.
The number of "Tajik"-language schools[11] underrepresented the number of Tajik speakers, and the schools that did exist were deprived

of Tajik-language materials (ibid.: 80). Thus, the dramatic shift in the counting of people according to nationality, Masov argues, was related to two factors. The first was the creation of Uzbekistan as a full union republic and of Tajikistan as a less "authentic" autonomous republic in the hierarchy of national territories. The second was that the outcome of the national delimitation was accompanied by locally introduced policies in Uzbekistan that made it much more beneficial to "be" Uzbek than Tajik, at least on paper.

Masov's argument, however, is tainted, both by his pro-Tajik stance, and, more importantly, by his assumption that there was an essential Tajik identity (or Uzbek, for that matter) to alter in the first place. For Masov, the fact that most residents of Bukhara spoke Tajik was evidence that they *were* Tajik. In fact, many people spoke both Uzbek and Tajik and, other than newly introduced economic and political incentives, had no obvious linguistic criterion for choosing an officially correct language. At least in the early 1920s, however, most city residents probably recognized the bureaucratic artificiality of declaring their nationality as Tajik or Uzbek. Soon enough, however, many claimed to be Uzbeks whose primary language (or "native tongue") was Tajik (Komatsu 1989: 132–33; Sukhareva 1958: 77–80). What is interesting here is that, at the time, how people identified themselves officially (i.e., in some form of public domain) became increasingly more significant. This applied to all of the main Central Asian nationalities. For example, Hirsch found that after the national-territorial delimitation, residents of some villages that ended up in Uzbekistan asserted their Kazakh identity and petitioned for the right to become part of Kazakhstan. In doing so, they appropriated the same national, economic, cultural, and geographic rationales which the government had used to create the republics. Hirsch notes:

The language of these petitions is particularly striking in light of the fact that before nation-territorial delimitation the population of Tashkent had used compound identities such as "Kazakh-Uzbek" and "Tajik-Uzbek." It was largely in conjunction with border-making and census-taking in the 1920s that the population of Tashkent had "learned" that "Uzbek," "Kazakh," and "Tajik" denoted separate national (as opposed to linguistic, kinship, or other) identities. (2000: 215)

This legacy seems to have continued seventy years later, after the demise of the Soviet system, but with mixed results: on the one hand, there have been clear attempts all along to eliminate the symbols and practices that people associate with certain identities; on the other hand, it was even more important to get the numbers right. Thus, there was a two-sided attack on national minorities, yet the two sides were not always coordinated. Numbers covered up practices and allowed for the reproduction of specific demographic claims; numbers also influenced policies that were designed for nationally homogenous populations or that were planned with the idea of homogenizing populations in accordance with administrative categories.[12]

The Tajik issue was addressed in 1929, five years after the first delimitation, when the Tajik Autonomous Republic was promoted to a full-fledged union republic. By 1929, however, it was already too late to repair the numerical "damage" to the corporate Tajik identity, all the more so because two major Tajik-speaking areas – Samarkand and Bukhara – remained in the Uzbek republic. It is important to note that the very fact of enclosing a sizeable Tajik-speaking population within the boundaries of the Uzbek republic made meeting the Tajik minority's linguistic, educational, and cultural demands economically unfeasible. This is especially true since the Russian language and a republic's titular language were given priority over third and other languages within the Soviet administrative-territorial system.[13]

Attempts by some Persian or Turkic-speaking urbanites and intellectuals to resist the territorialization and nationalization of Central Asian peoples utterly failed. In order to assure the preservation of aspects of Central Asian culture and identity, such as the Persian language, that did not fit into definitions of Uzbekness as it was coming to be defined, a Tajik identity and, ultimately, a territorial republic had to be established. While the process of collective identity formation always entails the assertion of "objective" boundaries between groups, the Uzbek-Tajik case illustrates that there was a particularly and blatantly political dynamic in the way national identities were formed in Soviet Central Asia. For example, because the more Persianized Tashkent (or eastern Turkic) dialect was adopted as the standard for the modern Uzbek language over more distant dialects, it was easier for Uzbeks (who had the upper hand anyway) to claim that Bukharan Tajik was really Uzbek (Turkic) with more Persian elements (Subtelny 1994: 52).

Little ethnographic research has been done on the topic of the complexity of Uzbek-Tajik relations today. According to the Soviet census of 1989, Tajiks comprised about 5% of the population of Uzbekistan. Based on ethnographic and informal interactions, however, many scholars argue that the "actual" Tajik population of Uzbekistan today is closer to 25 to 30 percent (e.g., Foltz 1996: 17) and that the numbers are lower because the political leadership in the republic maintains that most "Tajiks were simply Uzbeks who had adopted Farsi" (Mesamed 1996: 21). Since independence, the Uzbek government has pursued a deliberate policy of discouraging the learning and speaking of the Tajik language by limiting the number of Tajik-language publications and schools, mostly those in the cities of Samarkand and Bukhara, and by banning or refusing to register Tajik cultural organizations (Subtelny 1994: 55–56; Smith *et al.* 1998: 213). The question of who belongs to what ethnicity continues to be a largely political one.

As I mentioned earlier, language is one of the most widespread *cultural* markers of ethnicity. Yet, many self-identified Uzbeks in the capital city Tashkent, especially those who have studied or are from families who have studied in Soviet institutions of higher learning, speak more Russian than Uzbek. The majority of the population of Uzbekistan is able to communicate in Russian, if not as fluently as in Uzbek. I base this claim on three sources: Soviet census figures (Smith *et al.* 1998: 200); the results of an independent public opinion survey conducted in 1996 (ibid. 1998: 214–17); and my own extensive fieldwork and travel experience in Uzbekistan. The significance and relevance of language use varies from one function to another, and fluency itself is a fairly arbitrary assessment of spoken language ability. Thus, it is practically pointless to measure language ability based on one or two survey questions.

While there is no question about Uzbeks' official identity, the same is not true of Tajiks living in Uzbekistan. There continue to be cases of both Tajiks and Uzbeks, fluent in both languages, who have identified themselves as Uzbek in one moment or situation and Tajik in another. An example of this occurred during the course of a two-day visit at the house of relatives of an "Uzbek" friend of mine. The hosts were relatives of my friend's father, an orphan, whose own parents had been "Tajik." My friend, her father, and the rest of her immediate family identified as Uzbek and spoke Uzbek at home. The relatives, who lived in another city – Chust, in the Fergana valley – with a considerable Tajik-speaking population, identified as Tajiks when I asked about the Tajik community in the city. The next day, however, they assured me that they were *Uzbek* and that "We are all one nation." They spoke Tajik, Uzbek, and Russian. Schoeberlein-Engel encountered the same mixed uses of identity terms. He relates one telling encounter when he asked one companion "What is your nationality?":

On this particular occasion, my companion answered that he was an "Özbek" [Uzbek]. The reply was not surprising considering that we were in Tâshkent, the capital of Özbekistan [Uzbekistan] ... until I inquired further to learn that both of his parents were "Tâjiks," and furthermore that his first language was Tâjik, which he spoke much better than Özbek. (1994: 81)

Even to ask a family or individual's "native language" (*rodnoi iazyk*), a question many of the Soviet censuses posed in order to find out a primary language, is tricky. First of all there was much confusion on the part of both the respondents to and interpreters of the "native language" question on the census. It was not always clear whether native language referred to language spoken most often at home, language of one or both parents, a person's first spoken language, or the language associated with a person's national identity. Moreover, in urban and semi-urban areas many people live with their extended families sharing a courtyard house, or compound, i.e., living in separate rooms or sets of rooms around a common private, enclosed yard. Depending on the formal education, occupation, and travel experiences of the household members, it is not uncommon for them to speak different languages to different members, although everyone can always understand everyone else. I have also been in a one-family Uzbek home where the parents speak Uzbek and Russian to each other and to their children, and the children, depending on their ages, speak only Russian to their parents. The variation is great and demonstrates how language knowledge and use do not consistently correlate with identity.

Sukhareva's 1959 study (cited in Becker 1973: 161) of Samarkand *oblast'* (province) offers another telling example: the residents of two neighboring villages claimed to be members of the Chaghatay tribe and descendants of Uzbek nomads. Even though the residents of one village spoke Uzbek and those of the other spoke Tajik, members of Uzbek tribal groups living in areas surrounding these two villages referred to the residents of both villages as Tajik.

In Samarkand and Bukhara, where the issue of Tajik identity is a thornier one, language use and the possibilities for learning and preserving language outside of the home are highly politicized. This is especially true now that Uzbekistan and Tajikistan exist as sovereign states and neighbors whose potential claims on one another's territories, populations, and resources are based on decisions made in an era of pre-sovereignty. New states are often faced with threats to their legitimacy and outbreaks of civil war or inter-ethnic conflict. If the states are stable enough to conduct a national census, sometimes the census questions can be used to defuse conflict or refocus attention away from the kinds of cleavages around which conflicts arise. Such instability is unlikely to stand in the way of census projects in the Soviet successor states.[14] Nevertheless, the Tajik question poses a whole package of potential problems to Uzbekistan's borders, loyalties, and citizenships, as well as a challenge to its capacity to tolerate diversity in education, language, and other forms of ethno-cultural expression. Ironically, the Uzbekistan leadership has used the ongoing civil war in neighboring Tajikistan as an example of where inter-ethnic intolerance can lead.

Many scholars have argued that, despite Soviet attempts to categorize Central Asians as peoples divided into distinct national groups, traditional forms of social ties have prevailed, and that the Soviet-incubated nationalities failed to produce citizens loyal to the former Soviet Union (e.g., Fierman 1991; Olcott 1990). Scholars who use the failed transformation argument reproduce the flawed thinking of their Soviet counterparts, who took the traditionality of certain practices and beliefs at face value and claimed that they were nothing more than cultural survivals devoid of social meaning and logical context. Others contend that the Soviet legacy was a political system whereby the worst of "traditional" Central Asian and Soviet authoritarianism has prevailed at the expense of a more civic-minded communalism (Carley 1995: 304, on Uzbekistan; Huttenbach 1995: 338–39, on Azerbaijan). In any case, assessments of the success or failure of Soviet policies and whether those policies constituted a form of colonialism will not tell us what "traditional" or "postcolonial" or "national" identities mean in Uzbekistan today. Tensions between Uzbeks and Tajiks are not primordial, even if the rhetoric they employ is primordialist. While we cannot know how these tensions will develop, we can reasonably assume that the political actors involved will perform for and respond to a political culture that extends beyond the borders of the former Soviet Union.

If one looks at the role of numbers, counting, and statistics, as Peter Uvin (this volume) does in places like Rwanda and Burundi, there will appear to be little difference between colonial and postcolonial periods. The main change is that the technology of counting has become far more sophisticated and efficient and is increasingly under the guidance, if not control, of international agencies with international money. Census-generated knowledge is one of the more predominant kinds of state knowledge, all the more so as it involves the counting of ever more things. In the next section I shall explore the dynamics of counting knowledge within the context of Uzbekistan's emergence in a changing global arena of nation-states and international relations.

Global numbers and new states

The end of the Cold War has shaped a new social, political, and economic global environment for emerging nation-states which influences how state citizens align themselves. One of the prominent issues in this new environment is the relationship between national and modern identities. Shils (1963: 5), capturing both its ambiguous and constructed nature, defines modernity as "the idiom of progress, rational technology, collectivistic organization, social equality and populistic demagogy." The modern identity was once linked to movements for national sovereignty; now those movements and ideological orientations are struggling with the question "Which modernity"? Previously, states were divided between capitalist and socialist brands of modernity. Now that this is no longer the case, nationalist sentiments are much stronger, not because they *were* suppressed under socialist regimes, but because there *is* a greater sense of urgency about becoming a modern market and a democracy through national self-determination. Verdery (1998: 294), in discussing how national symbols, constitutions, and land and welfare reform in socialist societies were used to mobilize ethnic groups politically, points out that "in the formerly socialist world, transnational flows of capital and political interest turned nationalism into political capital". People relied heavily on such capital in Uzbekistan, but now there are a number of countervailing forces – alternatively based social networks, foreign aid, and international politics – which will no doubt reshape old interest groups and serve new ones. In this final section of the chapter I shall suggest how the introduction of global systems of categorization through international contact may be influencing "traditional" forms of social organization and religious practice – namely, the *mahalla* and Islam.

In newly independent and former socialist states such as Uzbekistan, global systems of counting and categorization are playing an increasing role. For example, both the Uzbekistan government and international and foreign organizations like the World Bank and international non-governmental organizations (INGOs) are currently setting up grant and loan projects targeted at the *mahalla*. Mahallas are urban neighborhoods or wards, run by local state committees, that oversee everything from the issuing of residency permits and sanitation and the distribution of welfare and scholarships to the building of mosques and the celebration of Islamic and state holidays. The *mahalla* has traditionally also been a form of local collective identity reinforced by shared occupational, ethnic, or religious affiliations. Given this broad range of activities and its history as an indigenous Central Asian institution predating Russian rule by centuries, the *mahalla* has come to be a remarkable synthesis of an informal social network and a state territorial-administrative unit (Abramson 1998).

As the *mahalla* becomes one of the primary small-scale administrative units through which the state governs, social ties may reorganize accordingly. Ironically, the new emphasis on *mahalla*s will transform them as institutions, yet the rationale for targeting them is that they play the unchanging and stabilizing role in Uzbek society of preserving valued traditions under the category of "national culture." While previously *mahalla* committee leaders played a central, if relatively informal, role in redistributing goods and services to the needy within their mahallas, recent state decrees and programs have increasingly shifted the burden of responsibility for determining neediness based on nationally standardized criteria onto these local leaders. Poorly trained in number-crunching, interpreting state policies, and in other requisite areas, the leaders cannot uniformly satisfy local needs and state demands.

As more and more neighborhoods are being transformed or incorporated into mahallas, in the administrative sense, the *mahalla* is becoming a new focus for enumeration – an enumerative *standard* for counting and measuring Uzbekistan's population and resources. Increasingly, each *mahalla* committee is in charge of maintaining information on welfare – the income, wealth, health, education, and other needs – of each of its resident households. Programs such as the World Bank's micro-credit projects, which target the *mahalla*, can only work if record-keeping of exactly this kind of information is instituted in order to monitor how its aid is used and to evaluate the benefits derived from such aid. But ultimately, for what purposes will this information be used? And how will the constructed categories required to accomplish such projects in the *mahalla* alter the way collective identities are constructed?

The issue of what role Islam as a religious category plays in Uzbekistan's political culture is one that the census has not defined. That is, the census has not yet become a forum for negotiating a Muslim identity. Nevertheless, other ways of counting have begun to play a larger role in influencing Islam's place in Uzbek politics. For example, the majority of foreign aid to Uzbekistan and foreign-supported development projects there have targeted non-religious organizations. To the extent that support for an Islamic identity in Central Asia is tolerated by the government, it is done so under the rubric of tourism (the restoration of old Islamic monuments such as medressahs and mosques), business (with countries in the Middle East, especially the wealthier Gulf states), or, more ambiguously, national cultural heritage.[15]

Anderson (1991: 169–70) discusses how in colonial Malaya and elsewhere, religion presented a particularly awkward problem for counting subjects. This was addressed through the ethnicization of religion as it was also done in the Soviet Union. While there is a common assumption in Uzbekistan that to be Uzbek is to be Muslim, the reverse is acknowledged not always to be true, given the presence of other Muslim nationalities such as Tajiks, Kazakhs, Kyrgyz, Tatars, and Turks. The debate over and design of new census categories will be significant, either way, in influencing the outcome of attitudes about Islam's relationship to Uzbek nationalism and national culture. For example, the continued omission of a religion question might communicate the state's desire to subsume Islam under nationality – e.g., if a person is Uzbek or Tajik, can it be assumed that he or she is also a Muslim? This connection between nationality and religion in Central Asia has been a common assumption for a long time and one which I have heard expressed numerous times during previous field research. The introduction of a religion question on a future Uzbek census might send a message of tolerance of religious (and ethnic) pluralism – that every individual will be considered a citizen of the Uzbek state regardless of religious belief. On the other hand, its introduction[16] could spark tensions focusing on national and spiritual loyalty, setting a precedent for making public and controversial what had safely been relegated to the private sphere. The once acceptable option for many Central Asians (in the Soviet and early post-Soviet years) – especially for those in official positions – of being both an atheist and a Muslim could be turned into a hotly contested issue. It is doubtful that a census question alone could challenge Uzbek citizens to rethink their identities. Nevertheless, how they respond to future census identity questions will likely echo and constitute the larger political question: not "What kind of Muslim are you?", but "What kind of Uzbek are you – secular or Muslim"?

Conclusion

At the beginning of this chapter I argued that the nationality category as used in the Soviet census and on other forms of official documentation helped instill in Central Asians a sense of belonging to a nationality and, over time, to a nation. Facing all newly independent states is the question of what kinds of knowledge its citizens must have in order for the state to function with some degree of unity. As I have tried to demonstrate, the census as a parapolitical technology for producing very specific forms of knowledge is a site of struggles over representation and for legitimacy. One type of knowledge, Handler suggests, must support the assertion of a nation's possessions in order "to meet the challenge of an outsider's denial of national existence" (1985: 211). This dual – internal and external – pressure compels new governments to undertake immediately the task of enumerating exactly what those possessions are and why they are significant. The census can be particularly important for a new state because it is the means by which a government can take inventory of its national human stock. Nation-state formation is not merely a matter of choosing flag designs, composing anthems, and lobbying for membership in the United Nations. The real cultural complexity behind national identity formation involves not only political legitimation through the public use of symbols, but also evidence that national identity has become a prime motivator in the types of choices and decisions citizens make. In other words, a unified national identity must inform, shape, and define citizen interests at least as much as regional or local, familial, and individual interests do.

At the same time, as the Soviet successor states emerge into a new global system of nation-states, ethnic and regional diversity must now be included among their national possessions. The press in Uzbekistan frequently cites figures conveying its national and cultural diversity. The independence day concert and other national performances held every year reinforces this message in staging a series of dances and musical numbers to represent each of the major national groups and provinces (*viloyat*) in the country. Uzbekistan may need a titular majority (to avoid the kinds of problems in Kazakhstan, Kyrgyzstan, and Latvia where titular identities, by census count, barely constitute a popular majority); yet, as Hannerz points out in discussing cultural complexity in the late-twentieth century, there are new transnational audiences for which nations must now perform:

There is some irony in the fact that even as the particular cultural emblems of national distinctiveness are indeed unique, the formula for distinctiveness is in large part transnational: a flag, an anthem. More importantly, the state cannot afford to engage only in a replication of uniformity. Not least through its educational wing, the state cultural apparatus also has a large part in the differentiation, the expansion and reproduction of complexity, deemed necessary for the conduct of the nation's business. (1992: 233–234)

In the cases of minority populations, a celebration of diversity that transforms them into Uzbek national possessions – "the peoples of Uzbekistan" – is a perfect example of a response to new nationhood within a global arena that incorporates traditions of Soviet nationality policy.

In this volume, our collective point of departure is the assumption that state-organized censuses (and the categories and numbers that constitute them) have had a significant impact on how people construct citizenship and collective identities. This impact does not stem from individual responses to census questions such as nationality, but from the ways in which those responses, collectively, are analyzed, inform state policies, are accepted as givens (social facts), and become the basis for political mobilization in pursuit of very practical ends (e.g., observation of religious laws, language use in public education, and access to jobs). The census, then, should not be seen merely as a state's instrument of oppression, silencing minorities in order to maintain the face of a culturally homogenous nation. Cultural categories cloaked by numbers constrain all political actors, and there is pressure for those acting on behalf of state governments to accommodate the social fact that nation-states are diverse and pluralistic societies.

NOTES

1 By "culture" I mean "the structures of meaning through which men [read: humans] give shape to their experience" (Geertz 1973: 312). Moreover, neither these structures nor their meanings comprise a closed or static system. Following from this, "[C]ulture does imply difference, but the differences now are no longer taxonomic; they are interactive and refractive" (Appadurai 1996: 60).

2 There are no neutral terms one can use to refer to the languages of this region. Suffice it to say that "Turkic" here refers to some of the languages of the Uralo-Altaic groups including contemporary Turkish, Azeri, Uzbek, Kazakh, Kirghiz, Turkmen, and others; "Persian" refers to Farsi, Dari, and Tajik, classified as belonging to the Indo-European group of languages. Prior to 1925, the terms Turki and Farsi were used to identify the two main indigenous languages spoken in Central Asia. After 1925, the words Uzbek and Tajik were used (Kocaoglu 1973: 155). As it is the central project of this book to question the political and cultural basis of classification schemes used in censuses, I shall not belabor the point that the same kind of scrutiny can be applied to the European system for the classification of world languages.

3 See Baldauf's (1991) discussion of the terms Chaghatai, Sart, Turkistani, Muslim, Turon, and various regional terms as viable alternatives to Uzbek. Also, long before the 1920s there were already movements of pan-Turkists and Jadids ("New School" reformers with a focus on Islamic education) to cultivate national and transnational consciousnesses in Central Asia under imperial Russian rule (Khalid 1998).

4 See Smith *et al.* (1998: 154–156) on internal passports in Central Asia.

5 According to figures from the 1989 Soviet census, Kazakhstan is the only union republic whose titular nationality did not enjoy a majority percentage of the republic's population. In this sense, Kazakhstan is similar to the titular nationalities of the vast majority of the autonomous republics and "lesser" territories, which also did not enjoy popular majorities (Bremmer and Taras 1993: 550–560). A titular nationality is the nationality after which a territory is named. Thus, Uzbek is the titular nationality and language of the republic of Uzbekistan.

6 The fact that the Malay census, for example, did not introduce self-identification until the 1947 census points to the high degree of sophistication of the Soviet planners in adopting the "subjective" approach as well as asking about nationality in any form.

7 Anderson also makes this important point in writing about East Asia under colonial rule, stating: "The real innovation of the census-takers of the 1870s was, therefore, not in the *construction* of ethnic-racial classifications, but rather in their systematic *quantification.*" (1991: 168)

8 The word parapolitical in this context comes from Geertz (1973: 275–77); "technology" is my contribution. For a more sophisticated contribution, see

Urla's discussion of our need to regard "the deployment of statistics as neither description nor pure propaganda but as a technology for the production of social knowledge and subjectivity" (1993: 836).

9 See Ingeborg Baldauf's short history of the rise and fall of the Soviet discipline of *kraevedenie*, or regionology, or as it was applied to the study of Uzbek people – *Uzbekovedenie*, or Uzbekology (1992). This "discipline" and the debates around it focused on the question of what constituted the Uzbek people.

10 "Sart" was a term for urban Turkic or Persian-speakers around the turn of the century. Russian ethnographers adopted Sart to distinguish between urban and rural populations, but dropped it during the Soviet period because its elitist connotation was incompatible with the development of a more inclusive socialist consciousness in Central Asia. Sart is almost never used in a social context today. For a more elaborate discussion of the history and cultural associations of the terms Sart, Uzbek, and others, see Baldauf (1991).

11 The medium of instruction was "Persian" in these "modern"-style schools which opened in the first decade of the twentieth century (Fragner 1994: 30).

12 Moreover, Masov's work is an excellent example of post-Soviet debates that take for granted (as objective truth) Soviet-era categories.

13 This two-language principle was reflected in the language question on later Soviet censuses, which asked first for "native language" and then asked for a second language from a list limited to the "languages of the peoples of the Soviet Union." This second language question was an indirect way of asking those not claiming Russian as a native language whether they were fluent in Russian as a second language (Silver 1986: 89–90).

14 Elsewhere, newly independent governments have refrained from conducting censuses for fear that publication of results reflecting certain inevitable demographic changes would ignite tensions. Lebanon, for example, did not have a census for more than three decades after independence for fear the results would reveal certain demographic changes that would undermine the existing system created to balance different religious interests (Geertz 1973: 275).

15 Little or no research has been conducted on this topic in Uzbekistan. For a similar kind of study of Muslims in China see Gladney (1987).

16 The only time a religious question was asked in a Soviet census was in the 1937 census. For a host of reasons this census was quickly discredited and redone in 1939. In the Soviet era, religion was not asked because, officially, it did not exist. Consequently, differences in religious belief between members of the same nationality were irrelevant. This meant that officially there were no differences in the identities of members of those groups even when, unofficially, ethnicity was significantly viewed in religious terms. For example, see Hirsch's discussion of the Muslim Ajars and Christian Georgians. Georgian politicians backed this argument because it allowed them to claim the Ajarians as Georgians (1997: 270). Soviet Jews, on the other hand, were not claimed by any group and, therefore, had to be redefined from a religious group to a nationality. In order to legitimize this political move, the Soviet government created the Jewish Autonomous Republic of Birobidzhan as a Jewish "homeland" with a Jewish population of about 2 percent. For a more general theoretical

approach, see Geertz's (1973: 275) discussion of Weiner's (unpublished) term "genocide by census redefinition" and Wallerstein's (1960: 129–39) "ethnogenesis by census redefinition."

REFERENCES

Abramson, David 1998, *From Soviet to Mahalla: Community and Transition in Post-Soviet Uzbekistan*, Ph.D. dissertation, Indiana University.

Anderson, Benedict 1991, *Imagined Communities: Reflections on the Origin and Spread of Nationalism*, 2nd edn, London: Verso.

Appadurai, Arjun 1996, "Number in the Colonial Imagination," in *Modernity at Large: Cultural Dimensions of Globalization*, Minneapolis: University of Minnesota Press, pp. 114–135.

Baldauf, Ingeborg 1991, "Some Thoughts on the Making of the Uzbek Nation," *Cahiers du Monde Russe et Soviétique* 32: 79–96.

1992, *"Kraevedenia" and Uzbek National Consciousness*, Papers on Inner Asia, No. 20, Bloomington, Indiana: Research Institute for Inner Asian Studies.

Becker, Seymour 1973, "National Consciousness and the Politics of the Bukhara People's Conciliar Republic," in Edward Allworth (ed.), *The Nationality Question in Soviet Central Asia*, New York: Praeger Publishers, pp. 159–67.

Bremmer, Ian and Ray, Taras (eds.) 1993, *Nations and Politics in the Soviet Successor States*, Cambridge University Press.

Brubaker, Rogers 1994, "Nationhood and the National Question in the Soviet Union and Post-Soviet Eurasia: An Institutionalist Account," *Theory and Society* 23(1): 47–78.

Carley, Patricia 1995, "The Legacy of the Soviet Political System and the Prospects for Developing Civil Society in Central Asia," in Vladimir Tismaneanu (ed.), *Political Culture and Civil Society in Russia and the New States of Eurasia*, Armonk, N.Y.: M.E. Sharpe, pp. 292–317.

Cohn, Bernard 1987, "The Census, Social Structure, and Objectification in South Asia," *An Anthropologist among the Historians and Other Essays*, Oxford: Oxford University Press, pp. 224–54.

Colas, Dominique 1997, *Civil Society and Fanaticism: Conjoined Histories*, translated by Amy Jacobs, Stanford: Stanford University Press.

Fierman, William (ed.) 1991, *Soviet Central Asia: The Failed Transformation*, Boulder, Col.: Westview Press.

Foltz, Richard 1996, "Uzbekistan's Tajiks: A Case of Repressed Identity?", *Central Asia Monitor* 6: 17–19.

Fragner, Bert 1994, "The Nationalization of the Uzbeks and Tajiks," in Edward Allworth (ed.), *Muslim Communities Reemerge: Historical Perspectives on Nationality, Politics, and Opposition in the Former Soviet Union and Yugoslavia*, Durham: Duke University Press, pp. 13–32.

Geertz, Clifford 1973, *Interpretation of Cultures: Selected Essays by Clifford Geertz*, New York: Basic Books.

Gladney, Dru 1987, "Muslim Tombs and Ethnic Folklore: Charters for Hui Identity," *The Journal of Asian Studies* 46(3): 495–532.

Gupta, Akhil 1995, "Blurred Boundaries: The Discourse of Corruption, the Culture of Politics, and the Imagined State," *American Ethnologist* 22(2): 375–402.

Handler, Richard 1985, "On Having a Culture: Nationalism and the Preservation of Quebec's Patrimoine," in George W. Stocking (ed.), *Objects and Others: Essays on Museums and Material Culture*, History of Anthropology, Vol. 3, Madison: University of Wisconsin Press, pp. 192–217.

Hannerz, Ulf 1992, *Cultural Complexity: Studies in the Social Organization of Meaning*, New York: Columbia University Press.

Hirsch, Francine 1997, "The Soviet Union as a Work-in-Progress: Ethnographers and the Category *Nationality* in the 1926, 1937, and 1939 Censuses," *Slavic Review* 56(2): 251–78.

2000, "Toward an Empire of Nations: Border-Making and the Formation of Soviet National Identities," *The Russian Review* 59: 201–26.

Hirschman, Charles 1987, "The Meaning and Measurement of Ethnicity in Malaysia: An Analysis of Census Classifications," *The Journal of Asian Studies* 46(3): 555–82.

Huttenbach, Henry 1995, "Post-Soviet Crisis and Disorder in Transcaucasia: The Search for Regional Security and Stability," in Vladimir Tismaneanu (ed.), *Political Culture and Civil Society in Russia and the New States of Eurasia*, Armonk, N.Y.: M.E. Sharpe, pp. 337–68.

Khalid, Adeeb 1998, *The Politics of Muslim Cultural Reform: Jadidism in Central Asia*, Berkeley: University of California Press.

Kocaoglu, Timur 1973, "The Existence of a Bukharan Nationality in the Recent Past," in Edward Allworth (ed.), *The Nationality Question in Soviet Central Asia*, New York: Praeger Publishers, pp. 151–8.

Komatsu, Hisao 1989, "The Evolution of Group Identity among Bukharan Intellectuals in 1911–1928: An Overview," *The Memoirs of the Research Department of the Toyo Bunko* 47:115–44.

Masov, Rakhim 1991, *Istoriia Topornogo Razdeleniia*, Dushanbe: Irfon.

Mesamed, Vladimir 1996, Interethnic Relations in the Republic of Uzbekistan, *Central Asia Monitor* 6: 20–6.

Olcott, Martha Brill 1990, "Central Asia: The Reformers Challenge a Traditional Society," in Lubomyr Hajda and Mark Beissinger (eds.), *The Nationalities Factor in Soviet Politics and Society*, Boulder: Westview Press, pp. 253–80.

Sabol, Steven 1995, "The Creation of Soviet Central Asia: The 1924 National Delimitation," *Central Asian Survey* 14(2): 225–41.

Schoeberlein-Engel, John 1994, *Identity in Central Asia: Construction and Contention in the Conceptions of "Özbek," "Tâjik," "Muslim," "Samarqandi," and Other Groups*, Ph.D. dissertation, Harvard University.

Shahrani, M. Nazif 1994, "Islam and the Political Culture of 'Scientific Atheism' in Post-Soviet Central Asia: Future Predicament," *Islamic Studies* 33(2–3): 139–59.

Shils, Edward 1963, "On the Comparative Study of the New States," in Clifford Geertz (ed.), *Old Societies and New States: The Quest for Modernity in Asia and Africa*, New York: The Free Press of Glencoe, pp. 1–26.

Silver, Brian 1986, "The Ethnic and Language Dimensions in Russian and Soviet Censuses," in Ralph Clem (ed.), *Research Guide to the Russian and Soviet Censuses*, Ithaca: Cornell University Press, pp. 70–97.

Slezkine, Yuri 1994, "The USSR as a Communal Apartment, or How a Socialist State Promoted Ethnic Particularism," *Slavic Review* 53(2): 414–52.

Smith, Graham, Vivien Law, Andrew Wilson, Annette Bohr, and Edward Allworth 1998, *Nation-Building in the Post-Soviet Borderlands: The Politics of National Identity*, Cambridge: Cambridge University Press.

Stalin, Joseph 1934 [1913], *Marxism and the National and Colonial Question*, New York: International Publishers.

Subtelny, Maria Eva 1994, "The Symbiosis of Turk and Tajik," in Beatrice Manz (ed.), *Central Asia in Historical Perspective*, Boulder: Westview Press, pp. 45–61.

Sukhareva, O. A. 1958, *K istorii gorodov Bukharskogo khanstva*, Tashkent: Uzbekistan SSR Fanlar Akademiasi.

Tishkov, Valerii 1997, *Ethnicity, Nationalism and Conflict in and after the Soviet Union: The Mind Aflame*, London: Sage Publications.

Urla, Jacqueline 1993, "Cultural Politics in an Age of Statistics: Numbers, Nations, and the Making of Basque Identity," *American Ethnologist* 20(4): 818–43.

Verdery, Katherine 1998, "Transnationalism, Nationalism, Citizenship, and Property: Eastern Europe since 1989," *American Ethnologist* 25(2): 291–306.

Wallerstein, Immanuel 1960, "Ethnicity and National Integration in West Africa," *Cahiers d'Etude Africaines* 3: 129–39.

Index

absorption, into Israeli society, 75–76
agricultural survey, in Burundi and
    Rwanda, 168–69
Albanians, in Macedonia, 21–23,
    22(table)
Alexis Carrel Foundation, 136
Algeria, 129–30
allophones, 107–8, 117 (n. 12)
American Anthropological Association,
    47–48
American Civil Rights movement, 44
American Indians, 53, 58
    early US censuses, 7–8
    increase in self-identification, 84
    inequality in eighteenth-century US
        census, 50
    racial categorization on birth
        certificates, 4
    US Census Race Categories 1790–2000,
        67(table)
    as vanishing race, 55–56
ancestry question
    defining ethnicity, 25–26
    ethnic groups in the US, 83–85
    Israelis, 76–77
    language identity and, 99
    losing ethnicity over time, 82
    US Census, 17–18
apportionment, as purpose of census,
    49–50
aptitude, as a construction of racial
    identity, 10–11
Arab American Institute, 59
Arab populations, 74, 77–78. *See also*
    Moslems
Arafat, Yassar, 78
Asia, Central. *See* Uzbekistan
Asian, as racial category, 58, 150
Asian-American lobbies, 58
assimilation
    of foreigners in France, 132–33
    of Jews, 74–75

language identity, 100–2
    linguistic assimilation in Belgium,
        105–6
    reversing language assimilation
        in Canada, 106–8
Australia, 8, 18
Austria and Austria-Hungary
    categorizing people of Czech
        descent, 28
    citizenship determination, 8
    Czech-German language dispute,
        100–2
    defense of ethnic identification
        in Austria-Hungary, 126
    identity formation through
        categorization, 32–33
    language of use as ethnic
        indicator, 26
    trilingual border area affecting
        census, 109–10
Azevedo, Fernando de, 63

Balfour declaration (1917), 78
Balkan region, 21
Banyarwanda people, 162
Basque people, 20
Belgium. *See also* Burundi and Rwanda
    Flemish speakers, 117(n. 10)
    French speakers, 117(n. 11)
    institutional denial of violence
        in Rwanda, 172(n. 6)
    language as categorization criterion,
        28–29, 94, 96
    linguistic assimilation, 105–6
    Ruanda-Urundi censuses, 149–52
    territorial aspects of language identity,
        31, 113–14
Bilingual Act of 1969 (Canada), 112
bilingualism, 113
    in Belgian schools, 31
    Flemish speakers in Belgium, 105–6
    politics of language use, 97–98

Ministry of Immigration and Absorption (Israel), 89(n. 3)
minority populations
British Race Relations Act of, 1976, 13–14
Canadian censuses, 14–16, 80
constructing nationality in Uzbekistan, 196
entitlement to social programs, 30–31
linguistic rights, 112–14
minority-majority electoral districting, 57–58
non-Jewish Israelis, 77–78
refusal to count specific nationalities, 23–25
Uzbek-Tajik identity question, 187–92
mixed-race groups. *See* multiculturalism
modernity, 192–95
Moslems, 74, 77–78, 130, 194–95
mother tongue, 27, 115
criticism of French survey categories, 134
defining nationality through language identity, 94–97
home language question in Canada, 118(n. 13)
Hungarian censuses, 117(n. 7)
as language indicator, 26
language of the group versus the individual, 109
versus language of use, 98–108
Tajik-Uzbek question, 190–91
two languages of use, 98
Mughals, 9
mulatto category, 11, 48–49, 51–56, 150
multiculturalism, 17–18
bilingualism, 98
Canadian ethnic interest groups, 82
collective identity and, 1
lack of multiracial identification choice in the US, 84
multiple responses in censuses, 85–86
multilingualism, 113
multiracial, as census category, 59

national character, 12
National European American Society, 59
National Institute of Demographic Studies (INED), 122, 130–36
National Institute of Economic Statistics (INSEE), 121, 130–35
nationalism, 1, 27
impact of language and territoriality, 114–16

inherited traits as authentic identity, 11–12
language identity, 92
state certification of collective identities, 3
territoriality of ethnic groups, 108–12
nationality, 3
Central Asia under Soviet rule, 176–87
constructing nationality through census questions, 195–96
as cultural community rather than bounded locale, 94–95
early Soviet Union, 103
French survey, 128, 133–34, 144(n. 4)
language identity and, 94–97
nature of social and national categories, 124
Tajik-Uzbek identity question, 187–92
Native Americans. *See* American Indians
Native Hawaiian or other Pacific Islander, 59–60
native language. *See* mother tongue
Negro, as US Census category, 56–57. *See also* Blacks
neighborhoods, ethnic differentiation in, 86–87
New Caledonia, 130
nonwhite, as racial category, 51–56
Nott, Josiah, 51

octoroons, 53
Office of Management and Budget (US), 17, 58–60
Official Languages Act (Canada, 1969), 15–16
OMB. *See* Office of Management and Budget
one-drop rule, 4, 34, 55–57, 59
Organization for Security and Cooperation (OSCE), 113
origin, country of
Canadian census, 80
defining ethnicity, 134
French census position on, 128
Israelis, 76–77, 89(n. 4)
multiple origins and memories concept, 138–39
race and ethnicity in US censuses, 83–85
versus self-identification, 85–86
OSCE. *See* Organization for Security and Cooperation